THE CITY OF
RAINBOWS

*A Colourful History
of Prince Rupert*

BLAIR MIRAU

Heritage House Publishing Company Ltd.
heritagehouse.ca

Cataloguing information available from Library and Archives Canada
978-1-77203-475-2 (paperback)
978-1-77203-476-9 (e-book)

Cover design by Colin Parks and Sara Loos
Interior book design by Rafael Chimicatti
Cover photographs: 1909 Dominion Day Arch, Prince Rupert, BC.
    Credit: J.D. Allen Photographic Company fonds. Prince Rupert City
    & Regional Archives. Colourized by Marilyn Carr-Harris.

The interior of this book was produced on 100% post-consumer recycled paper,
processed chlorine free, and printed with vegetable-based inks.

Heritage House gratefully acknowledges that the land on which we live and work
is within the traditional territories of the Lkwungen (Esquimalt and Songhees),
Malahat, Pacheedaht, Scia'new, T'Sou-ke, and W̱SÁNEĆ (Pauquachin, Tsartlip,
Tsawout, Tseycum) Peoples.

We acknowledge the financial support of the Government of Canada through the
Canada Book Fund (CBF) and the Canada Council for the Arts, and the Province
of British Columbia through the British Columbia Arts Council and the Book
Publishing Tax Credit.

28 27 26 25 24   1 2 3 4 5

Printed in Canada

CONTENTS

CONTENTS

PREFACE

WITHOUT THE RAIN, THERE IS NO RAINBOW

Since time immemorial, rain has defined life on Kaien Island, on the Pacific Northwest coast of North America, for Indigenous Peoples who call it home. Now the townsite of Prince Rupert, Kaien Island is home to the rainiest and cloudiest city in Canada: in other words, the perfect environment for rainbows.

But there is more to the climate of a place than the weather. The rainbow is also the perfect metaphor for Prince Rupert: a celebration of diversity and inclusion, a supernatural gateway between worlds, and a universal symbol for hope and calm after a storm. From the original Indigenous inhabitants to the European fur traders and salmon cannery owners and workers, the transcontinental railway, two world wars, and decades of boom and bust, Kaien Island has always been a rich multicultural trading hub that continues to weather countless storms. Now, with the third largest port in Canada, located at the end of both rail and road, Prince Rupert is finally realizing its potential to be a pot of gold at the end of a rainbow against the stunning backdrop of the remote wilderness of the Great Bear Rainforest.

Prince Rupert's story serves as a perfect example of how relentless optimism and tenacity can eventually ride the storm of bad luck and bad timing. Whatever the next chapter holds, we know the city's future will be built on its history: providing safe harbour for multicultural trade and exchange.

WHY I WROTE THIS BOOK

The stories we tell ourselves matter. For the last century, Prince Rupert's story has been one of unrealized potential: a grand destiny never quite able to be fulfilled.

Ever since the city's visionary and railway magnate Charles Hays perished on the ill-fated *Titanic* in 1912, it has been said that the hopes and dreams of Prince Rupert went down with him. But the claim that Prince Rupert is an orphan of Charles Hays ignores the entire

Indigenous history of the area and and many hundreds of years of multicultural exchange, both before and after the arrival of Europeans, that nurtured the community into what it is today.

Whether or not you believe in fate or destiny, the next chapter of Prince Rupert's story will undoubtedly be defined by the shared values that brought it this far: optimism, ambition, and resilience. The purpose of this book is to understand where Prince Rupert is coming from in order to articulate a vision of where the it may be going.

The future of Prince Rupert matters to me. I am a born-and-raised Rupertite, and my kids are the fourth generation of my family to call Prince Rupert home. After eight years serving on Prince Rupert's city council and more than a decade working for a local Indigenous Nation, I understand how our rich multicultural tapestry, close-knit culture of resiliency, and legacy of trade have defined this place since time immemorial. The seemingly random events and coincidences that have profoundly influenced the city's development make it difficult not to believe in fate and destiny. My only intent is to share with you the events, decisions, and people that have shaped the city that I know and love today, for good or for bad, in order to provide a guide on where it may be going next.

INTRODUCTION

UNWEAVING THE CITY OF RAINBOWS

Much as "colourful language" refers to something rude and offensive, a "colourful history" usually implies a dark dubious past. Prince Rupert's history is as defined by interesting and exciting things as it is by racism and prejudice. The story of this city is full of colourful characters, some amusing and extravagant, others morally reprehensible. There are those who undoubtedly contributed to progress while also having regressive and prejudiced attitudes. When I say that Prince Rupert has a colourful history, I am not trying to sanitize the past. Quite the opposite: my goal is to illuminate the complex series of events and people that have led us to today, without aiding and abetting the worship of icons or the formation of glossy pioneer narratives. In so doing, I hope to provide a pragmatic guide into tomorrow that lets us learn from both the successes and the mistakes of the past.

After Sir Isaac Newton first used the prism to reduce the rainbow to its individual colours, the poet John Keats apparently accused Newton of destroying the beauty of the rainbow. The evolutionary biologist Richard Dawkins eloquently makes the case in his book *Unweaving the Rainbow* that Newton's discovery actually was the key to unravelling a breathtaking and awe-inspiring poetry of complexity. Keats would probably have wanted us all to admire the City of Rainbows only for its natural beauty. But to be inspired like Newton and Dawkins means to dig deeper, discovering the hidden beauty in complexity by unweaving both the history and metaphor of the City of Rainbows.

R IS FOR RED AND RAIN

As the old saying goes, "no rain, no rainbow." This cliché is actually grounded in science. Humans can only see rainbows when there are water droplets in the air and sunlight shines through them at a low angle. Prince Rupert is the highest-ranked city in Canada for both the amount of annual rainfall and the greatest number of days with rain. Cities like Seattle, Vancouver, and London have earned popular reputations as "rain cities," but they are put to shame by

Prince Rupert, which receives twice as much as any of them on an annual basis. A newcomer in the early 1900s apparently said, "I was informed on arrival that it rained, on average, about fourteen months a year."[1] An American soldier who arrived during the Second World War remarked that "if it was not raining it had either just stopped or was about to begin."[2] And when future BC Premier Duff Pattullo first set foot on Kaien Island, he was told there were only two seasons on this part of the coast: the rainy season and August.

Prince Rupert is also the highest-ranked city in Canada for both the number of hours of cloud cover and least amount of sunlight. A South African family with a rare skin allergy to the sun chose to move to Prince Rupert because of the reliably cloudy skies.[3] This unique combination of rain and cloud makes Prince Rupert the absolute perfect environment in which to see rainbows. As the Hawaiian saying goes, "don't judge a day by its weather."

O IS FOR ORANGE AND OPENNESS

The Rainbow flag has come to represent the pride of the lesbian, gay, bisexual, transgender, and queer (LGBTQIA2S+) equal rights movements. In 2018, Prince Rupert became the first city in the country to adopt the RCMP Safe Spaces program[4] to support anyone experiencing anti-LGBTQIA2S+ hate crimes or discrimination. A local Prince Rupert Pride group hosts safe space events. And there is a rainbow bridge, rainbow bench, and rainbow staircase in town, painted with proceeds from the sale of RUP hats, which have a unique rainbow barcode design to promote the high school and middle school's gay–straight alliances. There is even a Pride Parade float in the annual local Seafest celebrations. While none of these individual initiatives prevent the bullying, name-calling, and harassment all-too-commonly faced by so many in the local LGBTQIA2S+ community, the progress and visibility in this small rural and northern community over the past few years stands in stark contrast to its neighbours.

Y IS FOR YELLOW AND THE POT O' GOLD

The old Celtic myth of the leprechaun who hides his gold at the end of the rainbow is sometimes told as a cautionary tale not to chase treasure that can never be found. For others, the idea of chasing rainbows suggests freedom to live life on one's own terms, with endless possibilities of finding or learning something worthwhile on the journey. Prince Rupert is the northernmost and farthest western terminus for Canadian National's North American railway. It is also the western endpoint of the Yellowhead Highway, quite literally the end of the line. There are countless stories of people who come to the city for a year and end up staying for forty, having found a place where they can be their genuine and authentic selves.

G IS FOR GREEN AND GATEWAY

In many traditional mythologies and cultures, the rainbow is a gateway between Heaven and Earth, between this life and the next, or between the past and present. The arch is a universal symbol of a portal. In Prince Rupert, the harbour serves as the direct ferry link to Haida Gwaii, Vancouver Island, and Alaska and is a stopping point for cruise ships from Washington, California, and Alaska. It is also the closest port in North America to the rapidly growing Asia-Pacific economies. Digby Island airport also connects Prince Rupert directly to Vancouver by air. Today, the railway and port are key to Prince Rupert's economy. Billions of dollars of goods—including but not limited to grain, coal, wood pellets, and logs—are shipped through the port every year. And as the Northwest Passage becomes increasingly accessible for shipping as polar ice melts, Prince Rupert is poised to become North America's Arctic trade gateway.

B IS FOR BLUE AND BEAUTIFUL

Prince Rupert is the only municipality in the Great Bear Rainforest, located between the Coastal Rocky Mountains and the North Pacific Ocean. Located in the heart of the temperate Pacific Coastal Rainforest, surrounded by estuary, fjords, steep peaks, lakes, streams, vigorous tides, and a well-protected shoreline, the stunning backdrop to Kaien Island is surrounded by tremendous natural biodiversity. The city is within the coastal temperate rainforest habitat of grizzly and black bears, eagles, ravens, wolves, orcas, dolphins, and humpbacks, and by an abundance of seafood, old-growth forests, and seemingly unlimited eco-tourism opportunities for the more than 180,000 tourists who travel to or through Kaien Island every year.

I IS FOR INDIGO AND INTERNATIONAL

It has been suggested that the rainbow flag was originally inspired by the 1960s peace demonstrations' Flag of the Human Race, which represented human diversity with red, white, brown, yellow, and black. Throughout history, the rainbow has been used as a symbol for peace and diversity: during the Protestant Reformation and the German Peasants' War in the sixteenth century, by Peruvian Indigenous Peoples in the eighteenth century and Sri Lankan Buddhists in the late 1800s, by the cooperative movement in the early 1900s, and against nuclear weapons in the 1960s. Prince Rupert is a microcosm of Canadian international diversity, with almost 40 percent of city residents identifying as Indigenous, including the Ts'msyen, Nisga'a, Gitxsan, Heiltsuk, Haisla, Haida, Métis, and more. Nearly 13 percent of the city's residents are first-generation immigrants, and another 17 percent are descended from immigrants from Vietnam, China, India, the Philippines, Portugal, Italy, and South Africa, and more.[5]

V IS FOR VIOLET AND VITALITY

The rainbow is an eternal symbol of calm after the storm. In most religions, the rainbow is a sign of promise for the future. Despite serious ups and downs, unrealized potential, false starts, and empty promises, the community of Prince Rupert has remained resilient. Years of weathering countless storms, both literal and figurative, have resulted in an adaptive and hopeful community. While the sense of optimism may be tempered by caution or skepticism, there is a liveliness, energy, and spirit that cannot be extinguished.

CHAPTER 1

TRADE, SINCE TIME IMMEMORIAL

"Long distance trade was a significant factor in the development and
sustaining of the cultural system in evidence at the Prince Rupert
Harbour site for over 2000 years before the coming of Europeans."

STEPHEN LANGDON

The study of history is basically the study of human civilization. Far
too often, the history of Canada's Pacific Northwest is told from
the perspective of the pioneer, who presents the region as a vast
unclaimed and unforgiving wilderness that was discovered and
tamed for settlement. Stories of adventures abound of enterprising men and women who escaped industrialized Europe to build
a new civilization in the pristine environment of North America's
wild west coast.

The history of Prince Rupert is no exception to this romantic
and selective re-telling of a seemingly wholesome tale. Outdated
or incomplete local histories brag of "thrilling tale[s] of hard work
and determined effort by rugged settlers,"[1] or claim that "the history of the north coast of BC is traced back to when the first [Euro-
pean] explorers were vying for control of the Pacific Coast of North
America."[2] Unfortunately, these pioneer accounts thoughtlessly place
thousands of years of Indigenous civilization into the fake category
of "pre-history," based on a flawed assumption that "real" history
somehow began with the arrival of Europeans to the western shores
of the North Pacific. As a result, Indigenous Peoples are far too often
treated as "an afterthought, or a tragic footnote, not significant players in their own right."[3]

This chapter is neither an ethnography nor anthropological history of the Ts'msyen Peoples. Instead, the purpose of this chapter is
twofold: first, to counter the erroneous claim that the history of Kaien
Island somehow only began in 1906 with the arrival of the Grand
Trunk Pacific townsite surveyors,[4] and second, to demonstrate that

the Ts'msyen were the first to create a hub for trade and exchange on Kaien Island, thousands of years before Europeans even knew that North America existed.

The deliberate failure of some history books to tell the full story ignores the experience of the Ts'msyen pre- and post-contact with Europeans. It also does a disservice to anyone who wants to understand the real details and complexities of what happened to allow a city to evolve out of the rainforest. Thousands of years before the earliest European explorers arrvied, the Ts'msyen and their neighbours inhabited the lands and waters surrounding Kaien Island in communities that pre-dated the "great dynasties of China and the blossoming civilization in Egypt, Babylon, India, Persia, Greece, Rome, Meso-America, and Peru by millennia" and not merely centuries.[5]

Without the thousands of years of deep connections between the Ts'msyen, their local ecosystem, and their neighbouring nations, the earliest Europeans would not have been anywhere near as profitable or successful in their ventures—and frankly may not have even survived. The keen trading abilities, natural resource management, and political alliances of the Ts'msyen were the bedrock for early European survival on the shores of the North Pacific Ocean.

LOCATION, LOCATION, LOCATION

Within the traditional territory of the Ts'msyen, Kaien Island has served as a common ground for millennia. The name Kaien translates from the local Sm'algyax language to "sea foam" or "foam on the waters," in direct reference to the unique reversing tidal rapids between the island and the mainland.[6]

Kaien Island is located just north of the mouth of the Skeena River, known by the Ts'msyen as Ksiyeen, which translates to "River of the Mist." Demonstrating the importance of the river to its original inhabitants, Ts'msyen translates as "people of the Skeena River" or "people inside the Skeena River." To the north of Kaien Island is the mouth of the Nass River, home to the Nisg̱a'a people. Slightly farther north is Southeast Alaska, home to the Tlingit. To the west is the archipelago of Haida Gwaii, home of the Haida. To the south are the territories of the Haisla and Heiltsuk. And in the Interior, numerous Nations inhabit vast and diverse lands. Wedged between two critical rivers and numerous cultures, Kaien Island is blessed with a unique geography and ethnography. Dominated by the Coast Mountains, it has some of the heaviest and most consistent rainfall on the entire continent, combined with high cloud cover. Over half the landscape is boggy muskeg,[7] which not only forms a significant part of the landscape, but the archaeological record as well.

ARCHAEOLOGY AND ADAWX

Archaeology is the study of ancient history through excavation and artifacts. The adawx (pronounced a'DOW-ach and translated literally as "truth telling") are the ancient Ts'msyen oral narratives and stories.[8] Passed from each generation to the next, adawx "collectively represent the authorized history of the nation."[9] I am not Ts'msyen, so I do not possess the cultural knowledge to interpret or use the stories. Therefore, any references to the adawx in this book will only be from authoritative sources. Archaeological methods and oral records are separate and distinct, but when woven together they have served an important function in revealing the earliest history surrounding Kaien Island.

The Prince Rupert Harbour has been described as an "extraordinarily rich archaeological record"[10] and a "flagship region in Northwest Coast prehistory with resonance across the archaeological world."[11] According to archaeological evidence, the Ts'msyen established ties to specific places about 8,000 years ago,[12] although recent work in the nearby Dundas Islands has extended that to 10,000 years.[13] Nearby salmon runs appeared by the early Holocene period,[14] and large-scale shellfish harvests by humans began around 7,000 to 8,000 years ago.[15] Gigantic shell middens (old dump sites) began accumulating in the Prince Rupert Harbour area approximately 5,000 years ago. Sixteen sites have been found with shell middens larger than two football fields in size, instead of one massive thirty-three-acre site.[16] These initial shell deposits helped create the ideal dry, well-drained locations that the Ts'msyen would return to over thousands of years.[17]

Analysis of obsidian imported from the Stikine River demonstrates that by 6000 BCE, "maritime life ways were well-established . . . and that long-distance trade was a feature of the cultural system operating at that time."[18] One of the most important archaeological sites in the Prince Rupert Harbour is the so-called Warrior's Cache, which demonstrates the occurrence of long-distance trade with "copper from Alaska, dentalium shells from the southern Northwest Coast, sea otter teeth from Haida Gwaii, obsidian from the Interior, and amber from Russia."[19] According to anthropologist Steve J. Langdon, "long distance trade was a significant factor in the development and sustaining of the cultural system in evidence at the Prince Rupert Harbour site for over 2,000 years before the coming of Europeans."[20]

The adawx undergirds the deep links between the Ts'msyen and what is now called the Prince Rupert Harbour, and shows that the historical connection is more profound than the adjacent environmental resources.[21] Generations of Ts'msyen continued to return to specific areas for important reasons other than food. Of the thousands of petroglyphs in the vicinity of modern-day Prince Rupert, two seem to mark the centre of the Ts'msyen world. They are within fifty metres of one another in the Metlakatla Pass and both depict the Raven. According to local Gitksan and Ts'msyen leader Art Sterritt, they represent "the primordial Raven as he first manifested himself as a raven with white feathers. After stealing the sun from the treasure box of the chief of the skies, Raven flew through the smoke hole of the house with the sun in his beak. He was turned black by the smoke and remains so today."[22]

Today's Prince Rupert Harbour was once the site of at least sixty-six known villages.[23] While there is contention around the exact timing, we know that between 3500 and 1500 BP (or around 1550–450 BCE), the populations of small and dispersed families grew. Houses became larger. The emergence of stone wood-working tools and knives gave rise to more evidence of plank houses,[24] which reflected long-term, multi-generational investment in particular locations.[25] These houses served as the foundation of social and economic organization by acting not just as protection against the elements, but also as storage for surplus wealth and markers of status and rank to outsiders.[26]

Early anthropologists initially labelled the Ts'msyen as hunter-gatherers. While they were undoubtedly experts at both, the term diminishes the profound complexity of Ts'msyen civilization. Not until relatively recently did archaeologists and anthropologists recognize that the Ts'msyen society prior to European contact exhibited many traits of the so-called agriculturalist society, including a high degree of economic specialization,[27] sedentism, food storage, plant cultivation, and highly specialized activities like controlled brush burns to encourage berry growth and entice deer.[28]

As early as 1050 BCE, the Ts'msyen practiced resource intensification, surplus production, and large-scale salmon storage on the Skeena River. The tools they used to catch, process, dry, smoke, and store fish demonstrate at least 3,000 years of processing large quantities of salmon. Some sources estimate the average Ts'msyen person in the area consumed 250 kilograms of salmon per year, equivalent to fifty to eighty salmon per person per year.[29] Beyond the natural abundance of salmon was the Ts'msyen Peoples' ability to leverage "extreme salmon specialization" into the development of permanent villages and system of exchange, with salmon becoming a form of pseudo-currency.[30] Any one of the five local species of salmon could be eaten fresh, raw, cooked, smoked on different types of woods for different lengths of time, or dried for varying periods to produce a variety of textures. Certain parts could even be boiled or fermented.[31] Some analysts have concluded that "salmon appears to have been more important in Prince Rupert Harbour than anywhere else on the coast,"[32] and that it should therefore be considered as essential to the Ts'msyen as the bison to the Plains Peoples or maize to Meso-Americans.[33]

Over time, the Ts'msyen's extensive harvests and processing and storage techniques resulted in such a surplus as to allow the strategic deployment of labour for other specializations such as carving, painting, singing, dancing, healing, hunting, fishing, and weaving. Each of these specialties required its own tools and materials—such as ropes, nets, baskets, mats, traps, masks, rattles, and regalia, to name just a few—which could then be bartered.[34]

The economic systems of the Ts'msyen and their neighbours in the region had a universally understood exchange rate and modes for different foodstuffs, materials, finished products, and services, "demonstrating characteristics of economic development not found in most other pre-capitalist economies lacking money."[35] More than half of household production was not used within the household, but put into distribution or trade.[36]

Unlike in European cultures, wealth in Ts'msyen culture was not for individual accumulation but for communal distribution. To the outside world, the culture of feasting, or the Potlatch as it is sometimes referred to, is the best-known and least-understood institutions of Ts'msyen society. Compared to the common settler-colonial notion of a feast as simply a big group meal, the feast is extraordinarily sophisticated in its rules, duties, and obligations, and was one of the central organizing principles of the Ts'msyen economy. In the absence of currency, the feast served as a universally understood cycle of reciprocity, which, in the words of Langdon, "permeated every aspect of Coast Ts'msyen society beginning with the naming of a child through the raising of a memorial pole after death."[37]

By approximately 350 CE, Ts'msyen society had advanced from hunter-gatherer survivalist egalitarianism. A ranked village had emerged at McNichol Creek, directly across the water from what is today downtown Prince Rupert, evidenced by the largest dwelling in the cluster of fifteen being double the size of the rest and having "a central hearth... a partially clay-lined floor and sea mammal remains... these attributes were only found in [that] house... this had been a chief's (or lineage head's) house."[38] Then, for a period of nearly 100 to 200 years, nearly all village sites in and around the Prince Rupert Harbour were abruptly abandoned, with only a handful of exceptions. A study of skeletons showed a violent era with 40 percent of adults sustaining fractures to the forearm, face, and skull; at least 60 percent of those fractures could be attributed to interpersonal violence.[39] Archaeologists can clearly demarcate a period of increased conflicts, site abandonment, and reoccupation.[40] Owing to the boggy muskeg environment, however, the Prince Rupert Harbour's archaeological record has been described as fauna-rich but artifact-poor.[41] As a result, many scientific methods and their corresponding conclusions are subject to fragmentation and subjectivity. Archaeology alone could not provide an explanation for such violence.

WAR WITH THE TLINGIT

There is an explanation that archaeology could not provide that the Ts'msyen adawx can. The Tlingit from Southeast Alaska invaded the Dundas Islands, Tuck Inlet, Stephens Island, and Work Channel.[42] Initially, they forced the various Ts'msyen tribes to retreat from many of their primary coastal occupations and into defensive sites up the Skeena River. The adawx records a Tlingit Chief conducting a series of raids on the Prince Rupert Harbour area from a fortification on Dundas Island.[43]

The unintended consequence of the Tlingit incursion into Ts'msyen territory was the formation of what later became known as the Nine Allied Tribes, which comprises the Giluts'aaw, Ginadoiks, Ginaxangiik,

Gispaxlo'ots, Gitando, Gitlaan, Gits'iis, Gitwilgyoots, and Gitzaxłaał.[44] Having moved up the Skeena River, "ancient clan bonds were rekindled as they rejoined their distant relatives. It is generally believed that the Nine Tribes' control and consolidation of their tributary watershed territories on the Lower Skeena were cemented during this period."[45]

According to the works of Charles Barbeau, considered a founder of Canadian anthropology, and William Beynon, a Ts'msyen Hereditary Chief and ethnographer, an incredibly decisive battle with the Tlingit took place on Kaien Island. One analysis claims this was "probably the most important shift in territorial control and ownership in the history of the Nine Tribes."[46]

The battle was initiated by a well thought-out and advanced tactical plan that involved luring the Tlingit warriors into a trap. A longhouse was built with a trapdoor to crush intruders and a platform in the rafters to hide men and spears. Inside, rotted logs were laid out under cedar mats as "sleeping" decoys and kelp was hung to imitate the sound of snoring. Outside, there were watchmen in the trees. As an early alert system, the tree branches were strung with caribou hooves that would rattle when disturbed and the ground around the fort was sprinkled with shells. After the lured Tlingit warriors entered the Kaien Island longhouse and mistakenly got their knives and spears stuck in rotted wood, the trapdoor was released, crushing several of the men. Arrows and spears were launched from the rafters. The ensuing panic and confusion among the Tlingit resulted in lost weapons and the accidental stabbing of their own men. The few who managed to escape were chased down, killed, or captured before they could reach their fortifications on Dundas Island.[47]

The Ts'msyen war leader Aksk and his eldest son Wi'hoxm "then organized all the Tribes into an alliance against the remaining Tlingit in the area. The ten[48] chiefs agreed and they lay siege to [the] fort on Dundas Island. They quickly defeated the Tlingit as there were very few of their fighting forces left."[49] The collective Ts'msyen triumph on Kaien Island and Dundas Island forced the Tlingit to retreat northward.[50] They would return to the harbour in the future, but in peace. The joint Ts'msyen defence of the Skeena against the Tlingit clearly enhanced the bonds between tribes, and marked a new period of integration and cooperation in Ts'msyen society.[51] With restored freedom and territorial independence, the Nine Allied Tribes established permanent settlements and a "new geopolitical core" at Metlakatla Pass.[52]

The wartime alliance not only forced the invaders back to where they came from but fostered a deeper political and socio-economic partnership that would profoundly change the complexion of the North Pacific Coast. Upon re-establishing their presence in Metlakatla Pass, at least nineteen villages were located within eyesight of one another, with smaller travel distances between them, demonstrating a higher degree of interconnectedness and social cohesion.[53] Beyond the enhanced defensive capabilities of such a strategic arrangement, the tighter grouping of villages allowed larger groups of people to travel together to harvest resources and over-winter.[54] Most importantly, with a greatly extended regional alliance, the Ts'msyen were able to dramatically expand their socio-economic trade networks across a much wider geography.[55]

GREASE TRAILS

While the physical wealth of the landscape contributed to Ts'msyen prosperity and defence, the economic and social outcomes generated through their new political alliances and kinship ties generated much more profound wealth through extensive trade.[56] Trade would ensure food security over an unforgiving winter, especially when certain seasonal resources experienced variability, and would provide a strong incentive to avoid hostilities; as populations grew, it was more efficient to redistribute surplus food than to go on raids. As trade networks grew deeper and longer, the effective carrying capacity of the entire region was increased. These well-utilized trade networks became known as the Grease Trails, named after the oolichan, one of the few predominant winter food sources and "one of the greatest natural sources of protein anywhere in North America."[57]

However, trade went far beyond the sharing of food for survival. Trade enabled the creation of more sophisticated tools, household goods, and hunting supplies. Exchange across longer distances could ensure certain items not available locally could be processed or have added value. And certain items had spiritual or ceremonial attributes or prestige attached, such as copper or regalia.[58] Trade advanced beyond subsistence to community-building.

Operating on a relay system on trails through challenging mountain terrain, cedar rope tumplines attached to headbands allowed the Ts'msyen to backpack heavy boxes of oolichan grease and other goods to trade in the Interior. Imported goods included "dentalium shell from Vancouver Island used in personal adornment, amber and jet from the interior used for beads, argillite from the Queen Charlotte Islands [Haida Gwaii] used for labrets... cold annealed native copper from Alaska, jade and greenstone for adze blades from tribes further south." Archeological remnants of these trade goods date back to the first millennium BCE and can be traced back hundreds of kilometres away in every direction.[59]

By 200 CE, between 6,000 and 8,000 Ts'msyen lived around the Kaien Island area in about eighteen villages.[60] Archaeologists have documented a pattern from this time, in which a rise in the trade of goods in sites paralleled lower incidences of warfare.[61] While violence was still an all-too-common occurrence across the globe at the time, numerous excavations in the Prince Rupert Harbour area collected over 18,000 non-weapon artifacts while only thirteen clubs were found.[62] Through extensive trade and political alliances, underpinned by a rich natural ecosystem, the Ts'msyen and their neighbours were able to spread their language, food, fashion, art, and technologies across thousands of kilometres in every direction.[63]

Prior to European contact, the Northwest Coast was one of the most linguistically diverse areas of North America, with at least sixteen different languages once spoken in the region.[64] Each community, from the Ts'msyen to the Nisga'a, Haida, Tlingit, Heiltsuk and more, has kept their own customs, beliefs, and taboos. Each has placed emphasis on different resources and places. And each responded to the arrival of newcomers in their own way. Generations of people within the different communities are not just related culturally, but genetically as well, thanks to sustained interconnectivity within what has been called the "North Coast Interaction Sphere."[65]

HOUSE AND HOME

Beyond the tangible benefits of trade, the increased intercultural exchange became crucial to ranked social organization, territorial ownership, and governance in Ts'msyen society.[66] Similar to the house-based societies of feudal Japan and medieval Europe, the Ts'msyen economy was comparable in that people organized themselves around a wider shared estate designed to outlast the lifespan of its inhabitants.[67] Economic activities were structured around house-owned territories and resources, and there was a universally understood social hierarchy.[68] In the Wa'ap, or house, all members of an individual house belong to one of four Clans: Laxsgiik (Eagle), Ganhada (Raven), Gisbutwada (Killer Whale), or Laxgibuu (Wolf). As Ts'msyen society is matrilineal, everyone is born into the Clan of their mother.[69] The Wa'ap is the core political and socioeconomic structure and is synonymous with both a physical dwelling and its inhabitants.[70] It is a shared identity, a social system, and what ties Ts'msyen groups to specific places, people, and stories.[71]

Ts'msyen law has a lot of the same characteristics as land title in the modern North American system: the right to exclude others, to use and allocate resources, to use title as compensation, or to share resources. As Langdon explains, "the Coast Ts'msyen economy is the most complex of any foraging population presently known in terms of the property rights institutions, which extend in certain nonmaterial areas well beyond property rights concepts and enforcement practices utilized in modern market economies."[72]

The feast system originally functioned as the "equivalent of Parliament, courthouse, land title office, banking and insurance systems."[73] In the feast hall, Chiefs exercised their authority and rank, not as individuals but imbued through their collective lineage. Through the process of feasting, claims and disagreements were settled and names and honours were bestowed. Ultimately, for a House to be successful, it must have been able to generate a sufficient surplus of resources to host a feast and provide numerous gifts to everyone in attendance, which would be converted into prestige.[74] The feast system still exists today and generally serves the same purpose, although it has evolved as a result of much Traditional Knowledge being lost with the passing of Elders and Knowledge Keepers as well as money being exchanged in place of other traditional goods.

The feasting culture of the Ts'msyen serves as a metaphor for their broader worldview and relationship with the natural world. The feast is a way to celebrate, a means to share, and a reflection of reciprocity. Amazingly, the archaeological record of the Prince Rupert Harbour does not seem to show any evidence of starvation periods, and some historians suggest that the feast culture may have role to play in this, as surplus food and other useful goods were continually redistributed throughout the communities. It is difficult not to draw a connection between this act of communal sharing and the spirit by which the

Ts'msyen managed their relationship with the natural environment. They coordinated themselves so harvests occurred according to the seasonal cycles of the lands and sea; their very survival was dependent on the health of their ecosystem.

The term "hunter-gatherer" is far too simplistic to describe the Ts'msyen. It diminishes their lived experience of building a stable, socially complex, artistically, culturally, and economically enriching society over thousands of years.[75] Some historians describe Ts'msyen society as the "epitome of the development of the hunter-gatherer-fisher,"[76] given the social and political complexity of the civilization that emerged around the Prince Rupert Harbour long before Europeans even knew it existed. When the first Europeans arrived in Ts'msyen territory in the late 1700s, they would unknowingly be entering a highly developed confederacy of independently wealthy communities. With approximately 10,000 Sm'algyax-speaking people, the Prince Rupert Harbour was one of the most densely occupied pre-European landscapes in North America. Bonded through shared natural resources, extensive trade, and political alliances, with the foundational cultural building blocks having been in place for thousands of years, the experience of the Ts'msyen cannot simply be written off as "pre-history."

The Ts'msyen relationship with trade is ancient. As noted earlier, a huge variety of goods was exchanged, sometimes across vast distances, in a complex system that involved sophisticated formal protocols, degrees of economic and artistic specialization, mediums of exchange resembling a form of currency, and regularly scheduled seasonality—all hallmarks of Ts'msyen trading society.[77] The sheer scale of trade occurring on and around Kaien Island prior to European contact was immense, whether that trade was measured in the number of items exchanged, the frequency, the wide range of goods produced, or the number of people and amount of time, energy, and resources required to produce and transport goods across hundreds of kilometers. Clearly, trade played a central and essential role in the Ts'msyen economy, culture, and way of life.

_eᴄ᙭ʙˀ_

Kaien Island did not become a multicultural trading hub as a result of European arrival. The Grease Trails were arguably as important to

Northern BC as the Silk Road was to China in its ability to connect different cultures over large distances. Landgon explains that trade was "essential to the functioning of Coast Ts'msyen society and that without it the fundamental and integral character of the society would have been different."[78] As a result, Kaien Island became an epicentre for trade on the Pacific Northwest Coast, with an "extensive trading system [that] had been in place since before the start of the Christian era."[79] Contrary to the incomplete pioneer histories of the area, it was the Ts'msyen and their neighbours who first utilized Kaien Island as a hub for trade and exchange.

CHAPTER 2

INTERNATIONAL EXCHANGE

1770–1830

> "[The North Pacific fur trade is] perhaps
> the most profitable and lucrative employ that the
> enterprising merchant can possibly engage in."
> CAPTAINS NATHANIEL PORTLOCK
> AND GEORGE DIXON, C. 1785–88

Unlike the stereotypical pioneer recounting of the settlement of Prince Rupert, the history of Kaien Island's development did not begin with the city's incorporation in 1910. Thanks to stable cultural systems of exchange built over thousands of years, the Ts'msyen and earliest European explorers and fur traders could exchange goods on their own terms, ultimately creating an international trading empire.

THE EARLIEST EUROPEAN EXPLORERS (1770–90)

In 1513, the Spanish were the first Europeans to lay claim to the Pacific Northwest Coast. Despite never having reached the area, and without fully realizing the ocean's expanse, the Spanish explorer Vasco Nunez de Balboa saw the Pacific near present-day Panama and claimed all the lands adjoining this "newly found" ocean for the Spanish crown. Over the next two hundred years, the territory of "New Spain" expanded as far north as the present-day Oregon–California border. Unbeknownst to all of the colonial powers at the time, this earliest claim by the Spanish set into motion a series of events that ultimately decided which European power would claim Kaien Island.

Russian expansion into Alaska in the 1700s forced the Spanish to push further.[1] In 1741, Vitus Bering's crew proved the separation of the Russian and American continents and also confirmed a sizeable sea otter population, instigating Siberian expansion eastward. In response, Spanish explorers were commanded to investigate Russian

encroachments and reassert the Spanish claim to the Pacific Northwest. They were given orders to treat all Indigenous people with
respect and to establish friendly trading relations with any they
encountered: "the natural inhabitants are to be treated affectionately,
with dignity and respect, and avoid conflict at all times."[2] The Span-
iards had obviously been forced to learn from previous colonization
attempts in South America that maintaining a friendship with the
Indigenous population was crucial.[3]

Between 1774 and 1779, numerous Spanish explorers set sail along
what is now the coast of British Columbia and Alaska, reaching as
far north as present-day Anchorage. However, they did not make
contact with Kaien Island and the Ts'msyen as all their ships sailed
from the west coast of Vancouver Island to the west coast of Haida
Gwaii without making landfall.[4]

Upon confirming an expanding Russian presence in Alaska, the
Spanish crews departed again after burying bottles with official doc-
uments along the coast, which at the time was still regarded as an
important way of asserting formal possession of an area under the
rights of so-called first discovery. Without traders or missionaries in
the region, the Spanish assertion was mostly ceremonial in nature.
In the eyes of the Spanish Crown, they had established the right to
colonize the entire Pacific coast. So in 1780, King Charles III of Spain
gave orders to prevent the Russian, British, and American ships in
the area from enjoying commerce with the Indigenous population.[5]
This would prove to be the trigger of an international dispute that
forever altered the European trajectory in the region.

With aggressive Russian expansion southward from Alaska and
Spain pushing northward from California, the major global maritime
power of Great Britain felt compelled to respond. In an attempt to avoid
being cut out of the prized sea otter trade, and still convinced of the
existence of a Northwest Passage, the British Admiralty turned to Captain James Cook. Their hope was two-fold: find the western end of the
Northwest Passage and establish a British presence on the North Pacific
coast. Cook's 1778 voyage marked a turning point in the economic and
social history of the region by opening up the Pacific Northwest to
British traders eager to participate in the sea otter trade.[6] While Cook
soon met his end on the voyage south in Hawaii, his crew found a
market in China for the few Indigenous items they had traded for. The
Chinese also paid extremely well for sea otter skins. By 1787, after the

journals of Cook's voyage were published, there were five British ships and six American ships operating along the Pacific Northwest coast.[7]

Under these conditions of competition between the Russians, Spanish, British, and Americans, what is widely regarded as the first European contact with the Ts'msyen occurred. A British captain named James Colnett, having previously served under Cook, was tasked with leading a private fur trading expedition in 1787. Sailing through the Hecate Strait and Dixon Entrance just south of the mouth of the Skeena River, Colnett and his crew encountered the Gitxaała only a few miles from their present-day village site. The Chief Seks welcomed the British in full regalia and invited them to a feast, where Colnett and his ship's officers were given honorary names as a means to formalize an alliance.[8] Colnett correctly concluded, based on a Nuu-chah-nulth engraved brass weapon in the Chief's possession, that there were already pre-existing Indigenous trade networks that were extending European artifacts northward well ahead of direct contact.[9]

At first, the large British ships were thought to be monsters, while the British crew, with their pale white skin, were viewed by the Gitxaała to be visiting supernatural spirits called "ghost people." However, this first impression did not last long after the two peoples shared a meal of rice, molasses, and bread.

According to the Gitxaała adawx, as told by matriarch Dorothy Brown, a Chief was making a fire on the beach:

da sa uks'niitsga gyet	the man suddenly looked out to sea
da gyaaks	way out on the ocean
naa la gyebn hagwilo'ga	a sea monster was rising out of the water
litxas waal ligigoo da nlax'oot	something was on its surface, on the top of it
Dawil luwanwantga gagoots dipgwa'a	They were worried
ada wil tkidawl ligigoo	when something was coming down from it
ada wil'niis dipgwa'a la wil logomk'ola gyet	when they saw that people were disembarking
ada wila bagayt ndeh dza wila huut	they looked for a place to escape

Ada wilt gididoxda
    K'mksiwah gwa'a
wilt hi'waada K'mksiwah
    Gitkaala
a siwaatgadil Tgwilaxgiilaxs

Ada wil gididoxs dipgwa'a
ada wil'nii goo wila waalt
Ada wila dii silaksis dipgwa'a

sm halguuyda 'wii halo'opxat

ada wil sagwaalga lak

...

Ada 'nii wil lik'adawl
    galmt'uu'tsk lax lak
ada lik'adawla dzamt
ada wil gwaanksa gwii
Ada wilt gingiins dipgwa'a
amawandit
lut'ilt'aaldida miyuupdida
    wil dm int txooxt
ada wil'ligats'gadza
    siwaatgadil biloos
Deya dipgwa'a
"K'a ksda gool waal dm gabas
    dipgwa'a"
ada wila hawsga 'yuutaga'a
"Saaban, wayei! Luunksm
    xsaan gwa'a"
deya ga'a
"Ada lat 'lig'ats'gadza lo'kagyet"

...

And then these white people
    caught up to them
the white people found the
    Gitxaala
at the place they call
    Tgwilaxgiilaxs
and when they caught up
they watched what they did
And then these people made
    a fire
they struck hard along the
    side of a large scraper
and the fire began to burn

...

And they put a black pot right
    into the fire
they put it into the fire to boil
and then it cooked
And they gave them food
they had them sit down
they served rice for them
    to eat
and poured over it what they
    call molasses
They said
"what food these people eat"

and one of the men said
"Saaban, wayei! These are
    dried maggots"
he said
"And they have poured the rot
    of people over it"

...

"A dm gabm" deya ga'a
 ada wil waals dipgwa'a
 txooxgat
 Gawdi gwii la leexgat
 ada wil gingiinda dipgwa'a
  da biscuit
 anaay gingiint
 Ada gik haws Saaban
 "Lat gingiinmda kabaa'lx"
  deya
 ada wil doxt dii dipgwa'a
 Ada wil gik goydiksa
  siwaatgadil hayooks'ontk
  'wiit'aa nika'nuunk
 ada wil hawsga captain ga'a
 ksgooxdida la 'ni'niit
  sm'oogits dipgwa'a waadas
  Saaban
 "Here" deyagu gwasga'a "Soap"
 Dawilt haws Saaban
 "K'amayt wilaay'anu
  K'mksiwaht" haw
 "K'amayt sahuutga na waayu"
  deya ga'a[10]

"Let's eat it" he said
 and this is what they did
 they ate
 When they were calm again
 they gave them biscuits to eat

 they gave them bread to eat
 And Saaban spoke again
 "They have given us ghost
  bread" he said
 and they took this also
 and they brought something
  else they call 'for washing
  hands'
 and the captain said
 to the leader, the one who
  was chief named Saaban

 "Here" he said, "Soap"
 Then Saaban said
 "already the white man knows
  me" he said
 "already he has announced
  my name" he said[11]

The same interaction as told by James Lewis of Gitxaała further explains that once Sabaan understood that the ghost people meant no harm, he led them to the village, where they were introduced to Chief Ts'ibasaa. Many Gitxaała were invited to board their canoes and follow the ghost people "to the huge monster, which had now folded its wings. When the Gitkaxaala [*sic*] arrived, they climbed aboard this monster, the abode of the ghost people."[12] After the chief of the ghost people gave presents of guns and ammunition to Ts'ibasaa, he hosted a feast in their honour, formally marking the first time Europeans and Ts'msyen exchanged cultures by giving names.

Although Colnett seems to have viewed the ceremony as nothing more than a trading encounter, for the Ts'msyen, trade and politics are inextricably linked.[13] The British ship spent two months in the area making major repairs, but unfortunately made little attempt to understand Ts'msyen law. Their attitude rested on their perceived cultural superiority over those who they viewed as "primitive savages." By picking berries, cutting down trees, and fishing salmon without permission or compensation, the Europeans were considered thieves by the Gitxaała's interpretation of property and theft. In response, the Gitxaała began taking small items from the British ship as compensation. Colnett's crew retaliated by launching an attack on the Gitxaała, killing multiple people and capturing a young woman. In his journal, Colnett recognized that if they had wanted to, the Gitxaała could easily have attacked and destroyed the British ship and even admits that they "would have been justified in doing so, as the British had fired on [them] first."[14] Thus began a new era of international relationships, rife with cultural dissonance and miscommunication.

INTERNATIONAL COMPETITION

There was some poetic justice when on Colnett's next voyage, his ship was seized and he was arrested by Spanish forces at Nootka Sound on Vancouver Island. The Spanish had previously received instructions to assert their sovereignty by preventing British commerce with Indigenous Peoples on the coast. When they discovered Colnett's ship was carrying a group of Chinese labourers and supplies intended for the construction of a settlement, the Spanish declared Colnett and his crew prisoners of war. While being escorted south to New Spain [California], the news of the arrest reached Europe, at which point "what had once seemed a minor incident... had now escalated into an international crisis."[15]

Known as the Nootka Crisis, the British parliament voted for war against Spain.[16] Spain launched an ill-timed appeal for naval support to their ally, France, just as the French Revolution was beginning. Without help, the Spanish chose to negotiate and reached a provisional, albeit slightly ambiguous, deal in 1790. The immediate crisis was averted by allowing the British to conduct commerce anywhere except within ten leagues of a Spanish settlement. However, the competition for other parts of the northwest coast remained undecided.[17] The main outcome from the Nootka Crisis was that, after 1790, the European understanding of sovereignty became a matter of occupancy rather than prior discovery. In essence, the British had forced the Spanish to allow the settlement of unpopulated areas of the Pacific Northwest without dispute. This was a principle which would become very important later after the United States took over New Spain and when the British and Americans would later fight over Oregon.[18] It would also have implications for the future of Kaien Island.

GEORGE VANCOUVER

Mired in conflict with the Spanish, the British Admiralty promoted a young George Vancouver with a three-pronged mission in 1791: negotiate additional treaty terms with the Spanish to settle claims to the Pacific Northwest coast; complete the coastal survey begun by his mentor, Captain James Cook; and search for openings for the Northwest Passage.[19]

Having previously served on two of Cook's expedition, Vancouver knew from British fur traders that Cook's map of the area north of 60 latitude was inaccurate since he had only sailed to the western side of Haida Gwaii and thus had failed to examine hundreds of kilometres of shoreline on the inner coast. As a result, there was still hope that any one of the missed inlets might lead all the way to the Arctic Ocean and provide the long sought-after short route to Britain.[20]

After Vancouver resolved the outstanding issues with the Spanish, he and his crew mapped the coast from Queen Charlotte Sound, going north into southeast Alaska. They utilized charts from Captain Colnett's earlier voyage, during which he had made first contact with the Ts'msyen. Despite Vancouver's reputation for careful and painstaking examination of the coastline, he and his crew were fooled by the presence of rocks and sandbars at the mouth of the Skeena and Nass Rivers. According to the ship's journals, the rivers "are the only two streams that had yet been discovered to the north of the river Columbia. These are too insignificant to be dignified by the name of rivers."[21] Unbeknownst to Vancouver, each river was hundreds of kilometres long and connected to thousands of square kilometres of tributaries and lakes, which had made Indigenous canoe travel deep into the Interior possible.[22]

One of Vancouver's survey vessels allegedly sailed through Metlakatla Pass in 1793 but reported that the villages around the inlet were deserted because the bark roofs of the houses had been removed. In reality, the roofs had temporarily been taken by the Ts'msyen to their other seasonal salmon encampments on the Skeena. Despite his horrible misjudgement of two of the Pacific Northwest's greatest rivers, Vancouver was the first to be able to state with certainty that no continental passage existed through the North. He also left an imperial stamp on the area by assigning nearly four hundred place names on printed maps, erasing many of the place names that the local people had used for centuries. As a result, his maps failed to show any of the numerous villages along the coast and completely neglected the harbour of Kaien Island, mistakenly showing the Ts'msyen peninsula extending across the mouth of the channel.[23] This mistake would be reprinted hundreds of times for nearly another century, leaving Kaien Island and its inner harbour protected from European incursion for a little while longer than the rest of the region.

BURGEONING FUR TRADE

By the time the details of Captain Vancouver's voyages were published in 1798, over twenty British and American vessels were plying the coast in search of lucrative trading opportunities. Three initial trading harbours were used at Big Bay, Tugwell Island, and Venn Passage, all within twenty kilometres of Kaien Island.[24] As the Ts'msyen grew accustomed to the presence of the Europeans, their skillful trading earned them a positive reputation. A former crewman of Captain Cook said that "they are very keen traders getting as much as they could for everything they had; always asking for more giving them what you would."[25]

Based on multiple encounters documented in ship logs, it was a seller's market. Ts'msyen traders knew if their asking prices were rejected, there would be another trading ship along soon willing to pay.[26] Having quickly learned that the Spanish, English, Russians, and Americans were competing with each other, they played groups off one another, holding onto furs and other goods to encourage competition until they could obtain the highest possible price.[27] They knew the Russians as the "Loosens," the Americans as "Boston Men" because so many of them came from the city, and the British traders as "King George Men."[28]

Thanks to their shrewd negotiating tactics, the Ts'msyen saw the price of fur quadruple. In a single month, Captain George Dixon obtained nearly 2,000 furs, which he subsequently sold for $54,875 in China (approximately $1.74 million in 2024 dollars). British captains Nathaniel Portlock and George Dixon wrote that the "inestimable value" of the fur trade on the Pacific Northwest Coast is "perhaps the most profitable and lucrative employ that the enterprising merchant can possibly engage in."[29]

Both the Ts'msyen and Europeans came from material and trade-oriented cultures, and they quickly discovered this common ground. The language of trade was understood easily across languages and formed the foundation for relationships. The exchanges were initially curiosities such as ornamentation, but soon the Coast Ts'msyen were utilizing European imports within the context of their own economies and culture, saving up trade goods and bartering for iron tools and other items that had pre-existing purposes in their society.[30]

Throughout these early days of international trade, the Ts'msyen proved themselves as intelligent traders, capable of driving a hard bargain and not the passive objects of exploitation that some might try to portray them as. The confidence with which they asserted their demands demonstrated the power dynamic between them and the Europeans at the time. By making a concerted effort, the Ts'msyen and their neighbours could have easily destroyed any of the visiting vessels, and the Europeans recognized this fact numerous times in their journals. Far from being victims, the Ts'msyen met the competitive international maritime fur trade and molded it to serve their own ends,[31] using their newfound surplus wealth to intensify their political capacity, status, and power through their feasting systems.[32]

BOUNDARY DISPUTES

In 1799, as more Spanish, American, and British ships began to arrive in larger numbers, the Russian Tsar, Paul I, asserted sovereignty over the Alaskan domain down to the 55th parallel, near the mouth of the Nass River. Even though it was still missing on all European maps at that time, Kaien Island was suddenly caught between disputes over the "ownership" of the Northwest Coast by four empires: the Russians southward from Alaska, the Spanish northward from New Spain (California), and the British and Americans wrestling for control of Oregon. All parties used the same argument of prior exploration to justify their claims. After another twenty years of competition, the Russia, under Tsar Alexander I, attempted to assert their domain even further to the 45th parallel (present-day Oregon) in 1821, issuing an edict that all foreign ships were forbidden to come within one hundred miles.[33]

Unsurprisingly, both Great Britain and the United States mounted immediate challenges. At that time, Captain Vancouver's erroneous charts were the only geographical source of information for the area.[34] The resulting Russo–American Treaty of 1824 set a border by demarcating a line along the Portland Channel near the mouth of the Nass River, with a boundary that followed the summits of the mountains parallel to the coast. Although the treaty provided more formal boundaries and temporarily reduced tensions, the vague language would later profoundly influence the chosen location for the future city of Prince Rupert. By 1825, Britain was the only European claimant to Kaien Island, sandwiched between American Oregon and the Russo–Alaskan panhandle. While Vancouver's cartography had missed Kaien Island, the Skeena River, and the Nass River altogether, without his charts, "it is conceivable that the northern boundary of Oregon might have been fixed at 54-40 North, and Canada would have no Pacific shores."[35]

Despite the European disturbance to their traditional ways of being, the Ts'msyen were resilient in absorbing the changes brought by the early Europeans. Trading relationships were mutually beneficial. New products and trade goods were introduced as sources of wealth and prestige. But the sporadic contact with explorers and fur traders had did not dramatically change the Ts'msyen way of life.[36] At this point, the most important development was the British formalization of international borders to the area, which would have major implications for Prince Rupert's birthplace. Unfortunately, the most radical change to the Ts'msyen was still to come with the establishment of the first permanent European settlement on the shores of the North Pacific.

CHAPTER 3

FORT SIMPSON

1836–61

"Fort Simpson was a very busy place; not only
as a a centre of trade but also as a vibrant
and often confusing social scene."

MAUREEN ATKINSON

Owing to thousands of years of sophisticated, complex, and dynamic socio-economic and cultural structures, the Ts'msyen were able to incorporate the earliest European explorers and fur traders within their daily lives and interactions, holding the greater power in their relationships. However, the transient nature of those earliest international relations would soon change abruptly as the fur trade began to develop into a full-fledged international export economy and the first permanent European settlements in the area were established.

Today, the communities of Lax Kw'alaams, Metlakatla, and Prince Rupert are the "political, economic and social hubs of Ts'msyen society."[1] Given that the Ts'msyen communities of Lax Kw'alaams and Metlakatla remain significant contributors to the region, it is impossible overstate or ignore their respective roles in shaping the development of Kaien Island and the North Coast. To give a complete history of Prince Rupert one must also examine the establishments of Fort Simpson (located thirty kilometres north and founded in 1831 before moving to its present site in 1834) and Metlakatla (ten kilometres northwest and founded in 1862).

This chapter is not meant as a definitive history of Fort Simpson (now Lax Kw'alaams). There are far more authoritative and detailed chronologies that examine the unique development of what was originally a small fur-trading fort into the nexus of Indigenous–European relations in northern British Columbia. For the purposes of telling the story of Prince Rupert, the creation of Fort Simpson allowed the British to gain a permanent foothold on the North Pacific Coast. It was also the first place that European missionaries arrived in the region, allowing for much more deliberate efforts to change or destroy the Ts'msyen way of life. Most importantly for the City of Prince Rupert, the advancement of British settlement provided the necessary springboard for the emerging colonial authorities to expand their influence into the region.

PELTS AND PROFITS

During the intense maritime competition of the late 1700s to the 1820s, the overland fur trade had also been expanding closer towards Kaien Island. The British Parliament granted the Hudson's Bay Company (HBC) exclusive trading rights with the Indigenous Peoples in all "unsettled" territories west of the Rocky Mountains in what was known as British North America.[2] The explorer Alexander Mackenzie reached Bella Coola in 1793 utilizing a Greease Trail, while Simon Fraser established the trading posts of Fort George (today known as Prince George) in 1806 and Babine Lake in 1822.[3]

Throughout the 1820s, the Ts'msyen were incredibly effective negotiators, playing the Russian, British, and American traders against one another to drive up fur prices. Americans, in particular, were paying higher prices on the coast than the HBC was in the Interior and had more high-demand goods to trade. To gain a competitive advantage, the HBC decided to establish a northern coastal outpost, sending their district superintendent of shipping for surveying. A Scotsman and former British Royal Navy-man named Aemilius Simpson evaluated different locations and settled on Nass Harbour because it was "the most productive part of the coast in land skins,"[4] and also partly because vessels could "lay at anchor within a pistol shot of shore, [so] the Indians can be easily kept at check."[5]

While overseeing construction of the HBC fort in 1831 Simpson died after a brief unknown illness and was buried just outside the new fort's walls. Within three years, the HBC had determined that both the fort and Simpson's remains were to be re-located[6] due to a number of reasons, namely: the lack of fresh water; poor protection from the cold winter weather[7]; the lack of direct access to the Interior; insufficient land to establish gardens to grow food[8]; being too far from the ocean; and difficultly for marine vessels to access. Likely on the recommendation of the Ts'msyen Chief Ligeex, the fort was relocated southward from the Nass to a Ts'msyen seasonal encampment site and was named Fort Simpson in honour of Aemilius Simpson. Despite having only visited the region himself for about a year, Simpson's name remained attached to the place for another 150 years before it was officially renamed Lax Kw'alaams in 1986.[9]

Once the HBC landing party was ashore on their new site, the adjacent rainforest began to be levelled to build makeshift structures. Within three days, the Ts'msyen arrived to meet the fur traders in their canoes. This must not have been unexpected as one of the first structures the fort men erected was a blacksmith's forge to produce axe heads for trade. Unlike the rest of the world, in the new Fort Simpson, masonry did not begin with stones and clay, but rather with the purchase of a canoe for the price of three blankets in order to fetch the necessary rock.[10]

Right from its inception, HBC employees at Fort Simpson relied heavily on the Ts'msyen and their neighbours for provisions. The fort's workers were poor fishermen and unsuccessful hunters, so in the early days, there was never fresh meat except for "a dubious roast of a porcupine or bear... fresh fruit and vegetables were rare... cattle brought in immediately foundered in the muskeg... however, [the Ts'msyen] enjoyed delicacies that the modern gourmet might envy and were teachers in good eating."[11]

Despite HBC policy that their forts should support themselves as much as possible, Fort Simpson was the least self-sufficient.[12] Even though they were ordered to develop gardens, it was never a practical possibility to produce fruit or vegetables because of the boggy and rocky terrain. So for its first few years, Fort Simpson only could exist because of its tolerant and patient hosts.[13] This fact was not lost on the HBC employees, as one remarked that when the Ts'msyen were busy participating in a feast, they "were joyful and peaceable disposed, none of [the] hunters can be prevailed upon to hunt deer of which we are sorely in want at present, neither do they fish; so that we have subsisted on salt provisions for the whole of this week; which is the longest interval we were without a fresh diet."[14] In another instance when the Ts'msyen temporarily travelled away from the fort, one man reported: "We have not seen the face of an Indian the last fortnight. It is, I believe, their feasting time, but with us the contrary. In order to participate in their joy we must receive a little more of the good things furnished by their woods and waters."[15] In other words, the first Fort Simpson employees survived only because of ongoing trade with the Ts'msyen.

PHOENICIANS OF THE NORTHWEST COAST

After only two seasons, the Ts'msyen and HBC men were out har-
vesting seaweed together in the waters surrounding the fort. Up to
four hundred canoes shuttled back and forth, paid in dried seaweed
papers as they unloaded before exchanging them at the trade shop for
various other European goods. In a single day, five hundred salmon
were landed at the fort. Even two decades after setting up the fort,
the HBC still depended upon fish and deer as their major source of
protein.[16]

During the early years of the fort, the Ts'msyen socio-political systems remained largely intact. The systems of exchange were simply
extended to include Europeans.[17] Standard units of trade became
well-understood, just as there had long been standard trade values
in the Ts'msyen economy: salmon were used as articles of commerce
and formed a sort of pseudo-tender.[18] Using their sophisticated
understanding of trading rights, the Ts'msyen were able to manage
how other Indigenous groups from the Interior could access to the
fort, and provided tributes for trading privileges. As a result of their
exceptional trading abilities, the Ts'msyen gained a reputation and a
nickname as the "Phoenicians of the Northwest Coast," a compliment
considering them among the greatest traders of their time.

The HBC had considerable self-interest and investment in protecting and preserving the Ts'msyen way of life in order to protect
their supply of fur and food. Therefore, there was little intrusion into
hunting and fishing grounds during the fur-trading period.[19] The
HBC also maintained a policy of detachment regarding Indigenous
affairs, observing a strict hands-off rule in matters of local customs.
However, this policy was sometimes bent towards peacemaking if
unrest would deprive the fort of its coveted furs. After all, furs were
the only reason for all the buildings, logging, shipping, and diplomacy
with the Ts'msyen.[20]

The most obvious factor contributing to the relative détente with
the Ts'msyen was that the Europeans were severely outnumbered.
Throughout the 1850s, while the non-Indigenous population of the
North Coast was incredibly diverse, it was minuscule in comparison
to the Ts'msyen and their neighbours. In recognition of this, HBC
employees heavily barricaded the fort, with armed guards stationed
day and night for weeks on end. However, the wooden tree trunk

palisades were almost as ineffective at keeping out the Ts'msyen as they were against the rain. Standing twenty feet high, maintaining the stockade became "an almost constant occupation for the next half century as the rain could rot the footing of a post in just two years."[21]

The multifaceted benefits purveyed by Fort Simpson gradually resulted in many Ts'msyen winter villages being abandoned in favour of proximity to trading advantages.[22] In the 1830s, thirty to fifty new post-and-beam houses were constructed around the fort while feasts were still being held around Metlakatla Pass to the south.[23] In 1835, it is estimated that there were 8,500 Ts'msyen people in the vicinity, with hundreds located adjacent to the fort. The first recorded feast was held at Fort Simpson in the summer of 1837.[24]

While the fur trade export economy certainly brought considerable wealth to the region, it also imported disease. The first smallpox epidemic to reach the Ts'msyen hit in 1836, carried to Fort Simpson on an American trading vessel from the Russian port of Novo-Arkangel'sk, Alaska.[25] Historians estimate that in less than a year, nearly 33 percent of the Ts'msyen population were killed by the infection.[26] The following year, fewer than half the usual number of canoes set out for the oolichan fishery: 340 down from 760.[27] This calamitous epidemic seriously threatened the Ts'msyen governance structure with the deaths of many Chiefs and matriarchs.

By the mid 1850s, over 2,300 Ts'msyen had become permanent residents at Fort Simpson.[28] As historian Maureen Atkinson explains in her 2006 thesis, "Fort Simpson was not only a centre of trade but also a vibrant and often confusing social scene." The relocation of the various neighbouring tribes to the fort would have meant that, for the first time living in the same place at the same time,[29] so new social processes had to be established. One such example is the account of a "joking feast" designed to reduce minor tensions between villages. William Beynon, a Ts'msyen Herediatry Chief and historian, is noted to have said in 1949 that for this event each village group would dress and speak as a caricature of a non-Ts'msyen group, such as the Gitxsan (Hagwilget), Scots, Japanese, Chinese, Haida, and Tlingit.[30]

INTIMATE RELATIONSHIPS

While the HBC chose to take a non-interventionist approach to disputes between Indigenous groups, their hands-off attitude did not apparently extend to their dealings with women. Only counting French voyageurs and local Ts'msyen women, at least fifteen marriages were documented in 1832.[31] And at least one of these was an outright trade alliance at the outset: the Ts'msyen Chief Ligeex married his daughter Sudaał to the fort's doctor John Frederick Kennedy as a diplomatic arrangement. Kennedy was part Cree and had recently become the first Métis man to be educated at a European university. As one of the first trained medical doctors on the coast, he was also the first clerk in charge of the Fort. The marriage forced a bond between Ligeex and the HBC, which in spite of temporary lapses, lasted as long as his life.[32]

Laans, Matthew Johnson, of the Gisbutwaada Clan of the Gispaxlo'ots describes the meeting and union of Sudaał and Kennedy:

> This beautiful daughter was sought by all the royal chiefs of the various tribes. But Ligeex would not entertain any proposals. On one of his trading trips he went with his family to the trading post of the Hudson's Bay Company just established on the Nass. He had much furs to trade. When he arrived there, the beauty of his daughter at once attracted a Dr. Kennedy, one of the officers connected with the Post, and the daughter of Ligeex and he were married.[33]

Henry Tate further described a conversation between Ligeex and Sudaal and the establishment of the new HBC fort:

> "Father, give a small piece of land to Mr. Kennedy, for I almost freeze to death here. Some men were frozen to death last winter." Then the great chief was speechless. He said, "I am afraid lest my child be frozen here next winter... my dear child, I have no land. This land belongs to all the tribes of the Ts'msyen. Only my camping place on Rose Island, where there are a few houses besides my own large house—I can lend this to your husband for some time." So she told her husband what her father had said; and the white man said, "Yes, I do not want to take land, but we will trade on it for a short time." Thus spoke Mr. Kennedy.[34]

Obviously, the promise of short-term use by Kennedy and the HBC has long since proved to be false. Yet at the same time, it is evident that these cross-cultural relationships were not just cold, calculated binary benefits. They were complex, mutually beneficial, and absolutely crucial to the success of trading ventures. With the Ts'msyen matrilineal kinship foundation, after marriage to fort employees, women and their children would join their husbands' households, but all lineage and cultural responsibilities remained an obligation. Therefore, children had a place in Ts'msyen society no matter where their father was from. While the Ts'msyen saw that their own relatives had food and shelter, the HBC employees could provide trade goods and delicacies, thereby increasing the social status of the family.[35]

Indigenous women who married HBC employees, as well as their children, played a tremendously important but largely unacknowledged role in fort development. They maintained an informal liaison between the fort and the surrounding encampments:

> They could predict the movements of the tribes because they had access to information ... the Ts'msyens would leave early for their fishing grounds, fearing a raid; the Massets would be arriving in a few days, bound on revenge. They could explain to the Ts'msyen the crazy actions of the Hudson's Bay people: the white men wasted so much time shovelling fish heads and offal out of the fort because they were sensitive to the smell; they brought all that water into the fort because they washed themselves and their clothes in their houses instead of in the sea or a lake; they worked all day long six days a week because their great chief to the south insisted upon it and would be very angry if they did otherwise.[36]

Clearly, in the earliest relations with the Europeans at Fort Simpson, Indigenous women played a crucial role as intermediaries, cultural ambassadors, and multi-lingual messengers. It is unfortunate that so many of their names and contributions were not recognized in writing.

INTERNATIONAL RELATIONS

Beyond intermarriages, one of the ways in which fort inhabitants and the Ts'msyen came to understand one another was in regard to matters of rank and social status. In the very class-conscious British ranks was a parallel to the Ts'msyen hereditary system. The Ts'msyen regarded the fort workmen as the officers' slaves. And in a way, they were not that far off: for HBC employees, a man was engaged under contract for years at a time, during which his life belonged to the company. According to one historian, "the stockade that kept the Ts'msyens out of the fort, kept [the HBC men] in... there were so many desertions and firings that there must have been a small colony in the Ts'msyen camp."[37]

While most of the HBC management and seamen were British, the company preferred the relatively poorer Highland Scots and Orkney Islanders for unskilled labour, making up over half their employee base. Sharing roughly the same latitude, they would have been accustomed to the coastal conditions of the North Coast and had some skill at fishing. For the Scots at that time, they were cheaper to hire than the English or Irish. North America offered a chance at a better life, free from the poor living conditions of the working class of the Industrial Revolution.[38]

As well, about one in five HBC employees were French Canadians. The "voyageurs," sometimes second- or third-generation company men, were the metaphorical backbone of the fur trade operation. And at that time, "bilingualism was not argued—it was practiced. Buildings were erected in French, salmon was salted in French, and a new clerk arriving at Fort Simpson had to learn fort French. There was also Christianized Caughnawaga Iroquois [Kahnawà:ke Mohawks] from the St. Lawrence River Valley, Prairie-born Metis, Indigenous Hawaiians, Japanese and Norwegian men who found themselves at Fort Simpson."[39]

By the 1850s, Fort Simpson had become a profitable success for the HBC, with fur trade profits exceeding any other HBC post along the Pacific coast. Trade relations were peaceable enough that up to five hundred Ts'msyen were allowed inside the fort walls at once, compared to a maximum of three at its beginnings. Ts'msyen women took over nearly all fur-related tasks from the fort men. When the canoes departed Fort Simpson for the annual oolichan run, HBC employees allowed the Ts'msyen to stow their belongings and, in preparation, "cleaned out every keg, cask and barrel that the fort could yield up."[40] But most importantly, Fort Simpson had become the central trading point of the entire region, visited by tens of thousands of people annually, including all Indigenous Nations in the region, American and European traders and merchants, and numerous British dignitaries.[41]

OTTER FAILURE

As the Indigenous economy was increasingly oriented around the international export of sea otter furs, European practices were impacted as well. While Indigenous Peoples "are cited as the supreme ecologists, nobody ever, ever attributed such leanings to the men of the Hudson's Bay Company."[42] The supply of sea otter skins eventually became so rare and desirable that the offer per skin was raised to eight blankets. So the HBC began a highly speculative method of acquiring furs by outfitting Indigenous hunting expeditions. The Ts'msyen could thereby set the terms of trading method and price. As a result, between 1839 and 1865, the price of furs skyrocketed: from one gallon of rum, two blankets, and some tobacco to thirty-nine blankets and three guns each.[43]

COLOURFUL CHARACTER: CHIEF LIGEEX

Ligeex (also spelled Ligaic, Legeex, Legex, Legaik) is a Ts'msyen hereditary chieftain name-title. During the fur trade period, the name was held by four different men.[44] At the time that the HBC set up at Fort Simpson in 1831, the title was held by a high-ranking Chief who had already been recognized as having built a monopoly of sorts over Skeena River trade.[45] It is likely a single Ligeex who was responsible for solidifying the trading monopoly from the 1790s to 1835,[46] giving him a "position of immense power, which he wielded with a tight grip."[47]

Ligeex's strategic diplomatic alliance with the HBC saw him marry his daughter to the first fort doctor the same year that the first fort was established on the Nass River. Ligeex subsequently made a landscape-altering gesture by offering re-location to his HBC son-in-law: "I have a place for you and your people. Come to Laxhlgu'alaams. Here we can visit you frequently and help you in many ways."[48]

And help he did. Ligeex played a central role in trade at Fort Simpson, holding the right to travel and trade on the Skeena. His influence is best demonstrated in the fact that no European travelled up the Skeena for the first twenty-five years of the fort's existence.[49] Many modern analysts now label Ligeex's rise to power as having united a regional hierarchy and reigned as a "paramount chiefdom."[50]

One of the title holders of the name Legaic,
who took the name Paul Legaic after conversion
to Christianity. PUBLIC DOMAIN

Ligeex's experience with the Europeans was also indicative of
the rapidly changing times. When he passed away in 1840, he had
already lost his wife, primary allies, prominent rivals, and his son and
chosen heir to smallpox.[51] The eventual heir to his name was unable
to maintain his trading authorities and would eventually change his
name to Paul Legaic upon his conversion to Christianity,[52] becoming
the first of several Christianized Ligeex title-holders.[53]

Despite having to confront the many negative impacts of European
contact, Ligeex was able to build and maintain important trade relationships, and also wield significant and unrivalled power and wealth
near the Skeena River. Without Ligeex, Fort Simpson may never have
been built at Lax Kw'alaams. Through political alliances and trade,
Ligeex was a central figure in the early geopolitics of the North Pacific.

The story of Ligeex's power and influence is told by Laans, Matthew
Johnson, of the Gisbutwaada Clan of the Gispaxlo'ots:

Wai Ligeex t'in habool gatgyet	Well now Ligeex he was the one who had the power
asga k'ala Ksiyeen	all along the Skeena
ada algatnaa	and there was no one
dm t'in goo k'ala Ksiyeen	who would go up the Skeena
gap ksgooga dmt ts'aaltisga	without first getting the permission

sm'oogit Ligeex
Ada dawaaltgal Gispaxlo'lots
na ts'aps Ligeex
guu t'in
da'axlga dmt k'ala goo Ksiyeen
Ada dzu dii waaldit
ada gap xk'eelt
asga sm'oogit
asgat wil k'ala goo Ksiyeen
Niitga sm'oogit
asga txa'nii 'wii k'ala Ksiyeen
Ada dzida waalsga ligik'oolda
   liksts'ap
ligi na wilaaysga k'oolda na
   ts'abm Gispaxlo'ots
adzit daatsga Gispaxlo'ots

adat ga hamoxgit asga
   sm'oogit
Ada dzila batsgat
da'alt hanwaaynt
asga ligioosga da'axlgat

asga k'ala'aks
Ada dzida 'wah waaldit
adat gooda na galdm'algyaxs
   Ligeex
at sn'naawt
Ada waal txa'nii
   liksgalts'ipts'ap
sm luutitga na gatgyetsga
sm'oogidm Gispaxlo'ots
Dzu'al dii heelda
   galts'ipts'apga
dzoogit asga k'ala Ksiyeen
a na gye'etsit asga Ts'ilaasu
ada alga dii waalt dzit goo
na gigyaani a Ts'ilaasu
ada algatnaal

of the chief Ligeex
Now it was the Gispaxlo'ots
Ligeex's tribe
who were the ones
who could go up the Skeena
And if they did so
they most certainly gave a gift
to the chief
for going up the Skeena
It was he who was the chief
over all the Skeena River
And if any other tribe

any relatives of the
   Gispaxlo'ots tribe
went in the canoes of the
   Gispaxlo'ots
they first gave a passage fee
   to the chief
and when they returned
then they gave a trading fee
for anything they had been
   able to get
while upriver
and if they didn't do so
then Ligeex's spokesman

went to demand payment
And all of the different tribes

greatly respected the powers
of the chief of the Gispaxlo'ots
Although there were many
   tribes
living along the Skeena
downriver from the Canyon
none of them had ever gone
upriver beyond the Canyon
and there was not one of them

dm t'in sila'wa'ata Gitksan	who traded with the Gitksan
Ksat Ligeex	Only Ligeex
'niisgat t'in sa'ayaawga	he was the one who made the law
dm ksat 'niitga	that he alone
dm sila'wa'atsga Gitksan	should trade with the Gitksan
Ada wilaayda txa'nii galt'ipts'ap[54]	And all the tribes knew this.[55]

Up until the 1860s, Fort Simpson had been "moderately insulated from the overt racism which had become part of the mainstream society as Europeans sought to define themselves as a colonial and civilized (thus superior) social entity."[56] The ethnic makeup, intercultural diversity, and multiplicity of languages brought about a much more fluid social organization in Fort Simpson compared to the continent at large. The fur trade had obviously brought significant change to the region, yet this was not dictated by the Europeans. Rather, a mutually beneficial symbiosis between the Europeans and Indigenous population brought about an international export economy. In so doing, "feasting became more intense so the [Ts'msyen] belief system and social values were reinforced."[57]

The early cooperative relationships during the fur-trading period were poor preparation for the impending disruptions set to arrive with the settlement frontier. While the Ts'msyen were used to decades of fur traders attempting to attune themselves to local customs, the coming confrontation with settlers and missionaries would see the accommodation of Indigenous Peoples within European communities replaced by assimilation.[58] The changes to the Ts'msyen way of life by the establishment and growth of Fort Simpson, in the words of historian and former Fort Simpson resident Helen Meilleur, "were like the outside waters of a whirlpool, circling imperceptibly at first, gaining in force during the 1840s and 50s, and spinning furiously into the vortex around the end of the 1860s."[59] It is no small irony that the success of the intercultural Fort Simpson trading hub would prove so lucrative as to accelerate the arrival of the emerging authorities of the colony of British Columbia and Canada, as well as the parties of God bringing the "good news."

CHAPTER 4

METLAKATLA

1862–70

"The Holy City."

The Ts'msyen set the foundation for the Kaien Island region to be a place of cross-cultural exchange. The first European settlement at Fort Simpson brought international trade less than forty kilometres away. The establishment of Metlakatla less than ten kilometers away, on the other hand, was a harbinger of the rapidly increasing pace of colonization. Fort Simpson, built in the early 1830s, came into existence a decade before Upper and Lower Canada were combined,[1] and more than twenty-five years before the colony of British Columbia was founded.[2] But by the time Metlakatla was under construction in the 1860s, what were formerly small pockets of white people had become thousands of white settlers drifting onto Pacific shores. The days of white immigrants being outnumbered by the Indigenous in the Pacific Northwest were quickly coming to an end. While the fur traders had built relationships with the Ts'msyen and their neighbours based on motivations to maximize profits, the settlers and missionaries had much more complex and far-reaching agendas.

FIRST FORT MISSIONARY

In January 1857, the Anglican Church sent an inexperienced twenty-four-year-old lay priest on a six-month sailing journey from England, destined for Fort Simpson. Upon his arrival in Victoria, the lay priest was greeted by James Douglas, the HBC Chief Factor and Governor of the Colony of Vancouver Island. Douglas advised against going to Fort Simpson as he wanted no religious interference in the fur trading protocols established on the North Pacific coast. Douglas tried to restrict itinerant missionaries to work only in major settlements, away from the unsupervised frontier.[3] After months in Victoria, the lay priest made such a positive impression upon Douglas that he was allowed to travel north to Fort Simpson, armed with a letter of recommendation from Douglas himself that he was to be "maintained at the Company's table in the same manner as any of the Company's officers."[4]

The young lay priest arrived at Fort Simpson in October 1857. The missionary hired a Ts'msyen man named Clah to serve as a cultural intermediary and to teach him the language. But after he refused an invitation to see what he called a "savage ritual dance," the missionary was issued an ultimatum: either he went to the dance or his words would not be heard. Reluctantly, he attended and quickly realized he had been ceremoniously placed in a seat of great honour: an elaborately carved and painted wooden backrest with a bearskin robe. Of this experience, he noted that "they [the Ts'msyen] would not be content until I took the chief place near the fire, and they always paced a mat upon a box for me to sit upon."[5]

After a few months, it became obvious that the young missionary was not there to barter, to buy or steal women, or trade for alcohol or guns. Instead, he claimed to be there with a message from the white man's god. Exactly one year to the day after his arrival at Fort Simpson, the young missionary asked Clah to seek permission of the nine Chiefs and to respect tribal customs to address people in their own homes. On that day, he spoke to approximately eight hundred Ts'msyen in their own language.[6]

Before the Europeans ever arrived, the Ts'msyen

> had an idea there was a Supreme Mysterious Being in heave when they worshipped. They offered up sacrifices to Him, putting in the best of their food in the fire. Before starting a fighting expedition against hostile tribes, they would fast all day, until nightfall [then] the chief would look up to the sky and ask for help in their under-takings. They... had great faith in fasting and prayers, so that when [they] learned the Gospel story, it was the older men who became the first converts.[7]

Although likely unintentional, the young missionary connected the Ts'msyen notions of god and the creation of the universe based on generations of oral history. In his journals, the missionary observered that "they believed that all men, animals, trees, plants and every growing thing had immortal spirits ... They too asked the immortal questions of who am I? Where is God? Whose sends the wind? Who sends the salmon? The Ts'msyens also believed in a Great Spirit above, a Heavenly Chief, known as Simoogit Laxha. They had a concept of prayer before eating."[8] The Ts'msyen could even identify with the Biblical story of the flood with a mountain as the place of refuge. Archaeological study of silt layers in the harbour around Kaien Island show indications of a large flood or tsunami that happened around 3000–1500 BCE.[9]

After the diplomatically arranged marriage of Chief Ligeex's daughter Sudaal to Fort Simpson's Dr. Kennedy, the Chief offered his large house to the young missionary to open his first school while a new schoolhouse was being built. The first few months were incredibly tense because of his refusal to stop ringing church bells during significant Ts'msyen cultural events. The young missionary's life was threatened by Ligeex before Clah intervened by flashing his pistol. Despite the disagreements, after only one year, Ligeex himself began attending the missionary's school, which would have added prestige and momentum.

From a status-oriented perspective, the missionary must have thought the Chief was a possible convert of great importance, while the Chief would likely have seen the missionary as an important addition to the Clan.[10] But it became apparent to the missionary that acculturating the Ts'msyen by demanding major cultural and ideological concessions was unsustainable, and that it was not possible to duplicate the British agrarian lifestyle at Fort Simpson.[11] Little could anyone have guessed that the conspicuous 5'6", 160-pound English missionary in his early twenties named William Duncan would later be described as having "left a deeper mark than any other single person on North Pacific Coast Indian history."[12]

THE "HOLY CITY"

It is not accurate to claim that William Duncan founded Metlakatla. As the name is a Sm'algyax word for "saltwater pass," Metlakatla was a longstanding and familiar gathering place for the Ts'msyen for thousands of years before Duncan's arrival. Metlakatla Pass played host to dozens of large Ts'msyen village sites before the modern-day Metlakatla was founded. However, we must acknowledge the role that William Duncan played in Metlakatla's reformation.

Not long after he arrived in Fort Simpson, Duncan began convincing followers of the need to separate the converted from the HBC's "gulf of vice and misery."[13] As early as 1859, Duncan proposed Metlakatla Pass as a location for a new settlement, recommended by Chief Seesklakkahnoosh, on a site about twenty-seven kilometers south, which had previously been abandoned by the Ts'msyen for the convenience of living closer to Fort Simpson.[14] While the site was rejected by the Anglican Church, Duncan earned the endorsement of BC governor James Douglas in 1860. After inspection, multiple scouting parties were sent to take down trees, dig ditches and plant potatoes in preparation for Duncan's flock to arrive.[15]

On May 17, 1862, a canoe arrived at Fort Simpson from Victoria bearing news of a smallpox outbreak that had already taken thirty Ts'msyen lives. Many more were headed home, forced to leave Victoria by the frightened authorities. Duncan took full advantage of the situation. He visited all the tribes, telling them that smallpox was a punishment for their sins and promised if they converted to Christianity, they would be saved.[16]

Only two days after people were stricken with the disease in Fort Simpson, Duncan and fifty of his followers left in six canoes. In Duncan's own words, "on that day every tie was broke; children were separated from their parents, husbands from wives, brothers from sisters; houses, land and all things were left."[17] Others would follow soon after. Within the first week, a fleet of thirty canoes arrived bringing two Chiefs and three hundred members of their Houses.

In Fort Simpson, as 500–700 people died (one fifth of the population), Duncan quarantined new arrivals to Metlakatla and vaccinated as many people as he could.[18] He also refused entry to those showing symptoms, drawing references to the plagues in Egypt.[19] At Fort Simpson, the sick were left untreated and the dead were left unburied. But in Metlakatla only five deaths were documented, leaving them as the only community on the entire coast to escape the epidemic relatively unscathed.[20]

With a newfound ability to attract new villagers, Duncan also began to leverage the Ts'msyen power structure to gain support by distributing food and gifts. Soon after the migration to Metlakatla, Duncan hosted a feast for 250 people. By demonstrating wealth and generosity, Duncan's action must have been perceived to undermine the Chief's authority because only a week later, the now-converted

Chiefs held a feast of their own with provisions donated by Duncan. As Atkinson explains, "whether it was intentional or not, Duncan had mimicked a fundamental principle of Ts'msyen social order."[21]

Duncan was explicitly trying to eliminate the Chiefs and cultural systems in Metlakatla. He kept the government of the village in his own hands, but did allow Chiefs a permanent position on the village council and shared half of the village taxes with them.[22] He hand-picked the constables and village council, but reserved the right to make final decision in all matters.[23] Despite most of his followers being unable to read or write in English, Duncan still had them sign a declaration to become residents by vowing fealty to Evangelical Christianity and the laws of the Queen of England and agreeing to fifteen commandments, which included giving up "Indian devilry," "calling in conjurers," and "giving away property for display" (that is, as part of the tradition of feasting).

By commanding the Ts'msyen to stop giving away property in a public way, Duncan was overtly attempting to eliminate the feast system. And yet, despite his best efforts to eradicate Ts'msyen culture, many Metlakatlans continued to participate in neighbouring ceremonies[24] and refused to give up ownership of longhouses in Fort Simpson.[25] While Duncan claimed that most high-profile convert, Ligeex (now Paul Legaic), had given up and forsaken everything by converting to Christianity, Ligeex's name was still called at feasts in Fort Simpson. He still maintained a home there and raised an eagle pole at a feast in 1866.[26]

Within the first year, Metlakatla's population reached 1,000 people. A sawmill, newspaper, salmon cannery, and trade shop were established. A ship was purchased for trade. The manufacturing of soap and clogs began on a commercial scale. By the 1860s, it was clear that the HBC no longer reigned supreme as the economic representative of Europe. Instead, "a new industrial regime slowly took over, accompanied by colonial society and government."[27] Unlike during the earliest formative years alongside the Europeans, when the Ts'msyen were full participants able to incorporate and adapt new things to their own use, events beyond their control were culminating in the south that were set to dramatically alter the physical, economic, social, and cultural landscape.[28]

The most notable development was the founding of the Colony of British Columbia in 1858 and the appointment of the HBC chief factor

James Douglas as governor. Having made a positive first impression on Douglas early in his career, Duncan travelled south to Victoria to petition to be commissioned as a magistrate. His request was granted and his appointment as Justice of the Peace for the North Coast region of BC gave him exclusive jurisdiction over eight hundred kilometers of coastline.[29] Thus marked the official arrival of British colonial authority to the North Pacific region.

When Duncan returned from Victoria with his newly bestowed powers, he was angry to learn that the deputy he had put in charge in his absence, Robert Cunningham, had gotten married to one of his most trusted students, Elizabeth Ryan. Allegedly, it was because she had gotten pregnant before marriage.[30] Cunningham had been sent by the Anglican Church to assist Duncan with Metlakatla's rapid growth. Duncan's unforgiving nature and subsequent lobbying saw Cunningham fired by the missionary society. This would soon prove to be a seminal moment on BC's North Pacific coast as Cunningham would go on to play his own unique role in settling the coastline.

From his new official bench, Duncan handed down sentences not found in law books, admitting "I have sometimes gone a little outside of the law,"[31] and that "I never allowed myself to stumble over the law when something good was to be accomplished ... being thus left alone I was obliged to act a little out of order."[32] Public whipping was for those found guilty of violence. A black flag would be raised to signal someone wicked was supposed to leave town. Duncan charged five innocent men as accomplices to a crime for not turning over the real offenders, just to set an example. When Duncan convicted two liquor traders to eight years of hard labour, the soon-to-be premier, Amor De Cosmos, wrote that Duncan was "thoroughly ignorant of the powers and jurisdiction of a magistrate ... missionaries are the most incompetent as well as the most dangerous persons to be entrusted with magisterial powers and responsibilities."[33]

Despite his unorthodox leadership, by 1874 Duncan had attracted enough followers that he could oversee the construction of a 1,200-person church in Metlakatla, the largest one north of San Francisco and west of Chicago at that time.[34] But Duncan's refusal to be ordained or provide communion precipitated a major religious schism, so the Anglican Church sent for a higher ranking bishop, William Ridley, to serve as Duncan's superior in Metlakatla. For the first time in twenty years, Duncan would be under direct supervision.[35]

Not long after Ridley's arrival, numerous grievances were levelled against Duncan; he was judged on his role as a magistrate rather than as a minister. His main trading interest was fueled by greed, and the community was being treated as if it were his personal property. There were allegations of forced marriages, unlawful imprisonments, and sexual misconduct thanks to Duncan's tendency to "warehouse" young Ts'msyen women in his mission house until they had reached a marriageable age.[36] Ecclesiastical arguments erupted over whether to allow the Ts'msyen to participate in communion, to make Sunday service mandatory, or to translate the preaching and gospels into Sm'algyax. Before long, Duncan publicly declared Bishop Ridley to be an enemy of Metlakatla.[37] He was eventually terminated by the Anglican missionary society and subsequently retired from his post as magistrate, although he remained in Metlakatla for a while longer.

Adding to Duncan's problems, at Bishop Ridley's request, the government attempted to survey plots in Metlakatla in 1884. The Ts'msyen viewed this as a secret plan to acquire their land, and protested by pulling up stakes and standing on chains. A naval ship was called in and seven people were arrested. Over one hundred people left the community as a result of the ongoing schism.

In response, a provincial commission was launched, which recommended completing the land survey, supported by military force if necessary. They determined that the source of disturbance in colonial settlement plans was the debate over land rights "inculcated in the Indian mind by some of the missionaries"[38] and that "the Indians would not do bad things unless they had bad teachings... the Metlakatlans say all the lands belong to the Indians. This is not true. White men who teach this are false."[39] Metlakatla was thus considered a danger to the peace of the entire Northwest Coast.

Prime Minister John A. MacDonald, who was also the superintendent general of Indian Affairs, directly weighed in on the dispute and concluded William Duncan was "refusing to obey the laws of the land," and was "so accustomed to unrestrained power that he lost his head altogether."[40] The federal government took the side of Bishop Ridley and BC. In just a few short years, Duncan had lost his control over Metlakatla to first the Church and then the State.

Shortly thereafter, he travelled to Washington, DC, in 1886. Aided by a wealthy American businessman, a public relations and diplomatic campaign was launched to secure land rights to establish a new Metlakatla, yielding an endorsement from US president Grover Cleveland to property on Annette Island.[41] In 1887, Duncan and six separate fleets of thirty to seventy canoes, fishing boats, scows, and rafts carried more than eight hundred men, women, and children across the international border into southeast Alaska.

COLOURFUL CHARACTER: WILLIAM DUNCAN

William Duncan, 70 years old, Seattle.
EDWARD S. CURTIS

William Duncan is a paradoxical and contradictory figure in history. Those who knew him labelled him an "old pirate," "cantankerous," "aloof, suspicious and vindictive." Yet somehow, others have said he "had fewer faults than any man [they] ever met"[42] and was "as close to a saint as anyone."

The first known record of William Duncan's existence was his baptism in England in 1832 as the "illegitimate son of Maria Donkin."[43] Born out of wedlock, a matter of deep shame in the Victorian era, he sought religious salvation through his Sunday school mentor, who was responsible for instilling the evangelicalism that would come to define Duncan's life.

Duncan left home after graduation and quickly found entrepreneurial success as a bookkeeper and salesman. After being recruited to attend the Anglican Church Missionary Society College, he wrote soon after arrival that "the students are not good enough, rich enough, polite enough, and intellectual enough for my pride. They do not reverence me as I was reverenced at home."[44] This pompous and solemn young man was quick to find fault in others, a trait demonstrated throughout his career.

His formative years through the 1850s were at the height of global missionary fervour, predicated on spreading "civilization" and Christianity. Upon arriving at Fort Simpson, Duncan judged the HBC men to be corrupt, greedy, and prone to drunkenness and lust, from which the Ts'msyen had to be separated.[45] Much like his own personality, Duncan's legacy of sixty years on the North Pacific coast is profoundly mixed.

As an Anglican missionary, Duncan played a critical role in advancing the Church's deliberate undertaking of cultural genocide. Yet, he was also one of the earliest campaigners for Indigenous land, fishing, and mineral rights. He was one of the first white men to raise concerns about the extractive nature of the industrial salmon canneries on Indigenous food sources, even though he personally profited from the industry. He deplored the treatment of Indigenous Peoples as children and wards of the state under the *Indian Act*, but he also chose to withhold communion from them because he believed the ritual was "higher than their experience and intelligence would warrant."[46]

In another contradiction, while he held up Metlakatla up as a "civilized" place of refuge, Duncan admitted in his own journal to, among other things: severely beating children, locking kids in cupboards for days, tying young people to posts all day, locking misbehavers in a solitary room for up to a week, and flogging kids for the sin of playing on a Sunday. And despite dedicating his entire adult life to building a utopian holy city, on his deathbed he remarked: "Don't bury me in Metlakatla, it will be a deserted village some day."[47] As well, contrary to his lifelong preaching against coveting wealth, Duncan died 1918 with a personal estate worth $146,159 (over $2.7 million in 2024 dollars).

But the single most confounding part of Duncan's existence is that while he continually stressed the critical importance of maintaining unity, he chose to lead not just one but two exoduses: from Fort Simpson south to Metlakatla, and then north to New Metlakatla, Alaska. His leadership broke up families for generations and resulted in countless personal feuds and grievances. And yet, both Metlakatla communities endure today. Over 150 years after he stepped off the boat in Fort Simpson, William Duncan's countless contradictions provide fodder for supporters and critics alike. Without question, Duncan left a profound and lasting influence on the North Pacific coast, and his story in Metlakatla is a testament to the complex interplay between religion and colonization as European settlement moved closer to Kaien Island.

COLONIZATION

One of the primary tools of European colonization and assimilation on BC's North Coast was the system of schools, particularly those run by the Church. Beyond William Duncan's mission, the Methodists arrived at Fort Simpson and opened two residential schools while the Anglicans established day schools at Metlakatla and Kitkatla, all of which operated until the 1960s and '70s.[48]

Horror stories abounded of abuse at local residential schools, designed to help keep the "unruly natives under control."[49] One missionary worker, Elizabeth Shaw, recounted her firsthand experience to her church:

> The minutest detail of every boy's life was supervised by somebody, and his thinking faculties were fairly superintended out of him... they all seemed to detest everything in connection with the Home... the slightest mistake on the part of the boys brought down the wrath of the authorities, and the severe floggings which were the almost inevitable consequences of wrong-doing seemed to me in many cases to be out of all proportion to the gravity of the offence... to keep them in a chronic state of fear, as these children apparently were, seems to me to be wrong and unnatural... I can truthfully say that I never was any place where I saw so little manifestation of love and sympathy as in that Mission House at Port Simpson.[50]

But the list of destructive influences of the time was not limited to religion: there were also smallpox, guns, alcohol, and prostitution.[51] In 1835, there were an estimated 8,500 Ts'msyen living in the region. By 1885, that number was down to 4,550.[52] The Ts'msyen word for "European" or "Caucasian" is "k'amksiwah," or driftwood.[53] Like driftwood, large numbers of Europeans were washing up on shore, seemingly out of nowhere, carried over great distances by the wind and waves. In much the same way that driftwood alters the landscape when it becomes affixed to wherever it touches down, European newcomers brought significant change to the North Pacific by drifting into and affixing themselves on Ts'msyen territory. "What had brought most newcomers into the area concerned material, not spiritual matters... it was the secular interests of fur traders... that brought Christian beliefs and instructors into the region in a more sustained way than had the fleeting contacts of the earlier naval explorers... only then, did the driftwood begin piling up on Ts'msyen shores."[54]

Unlike with the transient nature of the fur trade, the permanent settlement of Europeans on the North Pacific coast fundamentally altered the Ts'msyen way of life. Between disease, violence, residential schools, missionary fervour, and numerous other social ills coming ashore, the region would be unrecognizably altered in the span of only one generation.

COLOURFUL CHARACTER: ODILLE MORISON (NÉE QUINTAL)

Born to a French fur trader and a Ts'msyen midwife and healer at Fort Simpson in 1855, Odille Quintal was raised to become an extraordinary woman. When William Duncan first established Metlakatla, the Quintals moved with him so that the seven-year-old Odille could continue studying in Duncan's mission school. By the time she was a teenager, she had earned Duncan's trust to teach some of the younger students. From a missionary's standpoint, Odille would have been considered a star pupil given her literacy and academic abilities. Having grown up quadrilingual (English, French, Sm'algyax, and Chinook Jargon), she often acted as translator and correspondent for various dignitaries and missionaries, including the governor general Lord Dufferin during a visit to the region.[55]

At age 17, Odille caught the attention of Charles Morison, the head of the HBC at Fort Simpson. While William Duncan was in Victoria, the two got married, starting a partnership that would endure for over sixty years. Beyond serving as an intercultural intermediary, as an HBC officer's spouse and "Lady of the Fort," Odille was also tasked

Odille Morrison circa 1880, age 25.
PUBLIC DOMAIN

with being a diplomat and dignitary. This involved, among other things, playing host to the Canadian governor general or serving as a court-appointed interpreter.[56]

When William Duncan moved with his followers to Alaska, Odille chose not to follow. Instead, she remained with her husband, the man in charge of the HBC's Fort Simpson operations. She began working with Bishop Ridley to translate the New Testament and Anglican prayer book into Sm'algyax. Her translation work would become the basis for the first Sm'algyax practical spelling system. Unfortunately, it would also become a source of anger and resentment for her as Bishop Ridley never publicly acknowledged her contributions.[57]

In 1888, Odille worked in Port Essington as a translator and interpreter for anthrolpologist Franz Boas, lending her cultural knowledge to help him produce a written series of sixteen Ts'msyen proverbs. Within a year, she became the first woman of Indigenous descent to be published in the *Journal of American Folk-lore*.[58] Her continued correspondence with Boaz helped to tell the Ts'msyen story to the world, in addition to sharing artifacts and ethnographic information.[59]

Odille was an esteemed matriarch in both the European and Ts'msyen cultures to which she served as an intermediary. While her unique contributions to Northern BC have not been included in the "spate of celebratory pioneer narratives,"[60] at her funeral in 1933, North Coast minister Canon Rushbrook deemed her "the greatest woman Northern British Columbia has ever produced."[61] Odille's life story serves as a benchmark of how quickly the times were changing for the Ts'msyen. She was born in Fort Simpson, educated in Metlakatla, raised her children in Port Essington, and was then buried in Prince Rupert, a place her husband said created "infinite harm to the old historic Mission of Metlakatla."[62]

While the Ts'msyen easily understood and participated in the activities of the early European fur traders, the coming of western missionaries saw the demands of white people expand,[63] from trading goods and sharing cultures to forcibly transforming entire ways of life. The competition for exclusive jurisdiction over sea otter skins became a competition for saving souls. The inextricable link between Christianity and western civilization informed a new European view of the Ts'msyen. For nearly seventy years, the wealth and trading prowess of the Ts'msyen saw them recognized as the "Phoenicians of the Northwest Coast." But less than two decades after the arrival of the so-called good news at the first permanent European settlements on the coast, that perception had devolved to the "uncivilized heathen Indian."

With the fur trade waning at Fort Simpson and an industrial wage labour economy growing in Metlakatla, combined with robust Christian and government influence, the colonization of the north coast of British Columbia was well underway by the mid-1800s. No longer was this a place where Europeans were operating in Ts'msyen space, relying on them for sustenance. Instead, the latter half of the nineteenth century on the North Coast would come to be defined by the coming of a new justice system courtesy of the expanding colonial authorities. For the future of Prince Rupert, the stage was nearly set for colonization to begin in earnest.

CHAPTER 5

PORT ESSINGTON

1871–1902

"What a motley crowd you will find... what colouring,
what a Babel of tongues."

VISITOR TO PORT ESSINGTON, 1898

GOLD RUSHES NORTH

When the HBC was originally granted a trade monopoly by the British Empire, settlers were few and far between on BC's North Coast. However, this changed dramatically after a Haida man sold a twenty-seven-ounce gold nugget in Victoria for 1500 blankets in 1851 and a Skeena River Chief displayed a piece of gold at Fort Simpson in 1852.[1] An influx of Americans to Haida Gwaii came by way of California and Oregon. Miners, traders, merchants, soldiers, sailors, and all other types of adventurous and lawless people flocked northward. The recently appointed governor of the colony of Vancouver Island, James Douglas, urged British authorities to protect their sovereignty to avoid the Americans annexing Haida Gwaii for themselves.[2] Despite not having any physical presence on the islands, the British appointed Douglas governor and sent a guard-ship. The Royal Navy upheld the British territorial claim by requiring Americans to obtain a license to visit the islands, trade goods, or mine for gold.[3]

Less than seven years later, in 1858, the banks of the Fraser River were flooded by 30,000 gold seekers, prompting Governor James Douglas to again respond by stationing gun boats to control access. But this incursion saw the HBC lose control of their fur-trading monopoly, and forced Douglas—who at the time held a dual post as an HBC Chief Factor and governor of Vancouver Island—to resign from the HBC and focus exclusively on the new colonial government. The gravity of the loss of the HBC's monopoly was reflected in the steep decline in the sea otter pelt trade. By 1861, only eleven furs were traded at Fort Simpson.[4] That same year, gold was discovered in the Omineca region, about one hundred kilometres northeast of present-day Hazelton. Gold, not fur, was officially the hottest commodity in Northern BC.

Governor Douglas commissioned Major William Downie to undertake a systematic exploration of the Skeena River to investigate the potential for rail transportation. Downie was the first white man to do so.[5] At Fort Simpson, he hired a French voyageur and two Indigenous assistants, who managed to reach the confluence of the Skeena and Bulkley Rivers, nearly two hundred kilometres inland from the ocean. Afterwards, Douglas dispatched the message to the British government in London that

> the valley of the Skeena is thus shewn to be an available avenue into the interior of British Columbia, and will, I have no doubt, soon become a most important outlet... As a means of supplying the distant mining districts by a shorter and cheaper route than the valley of Fraser's River, its importance will soon be appreciated, and attract the attention of the mining and commercial classes; and I believe that the day is not far distant when steamers will be busily plying on the waters.[6]

This prediction soon came true. The British authorities quickly exerted control over the Omineca area, evidenced by officials issuing certifications, claims, water licenses, pre-emption records for land, settling disputes, issuing arrest warrants, holding small claims or police courts, convening inquests, holding prisoners for trial, and issuing contracts for bridge and road construction.[7]

COLOURFUL CHARACTER: JAMES DOUGLAS

Born in Guyana to a Scottish plantation owner and free woman of Barbadian-Creole ancestry,[8] James Douglas got an early start as a fur trader with the Northwest Company at the age of 15.[9] He quickly rose from HBC clerk to the highest field service rank by the age of 36. Douglas was responsible for negotiating with the Russian governor of Alaska for the boundary between Alaskan and British posts, which would later inform the eventual borders of Canada and the United

James Douglas, governor of British Columbia,
circa 1861. IMAGE A-01227 COURTESY
ROYAL BC MUSEUM

States. As the first British governor of Vancouver Island and Haida
Gwaii, Douglas's assertion of naval authority during the gold rush
era had a profound influence on the American–Canadian Pacific
borders we know today.

Most historians regard Douglas as the "Father of British Columbia,"[10] but in the North Coast region, his impact was more problematic
than paternal. Having married a Cree woman, he had established
many positive relationships with Indigenous Peoples as a fur trader.
But as Governor, Douglas put Joseph Trutch—a man who would later
be recognized on a list of the ten worst Canadians in history—in charge
of BC's lands and resources. Trutch reduced Indigenous reserve sizes
by over 90 percent, refused to recognize Indigenous land rights, and
alongside his brother-in-law Peter O'Reilly, oversaw arbitrary reserve
lines drawn all over the North Coast, including at Metlakatla and
Lax Kw'alaams. Douglas was also responsible for allowing William
Duncan to arrive and proselytize on the North Coast and also gave
him official colonial powers as a justice of the peace. As well, during
the 1862 smallpox epidemic, Douglas failed to institute quarantine
and instead approved a forcible eviction of Indigenous traders from
Victoria, costing countless lives on the North Coast.

In describing Douglas's legacy, historian Margaret Ormsby explains
that "against overwhelming odds... he was able to establish British

rule on the Pacific Coast and lay the foundation for Canada's extension to the Pacific seaboard. Single-handed in the midst of a gold-rush he had forged policies for land, mining, and water rights."[11] In so doing, Douglas was a singular force in constructing the colonial framework that gave British authorities a footing on BC's North Coast, laying the necessary foundation for further European settlement.

SMALLPOX EPIDEMIC

The 1862 smallpox epidemic is estimated to have killed one third of BC's entire Indigenous population, and the North Coast was no exception to the devastating spread of the disease. After the Haida Gwaii gold rush, a sizeable contingent of Ts'msyen, Nisga'a, Haida, Tlingit, and Heiltsuk people assembled for trade just outside Victoria. Immediately after the smallpox outbreak began, these 2,200 "Northernors" were given one day to leave by police, who threatened them with gunboats and barricades. The police burnt their houses and blankets and evicted them without making any attempt to quarantine or vaccinate them, simple steps that might have spared thousands of lives. As a result, the traders brought the disease back to their home villages. Smallpox has a two-week incubation period, and right on schedule, people became stricken with the disease after returning from Victoria. William Duncan later stated that between five hundred and seven hundred Ts'msyen died from smallpox in Fort Simpson that year.[12]

All aspects of life were affected, people were unable to catch and process furs, and there were fewer people available for food gathering and processing. The heavy losses of Chiefs and matriarchs seriously threatened the traditional Indigenous governance structure and created cultural voids. In 1866, less than half the number of canoes left Fort Simpson for the oolichan fishery compared to the 1830s.[13] By the end of the century, smallpox had claimed nearly two thirds of Indigenous lives in BC.[14]

After the worst of the epidemic had passed, in 1866 the British government consolidated the colonies of Vancouver Island, the Queen Charlotte Islands (Haida Gwaii), and the mainland. For the first time, British authority was asserted on BC's North Coast through the

machinery of government, including civil and criminal law.[15] Through
the strength of the British Navy, the colonial powers successfully
asserted their claim against the Americans to the north and south.[16]
By the late 1860s, it was clear that the influence of the fur trade
was waning as the accumulation of gold miners, fishermen, loggers,
surveyors, settlers, missionaries, and government officials arrived.

KLONDIKE ON THE SKEENA

Owing to George Vancouver's earlier mistake of underestimating the
mouth of the Skeena River, Kaien Island and its protected harbour
remained hidden from the Europeans on all maps and charts for
many years. The nearby waters, however, were bustling with traffic.
Just as James Douglas had predicted, by the early 1860s the Skeena
River emerged as a vital gateway to the Omineca goldfields. The
colonial government awarded a contract to two business partners to
upgrade a grease trail to a road to create access to the area.[17] Within
one year of the road being completed, the majority of travel to the
Omineca goldfields was via the Skeena. Those two business partners
obviously saw an opportunity to make more money. In 1871, the same
year that BC joined Confederation, they took out a pre-emption on
the south side of the mouth of the Skeena River and were given legal
rights to the land on the promise of settling it. The first European
community on BC's North Coast was born, named Port Essington
thanks to George Vancouver's maps.

One of the founding partners of Port Essington was Robert
Cunningham, the same man who had been fired as a lay priest a
few years earlier by William Duncan in Metlakatla. After his brief
stint with the Anglican Church, Cunningham found employment
with the HBC at Fort Simpson, rising to the position of chief trader.
He knew it would not be long before the new Canadian government
would learn of the region's big salmon runs, agricultural land, and
timber.[18] After pre-empting the land for Port Essington, Cunningham and his business partner Thomas Hankin began subdividing
lots and sold them to settlers. Three lots were sold to the HBC to
build a store that would serve as a mining and trading post, another
signal of the transformation of the local economy away from the
fur trade.

COLOURFUL CHARACTER: ROBERT CUNNINGHAM

Robert Cunningham, founder of Port Essington.
PRINCE RUPERT CITY & REGIONAL ARCHIVES

Born in Ireland in 1837 into an Anglican family, not much is known about Robert Cunningham before he sailed to Canada at age 25, other than that he was poorly educated, unordained, and an ex-prize fighter[19] who had apparently turned to religion after losing a number of teeth in the ring. Hired as a lay assistant to William Duncan in Metlakatla, he was fired for marrying one of his students and fathering a child outside of wedlock.[20] Cunningham then worked for the HBC at Fort Simpson for a few years before he was lured by one of William Duncan's deputies into illegally bartering liquor. Duncan had taken on the role of justice of the peace for the Colony of British Columbia, and he used his powers to convict Cunningham of rum-running. Labelling him a "foul sensualist," Duncan imposed a stiff fine, all but assuring that the HBC would terminate him.

Having married Elizabeth Ryan, a member of a prominent Ts'msyen family, Cunningham forged unique relationships with the Indigenous people of the region by encouraging his in-laws to build homes on a portion of the his newly claimed townsite.[21] Indigenous individuals were legally barred from holding land title in BC, so Cunningham set aside three acres of the property for the Kitselas and Kitsumkalum Peoples to build whatever they wanted for their own purposes at a cost of one dollar.[22] This seems to be one of the only "private reserves" ever created in Canada. Within a year, over one hundred Indigenous residents had to chosen to relocate. Cunningham also granted Anglican, Methodist, and Salvation Army missionaries small parcels of land for one dollar to build churches and day schools.

He established a salmon cannery, purchased a steamer, built a sawmill, store, hotel, town hall, and cold storage plant. Without any banks in the region, Cunningham issued his own currency made of brass.[23] He is said to have encouraged numerous hotels, brothels, and pubs to open up shop. Said one missionary, "all who lived at the place were more or less under his influence... the things he encouraged [created] the greatest difficulties in the spiritual advancement of the Church people at Essington."[24]

While his professional endeavours were quite lucrative, his personal life was marred by tragedy. Only one of his five children with Elizabeth Ryan survived to adulthood: three died in infancy and another drowned at the age of 17. His wife later perished in a canoe accident. Five years later, the 51-year-old Cunningham married a minister's 17-year-old niece within three weeks of meeting her. They would go on to have three children before his death in 1905.[25]

Having arrived on the North Coast as a lay missionary, Cunningham must not have come with the intention of making a fortune or starting a family. But on both counts, he got more than he bargained for. Between his economic endeavours, his left adequate financial support for his widow and children. And while he may have been fired from his first job in Metlakatla, that is where he was laid to rest.[26]

SPAKSUUT (SPOKESHUTE)

In the local Sm'algyax language, the Ts'msyen name for the site of Port Essington is Spaksuut (Anglicized to "Spokeshute"), which translates to "autumn camping place."[27] With the founding of Hazelton at the junction of the Skeena and Buckley Rivers in 1866, Port Essington developed rapidly thanks to the rise in freight traffic destined to the interior.[28] Hundreds of boats with miners, settlers, businessmen, and other officials travelled to Port Essington from the south before chartering Indigenous canoe crews to navigate the treacherous Skeena River currents with hundreds of pounds of supplies and gear. Even the HBC realized it would be more economical to supply its northern posts by utilizing Indigenous-led canoe expeditions, and eventually abandoned the long and arduous Fraser River route.²⁹

As the first new settlement on BC's North Coast after Confederation, Port Essington can claim many "firsts" for the region: the first hotel, town hall, and red-light district, meaning the first brothel and first bar, among others. While William Duncan's Metlakatla boasted the largest church north of San Francisco, much to his chagrin, Port Essington claimed the longest bar north of San Francisco.³⁰ One early visitor remarked that Port Essington was "a seething mass of humanity, with representatives of every race, and the vast majority of them in some degree of intoxication,"³¹ and that its streets were "among the lustiest of the north."³² Frequent brawling and even murder was not unheard of. Additionally, there was never consideration for the basic permanent fixtures necessary to building a community such as sewer, water, or electrical systems. Water came from rain barrels, and the tides beneath the boardwalks took care of the sewage and garbage.³³

The most transformative development for the area was the construction of the region's first salmon cannery and cold storage plant in 1876. Coincidentally, that was the same year that no gold was reported in the Omineca, marking the dawn of a new resource era. The gold rush was over, and salmon was set to take its place as the most in-demand commodity, much like gold had displaced the fur trade only a few years earlier.

The year 1876 was also a consequential one because the federal *Indian Act* reserve system was established by law. After nearly a century of mutually beneficial trading relationships, the advent of commercial salmon canneries and the *Indian Act* swiftly advanced the detrimental impacts of colonization into the North Coast. With Indigenous affairs now Ottawa's responsibility, Indigenous people could not vote or own land, so Cunningham privately held their land title in Port Essington.³⁴

Right before the emergence of salmon canneries, the Europeans in the region inhabited an Indigenous-governed space. In the mid-1870s, a visiting Methodist missionary remarked that "every mountain, every valley, every stream was named, and every piece belongs to some particular [Ts'msyen] family. This claim was recognized by all the white men... who rented small sites... for fishing purposes, and paid regular rent for the same."³⁵ So, almost immediately after

the establishment of Port Essington's cannery, the Canadian superintendent of Indian Affairs reported the concerns of Ts'msyen having
their rights encroached upon.

While the Ts'msyen sold fish to the canneries, they also demanded
payment for allowing fishing in their streams. They monitored and
sometimes even prevented fishing if the catch exceeded what they
thought was a fair return.[36] At first, canneries were almost completely
dependent on Indigenous people as a source of labour for both fishing
and shore work. Thanks to their ability to seize on the earliest economic opportunities of the industrial fishing and canning industry,
the Ts'msyen were described as the "most opulent aboriginal group
along the coast" and the "most advanced in civilization of all others
on the West Coast."[37]

The canneries then became an intricate part of the Indigenous
socio-economic ways of being. According to anthropologist Charles
Menzies,

> the canneries provided a nexus for Indigenous trade and created
> new avenues to maintain and develop ancient networks in the
> context of the emerging industrial economy. However, industrial
> development on the north coast also disrupted and inhibited the
> traditional economic system ... transform[ing] Indigenous into a
> dependent labour force.[38]

As dozens more canneries emerged around Port Essington, tensions between the Ts'msyen and commercial canneries reached a
point where twenty-nine white settlers, including Robert Cunningham, wrote to the lieutenant-governor: "We are too weak to hold
our own [against the Ts'msyen] and unless we are protected we will
be obliged to abandon our enterprises."[39] In response, the federal
government took swift and decisive action. In addition to sending a
gunboat in 1879 to demonstrate more "gunboat diplomacy,"[40] Canada
sped up the implementation of the *Indian Act* on the North Coast.

The concept of the food fishery was invented, essentially prohibit-
ing the sale of fish harvested from traditional sites or using traditional
technologies. By differentiating the Indigenous right to fish for food
or for barter, a false distinction was created between subsistence and
commercial fisheries.[41] Only white people could obtain independent
fishing licenses, and there were exclusive licenses only allocated to

canneries and processors. As a result, "only the canning companies, it seemed, could make money from salmon."[42] Within a few short years, Canada had effectively created a legalized, white-owned monopoly on commercial fisheries.[43]

The recently created Province of British Columbia followed suit. With Joseph Trutch in charge of BC Lands and Works, the provincial government denied the existence of Indigenous rights and title and enacted numerous prohibitions on land and resource ownership. After BC entered Confederation and Trutch became the first lieutenant-governor, his brother-in-law Peter O'Reilly arrived at the North Coast as the Indian Reserve commissioner, with the task of laying out reserves for the Ts'msyen and Nisga'a. Much like his newest family member, O'Reilly also refused to accept Indigenous entitlements or claims.[44]

Between 1880 and 1989, O'Reilly laid out far more reserves in BC than any other official. While he was appreciated by the colonial authorities for his efficiency, his almost total disregard for Indigenous views saw protest follow him almost wherever he went. As much as any one individual could be, he was largely responsible for the reserve map of BC,[45] particularly along the northern coastline.

O'Reilly's quick trip to the North Coast visit coincided with the rapid expansion of the industrial salmon canning industry, the establishment of permanent European settlements, and the first efforts by the newly formed colonial state to draw boundaries. He dismissed the idea that industrial canneries were interfering with Indigenous fisheries. He reduced the size of the Ts'msyen territorial claim because he felt that "so large an extent of country [had] no practicable use to them."[46] While he did eventually agree to create a 110-square-mile reserve south of Fort Simpson, the largest he ever allocated, O'Reilly only did so because he judged the land to be "for the most part, of a very worthless character."[47]

The local reaction to O'Reilly's 1882 land allocations was explosive and created a complex litany of complaints: reserve boundaries had been drawn wrong, allocated to the wrong people, cut people off from their own resources on which their livelihoods depended, and most fundamentally, O'Reilly had no right to allocate what was already owned.[48] A provincial commission was launched in 1884 because there were still acute fears of an "Indian war" that would dishonour the Crown. The resulting decision to allocate only ten acres per

Indigenous family was based on the commission's conclusion that the Ts'msyen had remained isolated from regulations and control for too long, and therefore, had no concept of land title.[49]

Soon after the reserves were laid out, the federal government issued a ban on the Potlatch, which came into force in 1885.[50] For the Ts'msyen, "without territory, a chief has no power. Without the ability to harvest, one does not have the ability to feast. Without the feast, names cannot be passed on."[51] In other words, the Ts'msyen Peoples' entire way of life was under serious threat by both levels of government.

THE SKEENA RIVER "UPRISING"

On May 8, 1888, the European settler fears of a "native uprising" were sparked when the first Gitxsan person, a man named Kitwancool Jim, was shot by a white constable near Hazelton, scared white people fortified in the HBC compound. They wrote directly to the BC attorney general, claiming, "our lives and property are in great, and we fear immediate danger."[52] A militia of seventy-two men with ten constables and the Provincial Police superintendent were dispatched. The militia set up camp at Port Essington under instruction from the BC Attorney General that they would be called inland if the superintendent and constables could not provide "relief of the white people."[53] While there, the gunboat made an additional stop in Fort Simpson to issue warnings about liquor and demonstrate its strength.[54]

After discovering the Gitxsan out fishing and the white residents "at liberty," the superintendent wrote back to the militia commander at Port Essington that matters were quiet, and that they should immediately return to Victoria. The episode was falsely labelled the "Skeena River Uprising," but the show of force was the largest that the northwest region of the province had seen up to that point.[55] And the message delivered was explicit: "law is the British law not the Indian law."[56] In the words of the police superintendent, "they seem now perfectly to understand our power."[57]

The Skeena River Uprising represented the start of a new era of colonial power in the region. In the following decade, the federal government began more aggressively restricting Indigenous fishing rights, reduced access to fishing grounds, barred Indigenous people from obtaining certain licenses, and established residential schools.

Federal Indian agents determined and controlled who had "status," the location and size of reserves, who could live on reserve, when and where children would go to school, and how traditional resources could be harvested.

Having been created under the colonial government's pre-emption laws, Port Essington was already unique. The settlement's inhabitants adhered to the land and resource regulations of provincial and federal officials. Contract law and taxes, not personal relationships, dictated economic exchange. Disagreements were settled in court, no longer by negotiation. Police constables collected taxes, fines, and fees for the fledging bureaucracy. Magistrates, inspectors, surveyors, insurance underwriters, and government officials were all dispatched to Port Essington. By the final years of the century, the North Coast had been brought into the emerging government regulatory regime.[58] The power dynamics and demographic balance in the province was rapidly and visibly turning. Indigenous people made up 52 percent of the population in 1881, but only 26 percent just ten years later.[59]

INTERCULTURALISM

As the industrial wage economy grew on BC's North Coast, so too did the need for workers. Mostly because the Europeans did not want to become over-reliant on Indigenous Peoples, they began bringing in low-paid Chinese and Japanese labourers.[60] All of the canneries in the Skeena region followed the same set up: the Europeans were administrators, clerks, mechanics, engineers and fishermen; Indigenous workers caught and cleaned fish; Japanese labourers who weren't fishing worked as carpenters and wood cutters; and the Chinese workers were mostly responsible for the canning.[61] With workers divided along ethnic lines, the physical and language barriers ensured that they could be played against each other for several decades, to the benefit of the European upper classes.[62]

Most Japanese issei (first generation) men came from poor farming and fishing villages and quickly formed fishing groups under a boshin (boss),[63] who negotiated a contract with a cannery. In exchange for a portion of their catch, the boshin took care of their accommodations, meals, clothing, and other services, including laundry and mail. In an unfamiliar environment with limited English abilities, the boshin system provided job security for the fishermen while also ensuring

the canneries received a reliable supply.[64] However, their quick success in the industry saw a rapid government response. Motivated by
appeals from white and Indigenous fishermen, as well as European
cannery owners, the federal government reduced hundreds of Japanese fishermen's access to fish by restricting them to harvest only
in specific areas and having processors bar them from obtaining
certain licenses.[65]

Similar to the Japanese, immigrant Chinese workers had "China
Bosses," who were contractors to the canneries and were responsible
for recruitment and the assignment and supervision of tasks. Chinese
workers made cans by hand and sorted and butchered incoming
fish with incredible productivity. Some had been documented to
have butchered up to 2,000 fish in a ten-hour workday.[66] The 1885
Royal Commission on Chinese Immigration shows 330 Chinese men
employed on the Skeena.[67] As the anti-Chinese movement in BC
grew, canneries along the coast saw the introduction of a new butchering machine called the "Iron Chink," a discriminatory name and
an explicit attempt to replace Chinese workers. While the machine
did speed up the slaughtering process, more Chinese workers were
ultimately needed in the canning process.[68]

Differences in language and racial prejudice must have been substantial cultural barriers for immigrants to the North Pacific coast,
but there were physical barriers as well. Communal and residential
networks were forged around mother tongues. The white elite lived
in large, fenced houses on the hill-slope away from the noise of the
canneries and the smell of offal. White fishermen boarded in the town
hotels and drank in the bars. The lives of Chinese cannery workers
revolved around the cannery butchering tables and bunkhouses. The
Ts'msyen lived in rows of huts rented from the canneries, and the Japanese fishermen also lived in blocks of cannery-built bunkhouses.[69]

The cultural and racial diversity among the people of Port Essington at the height of its population was a phenomenon for its
time. Many intercultural marriages yielded trilingual children who
spoke each of their parents' languages as well as English. One visitor
remarked: "What a motley crowd you will find ... what colouring,
what a Babel of tongues—Tlingits from Alaska, Haidas from the
Queen Charlotte Islands, Ts'msyens from the Skeena, Kawkiutls from
Vancouver, Chinamen, Japanese, Greeks, Scandinavians, Englishmen
and Yankees."[70] Similarly, a resident missionary stated that

human life at this village... is a conglomeration of races, and to one interested in the study of humanity most pleasing to watch... Indians, Japanese and Chinamen but while in larger towns and villages they are avoided and disliked by the whites, here... they enter into the totality of our lives, and wield their influence and play their part in it. It may be understood that we are a mixture, but to live amid such associations of human life and nature is to experience a life which can only be found in a few places.[71]

Fittingly, Port Essington saw the first large-scale integration of Indigenous children into the school system in BC, years before legislation technically allowed it.[72]

◦◦◦

By the turn of the twentieth century, Port Essington was one of the largest coastal settlements in BC north of Vancouver, with a seasonal population of 5,000.[73] Once gold supplanted sea otter pelts as the driving force in the European advance into northern BC, Ts'msyen economic and political dominance began to erode. The new missionaries, settlers, and forces of the Dominion of Canada and Province of British Columbia were not as malleable or reciprocal as the agents of the fur market economy. On the contrary, they were unyielding and aggressive, imposing far-reaching demands on the Indigenous population without compromise, whether that was giving up their language, their children to residential schools, or their traditional hunting and fishing grounds. The white man was no longer just a visitor to the shores of the North Pacific coast.

Fort Simpson brought international trade to the North Pacific, Metlakatla brought the church, and Port Essington, the state. Unlike in Fort Simpson, where disputes were directly negotiated between the HBC and the Ts'msyen, or in Metlakatla, where dictates were made by a single person (William Duncan), Port Essington drew upon the burgeoning judicial resources of the federal and provincial governments for its growth. It was not until the arrival of the industrial salmon canners like Robert Cunningham that the colonial administrative apparatus also arrived to the North Pacific. The short-lived, boom-bust experience of Port Essington, "the Klondike on the Skeena,"[74] was the final precursor to Kaien Island's emergence as a multicultural trading hub.

CHAPTER 6

FULL STEAM AHEAD
1903–7

"The entire north coast was searched, and every harbour sounded
before a final decision was made... the future metropolis of the
north coast will look out upon a harbour that is all that could be
hoped for... great are the possibilities of this new port."

GRAND TRUNK PACIFIC BROCHURE, 1912

THE STEAMER AGE

For an entire century, from the arrival of the first Europeans in the
late 1700s to the mid-1800s, the Ts'msyen had maintained a monopoly over Skeena River transportation by canoe freighting and guiding.
But once the Collin's Overland Telegraph company successfully chartered the first steamship 140 kilometres up the Skeena in 1865, that
longstanding monopoly was broken. Also known as paddle-wheelers,
a steam engine drove the stern paddles for propulsion, far surpassing
the limitations of oars or paddles. So when the Omineca Gold Rush
began, it suddenly became profitable for companies to charter and
build steamships. By 1891, the Ts'msyen "tariff of sixty dollars per ton
was declared ruinous by the [HBC], and they decided to build their
own steamer."[1] When the first HBC steamer *Caledonia* arrived at the
Skeena, it virtually collapsed the canoe freighting industry on the
river overnight, and with it, Ts'msyen control over the treacherous
Skeena transportation.[2]

The HBC had suddenly gained access to the trade for Haida Gwaii,
southeast Alaska, the Nass Valley, and the various places at the
mouth of the Skeena.[3] A single steamer proved to be so successful
that Forts McLoughlin, Stikine, and Taku were all abandoned as
Fort Simpson could now service the entire coast north of Vancouver
Island.[4] Robert Cunningham saw an opportunity to compete against
his former employer and bought his own sternwheeler, the *Monte*

Cristo, and poached the HBC's captain. Then the HBC built a second one, the *Strathcona.* Cunningham designed another, the *Hazelton,* and the HBC commissioned their third, the *Mount Royal.*[5] At one point, the rivalry escalated to a side-by-side race about 170 kilometres up the Skeena. Cunningham's *Hazelton* rammed the HBC's *Mount Royal* several times, causing it to lose control. The *Mount Royal's* captain responded by shooting his rifle at the *Hazelton's* captain. To rid themselves of the unprofitable and dangerous competition, the HBC eventually bought Cunningham's vessels and agreed to haul his freight for free.

Steamers would come to be used more in BC than anywhere else in North America for a number of reasons. With a flat bottom and shallow draft (the distance between the waterline and the boat's keel), they rode in the water like ducks, sometimes in depths of as little as six to eight inches. The wooden construction ensured they were buoyant and easy to repair. And utilizing a stern paddlewheel, the steamers could pass through narrow channels and dock easily without a wharf.[6] Once railway construction began in 1908, the Grand Trunk Pacific Railway construction firm made use of five sternwheelers to haul materials, supplies, and food for the first and hardest sections of track laying along the Skeena.[7]

The arrival of steamships and sternwheelers marked a watershed moment that heralded the end of Indigenous control over trade on the Skeena River, a real and symbolic loss of power. It was also one of the starkest juxtapositions of the European technological advantages and a showcase of the wide-ranging influence of burgeoning industrial commerce. Port Essington was the steamship's crucial base of operations given its strategic location at the mouth of the Skeena River, combined with the thriving local economy. While today steamboats may evoke romanticism and nostalgia for some, following fast in the wake of the Skeena steamships was the turbulent tide of colonization.

SETTING A TERMINUS

By the turn of the twentieth century, Kaien Island did not yet exist on European maps, owing to George Vancouver's earlier mistakes around the Skeena and Nass Rivers. When the Grand Trunk Pacific Railway surveyors began their work, it was naturally assumed that

Port Simpson would become the terminus for Canada's second transcontinental rail line. As the only active port on BC's North Coast with an adequate harbour, Port Simpson already had a hospital, multiple boat builders, a furniture factory, shingle mill, sawmill, multiple general stores, restaurants, a print shop, and a blacksmith shop. However, the provincial government had already sold most of the land around Port Simpson, leaving them nothing to negotiate with or leverage for public benefit.

So how did the rail line end up on Kaien Island instead of Port Simpson? The short answer is: the Klondike Gold Rush and Alaska Boundary Dispute.

Recall from Chapter 2 that the obscure 1824 Russo-American Treaty had set an ambiguous border near the forty-ninth parallel along the Portland Canal near the Nass River that "shall follow the summit of the mountains parallel to the coast."[8] After the United States purchased Alaska in 1867 from the Russians, the imprecise language in the treaty became a problem during the Klondike gold rush of 1897, which "brought the most concentrated mass movement of American citizens onto Canadian soil in all our history. In the space of fewer than 18 months, some 50,000 men and women... found themselves living temporarily under a foreign flag... almost everywhere, the Americans outnumbered the Canadians by at least 5 to 1."[9]

An arbitration process was launched in 1903 by the American and Canadian governments to settle the disputed Alaskan boundary. Given the remoteness of the area, the only maps of the region in use were the flawed admiralty charts of George Vancouver, so nobody knew what the true nature of the land was.[10] As a result, Vancouver's mistakes had profound geopolitical implications over a century later. With significant natural resources up for grabs, US president Theodore Roosevelt at one point threatened to send an occupation force to the territory. This threat, coupled with the arbitration panel ruling in favour of the US, infuriated the Canadian prime minister, Wilfrid Laurier.

Laurier had high hopes to surpass the Conservative-built Canadian Pacific Railway, which had reached the city of Vancouver only a few years before but was already limited thanks to a rapidly increasing population of immigrants and a growing economic output in the western provinces. Railways were highly politicized because massive government support was needed to construct them. The major issue of the 1904 federal election was whether the railway should be publicly or privately owned. Laurier's Liberals prevailed with a majority government to build an "All-Red Route," connecting Canada to the rest of Britain's empire, which at the time included Australia, New Zealand, pockets of Asia, the Middle East, and Africa.[11]

Owing to the Alaska Boundary Dispute, the prime minister suddenly found himself in need of a more southerly and easily defensible western terminus than Port Simpson for his new transcontinental railway. Enter Charles Hays, the general manager of the Grand Trunk Pacific Railway. Hays had some important inside information: the results of the Canadian Pacific Railway's original reconnaissance surveys had followed the Skeena River, but turned north before the river reached the sea.[12] So, when Hays approached Laurier about extending his railroad westward to the Pacific coast, he obtained immediate backing from the Laurier government, which wanted to build a railway to match or surpass the Conservative-backed Canadian Pacific Railway to Vancouver.[13] To fund the construction, the federal government committed $13,000 per mile on the Prairies, plus 75 percent of the actual cost of the mountain section.[14] At the time, the Grand Trunk Pacific (GTP) was slated to be the longest railway in the world, over some of the worst terrain ever encountered by builders. After the Panama Canal, the GTP project would be the largest construction project on Earth at the time.[15]

With the government subsidy confirmed, the GTP commissioned a survey at the mouth of the Skeena River to find a townsite with deep water access and wind protection. Kitimat was rejected because of the long, narrow channel required to reach it. One of the supposed reasons that George Vancouver did not ever venture into the waters surrounding Kaien Island is because of a rocky outcrop encroaching on the entrance to the harbour. After consulting coastal skippers and incomplete marine charts, the GTP surveyor sailed into the harbour and disembarked on the shores of Kaien Island in 1904.[16] On the surveyor's recommendation, Charles Hays and other GTP officials visited the following year. While enroute northward, the steamer carrying Hays' party struck a rock in heavy fog. Fortunately, the boat wasn't badly damaged and the rising tide lifted it afloat.[17] Unfortunately, Charles Hays's luck on the water would soon run out.

KAIEN ISLAND MAKES THE MAPS

An early GTP brochure campaign claimed that "the entire north coast was searched, and every harbour sounded before a final decision was made. The very satisfactory result is that the future metropolis of the north coast will look out upon a harbour that is all that could be hoped for... it has a mile-wide channel, and is sufficient in size to shelter all ships that are likely to come to it, great are the possibilities of this new port."[18]

Only four generations from first contact between Europeans and the Ts'msyen, the north Pacific coast had seen a lot of change, from the founding of Fort Simpson and Metlakatla to the creation of the first industrial salmon cannery on the Skeena. The stage was finally set for the development of Kaien Island. The settlement of Fort Simpson had proven that intercultural trading relationships based on reciprocity could maintain mutually beneficial advantages, but it had also brought violence and disease. Metlakatla was a living testament to both the potential and pitfalls of a hybrid bi-cultural value system. And Port Essington was the place where an entrepreneurial spirit and a tense blend of cultures came together in the new wage-based, boom-bust resource economy. All of these factors were set to be combined on Kaien Island, so it would seem fitting that the first dock on Prince Rupert's new waterfront was built with piles bought from Metlakatla, with a pile driver rented from Robert Cunningham in Port Essington.[19]

Without the cunning trading prowess, political alliances, and natural resource management of the Ts'msyen, the first permanent European settlement at Fort Simpson would likely have failed. Without Fort Simpson, it's possible that William Duncan may not have gathered enough followers for a new settlement, or he may not have moved to the north coast at all, which would have meant there would be no Metlakatan "holy city." If not for successive gold rushes on Haida Gwaii or the Fraser, Omineca, and Klondike rivers, the colonial government may not have established authority at the mouth of the Skeena River. The Industrial Revolution was necessary for salmon canneries to bring thousands of settlers to the north Pacific coast. And, finally, it took the Alaska Boundary Dispute, Wilfrid Laurier's election, and his friendship with Charles Hays for Canada's second transcontinental railway to have ended up on Kaien Island. This unlikely series of events culminated in Kaien Island finally making the map, correcting George Vancouver's century-old oversight and laying the foundation for development to begin in earnest.

THE LAND QUESTION

With Kaien Island selected as the railway terminus, Charles Hays and the GTP required land to start building. After being denied land grants by the provincial government, Hays formed the GTP Development Company and purchased 10,000 acres for a townsite in 1905. But before architects could lay out the city, Hays had been advised that the GTP railyards and wharves would require an additional 14,000 acres from Ts'msyen reserve land, the boundaries of which had been drawn by the Indian agent O'Reilly just over a decade previously. The GTP legal agent was sent to negotiate with Metlakatla with the stated objective of "securing Indian rights first" before dealing with the provincial government. At that time, provincial consent was required for reserve land transactions.[20]

Unfortunately, few records have survived about the land negotiations. What is known is that the participants included the GTP's legal agent, the Indian agent, and a local Anglican bishop. Metlakatla initially refused to sell the whole parcel of land to the GTP. After a week of negotiations, the GTP offered $5 per acre, received a counteroffer of $10 per acre, and settled on $7.50 per acre for 13,567 acres, with one half of the proceeds to be paid immediately to Metlakatla and divided evenly amongst its membership. Although the decision was described as being unanimous, the vote was not taken until 2 AM after several meetings.[21] As historian Patricia Roy explains, with the "combined forces of God, the Law, and Business, they acquiesced to the sale."[22] The costs of land purchases was not always the same in other placed where the railway would pass through. In comparison, the GTP paid over $115 per acre in Prince George, plus offered additional lands in compensation.[23] Despite the disparity, the local Indian agent concluded that "it was an excellent bargain from which Native people could use every cent in repairing and furnishing their houses."[24] A 2023 legal settlement gave Metlakatla the maximum possible award of $150 million after determining the accurate market value was $31 per acre, and that the federal government had engaged in financial wrongdoing.

Along the GTP's route, the company had gained an evil reputation with its numerous high-handed and often illegal actions. A BC
judge would later say of the GTP that the company was not above
"a breach of faith of the worst character to achieve its ends, or of
obtaining land through the grossest deceit."[25] Unsurprisingly, the
GTP did not immediately pay up the first half that was promised to
Metlakatla, in part because it was technically illegal. To complete
the agreed upon transaction, the company had to first convince the
federal government to amend the Indian Act. Down payments on
"surrendered land" could not exceed 10 percent, and any reserve lands
"surrendered" automatically reverted to the Province. While the GTP
successfully lobbied the federal government to increase the maximum
down payment to 50 percent a few months later, the Province claimed
the "surrendered" reserve lands for itself and issued an eviction notice.
Provincial representatives argued that the GTP could not buy the land
since the Ts'msyen technically did not own it, and therefore, could
not sell what was held in trust by the federal government.[26]

In response, the GTP offered the Province one quarter of the profits
and waterfront lands if they agreed to extinguish Ts'msyen reserve
title, arguing that the land was worthless to the Province. Yet the
Province's valuation was $4 million for half the reserve lands, about
fifty times higher in value per acre than what the GTP had offered
Metlakatla,[27] adding that the railway had to begin building eastward before 1908 or there was no deal. While Charles Hays agreed
to the condition, his decision later spelled disaster for the railway
company. During the months-long dispute, the GTP convinced the
Indian agent to withhold the money from Metlakatla until a deal was
reached with the Province. A provincial commission would later find
that Metlakatla's "surrender" of 10,458 acres would constitute over
20 percent of the total Indigenous land sold in the entire province.

KAIEN ISLAND INVESTIGATION

News of the Ts'msyen land sale broke as the provincial government
was already embroiled in an investigation into the sale of an additional 10,000 acres around Kaien Island. The GTP had disguised
their acquisition by using an agent, paying only $5.20 per acre to
an intermediary to mask the transaction. But when their agent
staked out both sides of Tuck Inlet with "GTP" labels, a group of

South African veterans attempted to file for over 1,000 acres on Kaien Island, overlapping the GTP's claim in an attempt to financially benefit through land speculation. The Province rejected the request on suspect grounds, which led to them being sued by the prospecting South Africans, prompting a formal inquiry called the Kaien Island Investigation.[28] The inquiry determined that there were significant irregularities and illegalities in how the provincial government was transferring lands to the railway. However, the GTP was able to preserve the lands it had acquired at an incredibly low cost, meaning townsite development could begin.[29]

A name was needed for the new city, so the GTP hosted a nation-wide contest. Despite not meeting the naming criteria of two syllables or fewer, and being "distinctly Canadian," GTP officers selected a three-syllabled entry that was the namesake of a man who had never set foot on the North American continent: Prince Rupert of the Rhine.

COLOURFUL CHARACTER:
PRINCE RUPERT OF THE RHINE

Recognized as the first Governor of the Hudson's Bay Company, Prince Rupert was known as the "Prince Robber," the "Duke of Plunderland," the "Bloody Prince," or even the devil himself. He had even been described as "perhaps the most hated man in England" during his lifetime.[30]

Born in 1619 to Frederick V of the Palatinate, or the Winter King of Bohemia, Rupert spent his childhood in exile after his family lost the throne before his first birthday. Drafted into military service at the age of twelve, he had a long and colourful career as a soldier. He fought in the both Thirty Years' War and the Eighty Years' War, before being captured and imprisoned twice. After release, he joined the English Civil War, quickly rising ranks to become the general of the Royalist army by the age of twenty-four.[31] During this time, the earliest use of the word "plunder" in English, coming from the German "plundern" (literally "to rob household goods"), is associated with the activities of Prince Rupert's forces.[32]

After the Royalists' surrender in the First English Civil War, Rupert was banished from England. He then fought for the French

Prince Rupert, circa 1650. PUBLIC DOMAIN

king Louis xiv in the Franco-Spanish War as a mercenary in command of all the English in France.[33] He miraculously survived being shot in the head, followed by the medieval procedure of trepanning (burrs drilled in the skull), before returning to England for the Second English Civil War as a navy admiral, despite having no naval experience.

To raise money for his fleet to retake England, he persuaded his mother to pawn her jewellery and began ordering his crew to pillage from other ships. Sailing down the Iberian coast and the Mediterranean, capturing and looting as they went, Rupert commanded his forces to resort to trickery: flying the wrong flag to attract supposed friends and luring officers away from their ships before overwhelming them. After surviving a major shipwreck that claimed the lives of over 300 of his men, he plotted a course for West Africa to avoid an enemy fleet that had been sent to hunt him down.[34]

Off the coast of modern-day Mauritania, Rupert took a young Indigenous boy as an "exotic servant" before sailing up the Gambia River, where "relationships with the Indigenous people proved fraught."[35] Multiple skirmishes and hostage-takings culminated in Rupert taking an arrow to the chest. He ordered his crew to sail for the Caribbean to continue plundering the English and Spanish, which resulted in a small mutiny. With his "ragbag fleet of warships," Rupert's forces captured multiple merchant ships and killed a handful of sailors before returning to France. After four years of piracy, Rupert returned with a disappointing haul, causing suspicion that the "financial accounts of his spoils were less than honest." This made worse not only by his refusal to hand over the proceeds to the British king, Charles II, but also by his insistence that the king also pay the expenses of his voyage.[36]

At 33, aged by a life of conflict and without enough money to match his princely birth rank, Prince Rupert began engaging in scientific experimentation. As one of the founding members of the Royal Society, the oldest scientific institution in the world, he made a wide range of impressive discoveries and inventions from his experiments,[37] including: a precursor to tempered glass, known as "Prince Rupert's drops"; a cannon, the "Rupertinoe"; a geometric concept, "Prince Rupert's cube"; and a brass alloy used as imitation gold, "Prince Rupert's metal." And on top of fabricating a gunpowder ten times stronger than anything of his time, Rupert also created a gun that fired high-speed rounds, installed rotating barrels on a handgun, and built an explosive charge that could travel through water—the early precursors to the machine gun, revolver, and torpedo.

While Prince Rupert's scientific contributions are impressive, his morals were not. Having previously discovered goldfields in West Africa, Rupert became one of the first two patentees and councillors of the Royal African Company. Formed with the principal goals of acquiring gold ore and slaves, the Royal African Company shipped "more enslaved African women, men and children to the Americas than any other single institution during the entire period of the transatlantic slave trade."[38]

When Prince Rupert retired from the military, he was appointed by Charles II as constable of Windsor Castle. It was here he encountered two Frenchman who claimed that New France (modern-day Quebec) was the key to finding the Northwest Passage and unimaginable wealth. Prince Rupert secured investors and formed a syndicate that funded a voyage across the Atlantic in 1668. Demonstrating Prince Rupert's importance to the mission, the nearest freshwater source found after reaching the Hudson's Bay was immediately named the Rupert River by the crew. So too was the first fort eventually named after him.[39]

The excursion proved that lucrative trade was possible in the New World. In quite possibly the most lopsided deal in recorded history, the King Charles granted Prince Rupert the governorship of the newly chartered Hudson's Bay Company, with a trade monopoly of every tributary that flowed into the Hudson Bay. Covering over 3.8 million square kilometres, or one third of modern Canada, five times the size of France, the territory claimed by the company was named "Rupert's Land." On paper, one of the largest empires in human history was instantaneously created in exchange for just two elks and two black beavers per year from the company as tribute to the British king.[40] Prince Rupert helped build the foundation of an enormously profitable colonial trade empire by the time of his death in 1682. The company remains the world's oldest surviving commercial enterprise, which at its height held territory ten times the size of the Holy Roman Empire.

There is a diverse array of descriptors that fit Prince Rupert of the Rhine: prince, exile, cavalier, pirate, plunderer, renegade, inventor, or even renaissance man. Even in the face of concern about his immoral character, the officers of the Grand Trunk Pacific believed Prince Rupert still met their criteria for being "distinctly Canadian." While he undoubtedly left a mark on the country through the HBC, Prince Rupert's life was as colourful as the history of the city that now bears his name.

CHAPTER 7

THE TIP OF THE RAINBOW
1908–12

"Picture Prince Rupert, the golden city which is being built at the rainbow's tip. when it has been painted and pictured and painted again, and the west-bound traveller, watching from the window of the train... rounds the shoulder of the last mountain and has flashed before him the real thing, he will own to a feeling of disappointment, not with the picture, but with the poor painters."
CY WARMAN, GRAND TRUNK RAILWAY ADVERTISEMENT, 1908

ON TRACK

With Kaien Island officially secured as a terminus for his railway, Charles Hays launched a global charm offensive with widespread advertisements of the promise of a new major port metropolis set to grow to 100,000 people and rival the likes of Vancouver and San Francisco. Designed to attract outside investment, Hays and the GTP hired a publicist to begin marketing "the Dream City, a paragon of perfection," the "Canadian City of Certainties," "Gloucester of the Pacific," and the "Norway of North America."[1]

Hays confidently predicted that, as the nearest port to Asia,

to this new port will come the ships of the Seven Seas. Ships of the East, laden with silk and rice, will soon be riding at anchor in this splendid harbour, to sail away laden with lumber; ships from the West with the wares of the West; ships from the shores of far-off continents, trading through the new and picturesque port of Prince Rupert.[2]

The railway also made the bold predictions that the new city would have 50,000 residents by 1920 because, "unlike an oil town or a mining camp, its stability, its fortune is, by reason of the railway and the richness of the surrounding country, already assured."[3] In other words, Prince Rupert was their pot of gold at the end of the line.

To support these grandiose and exaggerated claims, Hays hired his daughter's new husband, George Hall of the Brett & Hall landscape architecture firm from Boston, to design a city that could rival any international metropolitan destination. This act of nepotism resulted in a sweeping townsite plan laid out in the City Beautiful style, which aimed to maximize an aesthetic defined by grand monuments and boulevards, symmetry, and public spaces. By its very design, Prince Rupert was intended to embody the values of a British society.[4]

At the turn of the century in Canada, the best way to promote new railway lines and increase potential profits was to develop railway stations and hotels. To pay for his grand promises, Hays and the GTP embarked on a massive building program, buying 45,000 acres along the rail line and laying out 120 new towns along the route named from A to Z.[5] In existing major urban centres, new landmark buildings were constructed inspired by French Renaissance architecture. The Chateau Laurier in Ottawa was fit with ornate gables and Belgian marble floors. The Fort Garry Hotel in Winnipeg was the tallest structure in the city when it was completed, and one of the first hotels where each room had its own bathroom and luxury tub. In Edmonton, the Hotel MacDonald was designed with countless "pilasters, balustrades, balconettes... cornices, arches and keystones."[6]

Fitting into this, a central feature in the Brett & Hall town design was a grand hotel designed by famed architect Francis Rattenbury, the man who had designed the BC Legislature, the Empress Hotel (commissioned by rival company Canadian Pacific), Government House, and the Vancouver Art Gallery. Planned to be twice as high as the Empress in Victoria, the Chateau Prince Rupert was to serve a fleet of the world's largest ocean liners and act as the official railway terminus.[7] The extravagance, opulence, and grandeur of the chateau-style hotels across Canada were all chosen by Hays himself, and the Chateau Prince Rupert was to rival or even surpass them all in this respect.

Contrary to the values of the utopian and grandiose city plan, however, the GTP enforced very strict commercial requirements, retaining effective control of the entire waterfront for the rail yard and wharves, and securing a kind of hegemony that (mostly) still exists today. The GTP General Manager wrote, "the rail way company's requirements at the waterfront are paramount, the townsite secondary."[8] The GTP's designs would prove so sweepingly effective that an aerial map of the City of Prince Rupert today is immediately recognizable beside the original 1907 Brett & Hall plans. As a result, the present-day community has inherited a purposeful lack of public waterfront access in favour of the railway and port complex.

MAKING IT OFFICIAL

As a "company town," no one could independently move to Prince Rupert, at least not legally. Permission had to be sought from the general manager of the GTP, who lived in Montreal. But thanks to the GTP's glitzy marketing and promotional campaign, hundreds of unordinary characters were attracted to Kaien Island on the promise of building a new civic utopia. In defiance to the GTP's repeated warnings to stay away, a Scottish prospector named John Knox staked out a miner's mineral claim on Kaien Island. He then granted anyone who applied permission to live on his claim. Soon, a little village known as Knoxville developed, which surely would have irritated the GTP. By the time the railway survey party arrived to build a wharf and railway headquarters, they found a population of nearly 1,000 "squatters" and 150 businesses, a rag-tag group of individuals living in a makeshift tent-town, three quarters of which were on John Knox's claim.[9] The first local newspaper reported that "the village does not have a boss, either political or landowning, and residents enjoy the utmost freedom, paying no taxes... and worship God every man after his own fashion—may the Mineral Act never be repealed or changed!"[10] When it came time for the construction of the waterfront railway yard and Knoxville's inevitable eviction, the headlining article in the local newspaper read that "war was openly declared" as dynamite wrecked a building and windows were smashed before the violence was quelled.[11]

Beyond attracting lively newcomers, the GTP's aggressive salesmanship set off a speculative boom as land auctions began carving lots out of the rainforest for buyers from all over the world. In another not-so-subtle act of nepotism, Charles Hays' brother was appointed as the GTP Development Company's sole land agent. David Hays personally brokered nearly $600,000 worth of real estate for the company (over $18 million in 2023 dollars). Corner lots in the downtown sold for as much as $50,000 ($1.67 million in 2023 dollars), and the first 1,200 lots were sold to outside speculators, resulting in criticism that the company was doing "fancy work for vested interests."[12] But once locals could bid, the newspaper recounted that "people crowded into the harbour... they were intending to make their fortunes out of the muskeg and mud and the people and the ships and the railway... hardships were laughed away for all could see the rainbow with the pot of gold."[13]

By the time the first lot sales were completed at the end of summer in 1909, the population of Prince Rupert had more than tripled to 3,000 people.[14] Widespread advertisements for clearing contractors brought people of many nationalities and religions together to cut down trees. Before long, most of Kaien Island was entirely levelled, with only "stumps of all sizes left in a sea of muskeg on the hilly shores."[15] But this was no easy task, as a long pamphlet described:

> You walk out on the stump ranch you notice a peculiar springiness to the ground—watch out—later on you will realize the true meaning... you patiently excavate around the stump until the spreading roots are bared... you then cut all the visible roots cleaning in two and, standing back, you give the stump a shove with your foot expecting to push it out. Not so fast! Instead you find there is the secondary root system, the members of which are nearly all larger than the stump. You cut these, and then you start to pry... after several minutes of hard work the stump comes out with a juicy sucking sound... festooned with dripping muskeg. You proceed just the same with the others... note all the time that the springiness is decreasing and that instead your shoes are being pulled off... at last you are finished, and you look back with pride, dimmed somewhat with the knowledge that instead of a stump ranch, you are now the proud owner of a muskeg swamp. This will require several drainage ditches to make it serviceable. And then you remember that the back yard still hasn't been touched.[16]

The construction of government docks, major streets, wholesale distribution companies, and the railway meant that Prince Rupert quickly had better access to both goods and services than the nearby communities. Even the unofficial mayor of Port Essington chose to relocate his business to Prince Rupert.[17] In 1910, Prime Minister Wilfrid Laurier visited Prince Rupert for its official incorporation.

He remarked, "I have no doubt that someday Prince Rupert is destined to be one of the great cities of the North American continent... probably never before has there been so much money and time expended in the planning of a new city."[18]

ONE CORPORATION TOWN

While most cities grow organically over time owing to their natural advantages, Prince Rupert's site was selected by a transportation company for its deep harbour and proximity to another continent. Furthermore, a "made-to-order" city plan that largely ignored the topography meant the cutting of rock bluffs and removal of bogs. The first streets were built on stilts above the muskeg while rock bluffs and hillsides were blasted and levelled. Approximately 306,000 cubic metres of rock had to be removed just for the rail yards.[19] As a result, Kaien Island's physiography required much more capital than the average city to grade streets and install sewers and water supply. City building is expensive. But building a fully planned-out city that did not take into account the rocky bluffs and deep muskeg required a lot more money and debt.[20]

The first elected head of the city's finance committee, Duff Pattullo, moved to establish public services as quickly as possible in order to attract investment. He helped persuade the provincial government to grant the city water and power rights on Woodworth Lake (which is still used to this day). He tabled the first municipal budget built on large-scale debt spending and a flat tax on all unimproved properties to fund lighting, streets, and other public improvements. He gave city project labourers a 17 percent hourly wage increase and instituted an eight-hour workday.[21] However, while Pattullo's plan was endorsed by the majority of the city council, it ran afoul of the GTP.

Despite being labelled as the "father of Prince Rupert," Charles Hays was not inclined to provide financial support for the newborn city. When the first municipal tax bill of $105,000 came due, Hays and the GTP objected as they felt they should be given a total exemption, taking the position that the city would not have existed without the railway. Hays demanded to be exempted from taxes for fifteen to twenty years and threatened to discontinue all work on the railway projects in the city, including the rail itself, the hotel, the cruise terminal, and the dry dock. Hays pressured the city's only bank into withholding funds from the new municipality and prevented the city's bonds from being advertised. He even threatened to move the proposed railway terminus and dry dock to Port Simpson. After four years of GTP development on Kaien Island, this threat was preposterous,[22] especially given that the dry dock itself weighed 20,000 tons, the largest on the entire Pacific coast.[23]

Duff Pattullo stood firm against the intimidation and went to the papers saying that "the GTP does not own the country; the country owns the GTP."[24] Eventually, the railway presented a counteroffer of $5,000 a year, to which one of the local newspapers retorted that the offer was "a joke, although not a very funny one since it would mean that the citizens of Prince Rupert would have to carry almost the entire tax burden."[25] The dispute saw accusations of socialism and disloyal agitators, and drew public criticism that Prince Rupert was in danger of becoming a "one corporation town." In the end, the city council and the GTP agreed to an annual levy of $15,000 per year for ten years, with the GTP providing to hundred feet (sixty metres) of waterfront and sixteen lots to be used for parks and public buildings.[26]

The animosity between the GTP and municipality spilled over into the local elections the following year when the entire incumbent city council lost their seats, except for Duff Pattullo, who was now fondly known by locals as "Finance Minister Pattullo." At the next election, Duff Pattullo campaigned for the mayorship on a platform of establishing an eight-hour workday and raising minimum hourly rates by 10 to 15 percent for the city writ-large. He won with two simple slogans: "Cut the peanut politics and get together to boost Prince Rupert" and "Provide plenty of work at good wages."[27] The former still resonates with local "Rupert boosters" today, while the latter would later reverberate around the entire province some twenty years later.[28] Duff Pattullo would go on to become MLA of Prince Rupert in the 1916 election and would sit as a member of the Legislative Assembly representing Prince Rupert for nearly 30 years, first as Minister of Lands, then leader of the Opposition, and finally as Premier.

The GTP's efforts to quash local opposition had failed, and it is estimated that delaying the works during the dispute costed them more than $50,000 ($1.4 million in 2023 dollars). According to an assessment by railway historian Frank Leonard, "fault can be placed nowhere other than with [GTP] President Hays."[29]

LABOUR RELATIONS

The infant city had a working class that was largely non-British, working for low wages in poor conditions to clear the land and prepare the civil works. Conversely, virtually all of the local authorities were of British origin. So it's no surprise that when the Prince Rupert Industrial Association was formed, nearly a thousand people who joined with the founding members came from the United States, Scotland, Sweden, Spain, Serbia, Ireland, Italy, and Montenegro.[30]

In 1911, when a private street contractor refused to match the new minimum wage enacted by the municipality, the Prince Rupert Industrial Association launched a strike. The road building company responded by importing replacement workers. Unsurprisingly, a riot broke out. Five hundred men attacked a twelve-metre cliff where the private contractors were building a new road. Fifty-six workers were arrested by the police, despite the police being outnumbered twenty to one. Two police officers were injured, and three people were shot.[31]

The new Conservative-led council panicked and called a secret meeting at the offices of the GTP's main contractor, Foley Welch & Stewart. The company had earned a slogan from critics: "Frig 'em, Work 'em and Starve 'em." This was partly because they issued time cheques instead of cash, with uncompetitive wages.[32] The council discreetly called on the federal government to send the HMS *Rainbow* to suppress the strikers. The *Rainbow* was a heavily armoured and significantly gunned Royal Canadian Navy cruiser that would later be ordered to intervene in the infamous *Komagata Maru* incident. Although the strike was eventually a failure, and fourteen of the ringleaders were eventually tried in Victoria,[33] this legendary strike is now known as the Battle of Kelly's Cut. The influence of the labour movement in the city has lived on ever since.[34]

The GTP had a vital interest in keeping wage levels low in Prince Rupert during a time of acute regional labour shortages. Even before the strike, their bad pay and terrible camp conditions on the remote Skeena River route had caused a high desertion rate to the comfort of the newfound amenities in Prince Rupert. The GTP helped to import professional strike-breakers from the US who shepherded men through picket lines and publicly vilified strike leaders. They even went as far as having their contractors meet incoming ships outside of Prince Rupert in order to take men directly up the Skeena to work camps to avoid the risk of losing them.[35]

The GTP's intervention in the strike did see men return to work and wage levels stagnate for years. However, their "win" came at a significant cost. In addition to losing almost an entire construction season, the GTP was now on the hook for debt repayments. A later analysis by railway historian Frank Leonard showed that if the GTP had paid the requested daily rate of $3–4, they would have saved $4.5 million in interest costs. After four years, less than 321 kilometres of track had been laid westward.[36]

Charles Hays visited in 1912 and disputed the concerns that low wages, poor camp conditions, sketchy accommodations, and bad food were contributing to the labour problem. In his own words, the problem was that workers themselves were "a class who like to be where they can spend half their time in palaces of amusement."[37] While Hays had absolute control over the circumstances of the labour shortage caused by his own orders, there is no evidence that he ever considered offering a more conciliatory labour relations policy.[38] Instead, the GTP pressed further.

Said the leader of the Prince Rupert Industrial Association, when it came to the GTP, the "court and the lawyer's office is a regular trail."[39] First, the company lured new workers with false advertising of wages of $3.50 to $4.00 per day, while in reality only paying $2.25 to $2.50. Then, in an attempt to induce more men to move to Prince Rupert to replace the strikers, the GTP offered paid transportation—but with a catch. They inserted a clause in the contract that released the company from liability for all injuries, even those caused by company negligence. This allowed the GTP legal department to begin claiming contributory negligence, which could diminish the company's liability and damages paid, in cases where an employee was injured or killed.

There are many egregious examples of the GTP's underhanded tactics in early Prince Rupert. When a brakeman lost a leg after being knocked off a car in a freight yard, while still in a state of shock, the employee was immediately approached by the GTP agent to sign an incident statement that no one was to blame. In another incident, they rejected the claim of a worker who was injured falling off a roof on a project that the GTP directly supervised. And when a GTP clerk was killed helping a client, the company held back compensation to the employee's widow, claiming he had gone beyond the terms of employment in helping their customer. But perhaps most disgustingly, when a GTP labourer was crushed to death between a pile driver and a dock, the subsequent inquest found that the pile driver operator had not whistled before moving. The company refused to pay $3,000 in compensation to the employee's father, who then sued them. In response to the suit, the GTP hired agents to spy on the man, threatened him, and then coerced him into a settlement of only $850. For this so-called success, the hired lawyer responsible became the GTP's new legal agent in Prince Rupert.[40]

RACE RELATIONS

The earliest European settlers in Prince Rupert bragged that every new Rupertite had come from somewhere else. Of course, this statement ignored the entire Indigenous population. There are no records of Indigenous people purchasing land in the early days of Prince Rupert. Local newspapers explicitly refused to print articles supporting Indigenous rights and title and only mentioned Indigenous people anonymously. Numerous stores and restaurants refused service. Many jobs or companies would not hire. The city council rejected the Indian agent's request to establish a hostel to increase the amount of trade with Indigenous people, saying "the object should be not to attract them to Prince Rupert but to keep them away."[41]

As bad as the prejudice was, Indigenous people resented being treated like Asian immigrants.[42] Between 1906 and 1909, the GTP had forty-two Chinese labourers mostly doing menial work. But by 1911, there were about 150 Chinese people in Prince Rupert; some had started their own businesses, including contracting to the railway. As the anti-Chinese movement was growing across BC and Canada. The local police chief referred to them as "little Chink devils." When two Chinese families bought two buildings on one block and opened laundries, the all-white city council passed bylaws restricting their location and operations, and instituted intrusive monitoring and enforcement.[43] One local newspaper claimed that the Chinese quarter was full of "filth, immorality, and drunkenness,"[44] while another paper regularly featured anti-Chinese advertisements.

Similar vitriol extended to the Japanese, who had arrived as fishermen but were lumped in with the Chinese by the white majority as "Asiatic labour." White and Indigenous fishermen had successfully joined forces to stage a strike that called for the reduction of fishing licences to the Japanese. In addition to many losing their licences, Japanese fishermen were also restricted to specific areas, barred from being skippers on herring seiners, prohibited from salmon seining, and even dictated to whom they could deliver their catch.[45] At one point in 1907, the number of local Japanese labourers had grown to 125, nearly one third of Kaien Island's population at the time.[46]

The BC premier, Richard McBride, personally reminded Charles Hays of his government's policy of "retaining this Province as a white man's country," and induced the GTP to sign a legal agreement with the provincial government in 1903, which stipulated that white labour should be used exclusively unless they could prove the impossibility of doing so to the government's satisfaction.[47] However, this had little effect on the GTP's hiring practices. By 1909, despite the fact that wages in BC had risen 30 percent, Hays took the position that the company should pay rates as close as possible to the 1903 agreement, saying "we will take every kind of labour we can get... if white workers would not work for the wages we are paying, we will employ any kind of immigrant."[48] Hays even went as far as asking Premier McBride to import Asian labourers under bond,[49] a form of temporary indentured servitude. While it was clearly not corporate benevolence or a desire for diversity behind the GTP's hiring practices, Asian immigrants continued to find employment with the company and were allowed to locate their businesses on GTP land.

If you were Chinese, Japanese, or Indigenous in Prince Rupert in the early 1900s, you legally did not have the right to vote, run in elections, buy land, or qualify for the most high-paying jobs. The Prince Rupert Pioneer's Association and Prince Rupert Board of Trade both declared that only white people were eligible for membership. Additionally, their membership cards even had a statement in red ink that employers of Asian labour were not eligible.[50] A local group was formed called the Society of White Pioneers, where the only membership requirements were to swear an oath to oppose "Asiatic Coolie Labourers" and not to vote for anyone who did business with Asians.[51] White children were taught in separate schools, while entry-level English programs were only made available to immigrants from Scandinavia.[52] Despite the city erecting a welcome arch that read "Come One, Come All, Let 'Em All Come," it was abundantly clear that only a certain complexion of people were to receive a hospitable reception.

RELIGIOUS RELATIONS

While there were clearly racial and class disparities, there was also an incredible number of active religious groups in the early days of Prince Rupert. By the time the city was officially incorporated in 1910, the Anglicans, Presbyterians, Roman Catholics, Salvation Army, and Lutherans had constructed their own churches. There were even forty early Jewish residents who formed the Beth Israel congregation. Within just a couple of years, the Anglicans, Methodists, and Baptists had all erected their second churches,[53] and after an influx of Scandinavian fishing families had settled, the Lutheran congregation began switching between Norwegian and English every week. Said the local Member of Parliament, "we have little if any religious strife; the people live in amity, one with another, and they allow their neighbours to have such religious opinions as their consciences dictate. Their action in that regard might very well be copied in other parts of the world."[54] This foundation of religious pluralism has extended into the current century. Beyond the earliest arrivals, Jehovah's Witness, Pentecostal, Mennonite Brethren, Seventh Day Adventist, United, Native Revival, Church of Christ, and Sikh communities all have an active presence in the community today.

"PIONEERS"

While there was a significant amount of diversity right from the beginnings of the city, it obviously did not translate into inclusivity or harmony. Prince Rupert was far from a civic utopia. While it may be easy to romanticize the period under the guise of "pioneering," Prince Rupert was by no means a futuristic metropolis. While other cities in the Lower Mainland and Vancouver Island had decades of experience with municipal water and sewage systems, Prince Rupert was much closer to a wild west frontier town. The early community garbage disposal system was a large barge with a central trap door and high sloping sides, moored at the waterfront. When filled, the garbage boat was towed out to sea and the trap door opened. For obvious reasons, it was often nicknamed the "sniff yacht" or "floating lavender box." To deal with sewage, the city purchased a thousand night soil cans that were carried around the streets on a horse-drawn cart, nicknamed the "Honeywagon." Three men would empty the

Honeywagon's waste buckets six nights a week. Additionally, rats plagued Prince Rupert so badly that the municipal government had to reach out to Britain's Royal Institute of Public Health for advice.[55]

It was not just public services that lacked sophistication in Prince Rupert's early days, but also public safety. The local militia, called the "Muskeg Scouts," carried no arms and wore civilian trousers with their uniform jackets. The local chief of police also had to serve as game warden, mining recorder, health inspector, justice of the peace, and notary public.[56] Police chief William Vickers was once asked if there was anyone in jail who could be a deckhand to aid a ship that had recently lost a crew member due to desertion. The ship legally required one more person on board, regardless of their experience or competence as a sailor. Without anyone in jail at the time, Vickers replied, "Now if there's no one in the jail who should do, surely in this town somewhere there's a character who should be in jail." A drunk transient couldn't give a proper account for himself was arrested and released on the condition that he get out of town immediately. When the man was driven to the wharf and dumped over the railing of the ship, the captain looked at his limp new recruit and said, "I'll be damned ... that's the [expletive] who jumped ship."[57]

❧

By 1912, the infant city of Prince Rupert had a uniquely diverse population of more than three thousand souls with origins from Metlakatla to Montenegro and everywhere in between. For those who followed the railway to the Golden City at the tip of the rainbow, Prince Rupert was a new place that represented many things: a pot of gold at the end of the line, a gateway to a new world, and a promise for the future. Beyond the natural splendour of its surroundings, the community of Prince Rupert had a strong sense that they were destined for greatness. However, that spirit would soon be tested by a series of unfortunate events and rash of bad timing.

CHAPTER 8

A TITANIC LOSS

1912–14

> "The trend to playing fast and loose with larger
> and larger ships will end in tragedy."
> CHARLES HAYS, APRIL 14, 1912

UNSINKABLE DREAMS

In April 1912, Charles Hays was in London, England, to convince the GTP board of directors to invest even more money to continue his ambitious railway and hotel construction plans. He won tentative approval to continue with his plans, albeit with his trademark flair for exaggeration. Even though Hays had negotiated a sweetheart deal with the Laurier government to only pay interest on the government construction loan charges for the first seven years, he flagrantly misrepresented the terms of the deal to win over his nervous shareholders, claiming the GTP would face no charges at all for ten years.[1]

While Hays was in England, part of his business dealings brought him in contact with the chairman of the White Star Line, Bruce Ismay. Years prior, one of the people who recommended Hays to the GTP was financier J.P. Morgan, who now controlled the White Star Line.[2] Hays wanted the luxury cruise line to bring travellers from Europe and Asia to his dream city of Prince Rupert. Ismay extended an invitation to Hays as his personal guest aboard the RMS *Titanic*, the largest and fastest ship in the world at the time, which was about to embark on its ill-fated maiden voyage. Hays gladly accepted the offer because he was anxious to get back to Canada. The gala opening of his grand new hotel, the Chateau Laurier in Ottawa, was scheduled for April 26 while the *Titanic* was scheduled to depart on April 10.[3]

On the eve of the tragedy, Hays allegedly made a prophetic remark. While engaged in a conversation about the advances in transportation, he criticized the way steamship lines were competing to win passengers with bigger and ever-faster vessels, saying, "The trend to playing fast and loose with larger and larger ships will end in tragedy."[4] Later that night, the "Ship of Dreams" became a place of nightmare after it struck an iceberg, ultimately resulting in the deaths of over 1,500 souls.

The same hubris that defined Hays's railway career may partly explain his untimely demise. One of his acquaintances who survived the sinking said that Hays did not show any fear after the *Titanic* hit the iceberg, reportedly telling his daughter as she was getting on a lifeboat, "This ship is good for eight hours, and long before then help will arrive."[5] Apparently, she was so reassured by her father's demeanour that she didn't even kiss him or her husband goodbye. The *Titanic* sank in less than three hours. Hays drowned in the disaster and his body was recovered eleven days after the sinking.[6]

IN HIS TRACKS

The demise of Charles Hays on the *Titanic* dealt a huge blow to his company and the city of Prince Rupert. W.H. Biggar, the former head of the GTP legal department, stated: "but for [Hays's] untimely death ... I believe that the GTP today would have a very different story to tell."[7] Newspapers ran countless headlines resembling the theme that it was "the Iceberg that Shook Prince Rupert."[8] Local historian Dr. Richard Geddes Large concluded in 1960: "the Grand Trunk Pacific Railway and the City of Prince Rupert were "entirely the children of his brain ... with his death, the inspiration was gone."[9]

It has been said that when the *Titanic*, the "Ship of Dreams," sank to the bottom of the Atlantic, so too did the dreams of Prince Rupert. Charles Hays carried his plans in his hip pocket; it would have been impossible to estimate just how far the effects of his sudden demise would reach.[10] His son-in-law noted that Hays's plans "will never be known as they perished with his brain ... it will take months just to gather together the threads."[11] Throughout his career at the GTP, Hays had explicitly refused to delegate authority to others on the grounds that he and his general counsel were the only ones who understood government relations. Said Rivers Wilson, the president of the GTP's parent company, "the GTP had become a one-man management, undivided, and practically uncontrolled."[12]

In a strange coincidence of timing, the same day that news of the *Titanic*'s fate first broke, it also was reported that the city of Prince

Rupert had reached its borrowing capacity. As a result, the city council was forced to cut staff, salaries, and projects.[13] As plans for Prince
Rupert were being abandoned one by one, it was being written in
the press that "Prince Rupert never attained that Impossible Dream
as Hays saw it ... never developed to its full potential."[14] An all-too-
common refrain became that Prince Rupert was orphaned with the
loss of its founding father.[15]

Without a doubt, the death of Charles Hays was a symbolic loss
of optimism for the future. However, while building up the life story
of a visionary founder makes for a compelling tale, it incorrectly pro-
motes the myth that Hays's successors somehow lacked the ability to
steward his dreams of grandeur for Prince Rupert into reality. Quite
the opposite: Hays's death revealed the financially ruinous position
the railway, and by extension the city, had been left in because of
his decisions and actions. Ironically, this left Hays's successors in
the metaphorical position of re-arranging the deck chairs on the
Titanic in trying to salvage the GTP's prospects. Less than five years
after Hays's death, the GTP defaulted on loan payments to the federal
government and was nationalized.[16]

SUNK COSTS

The collapse of the GTP after 1912 has commonly but inaccurately
been attributed to Hays's untimely demise. However, thanks to the
benefit of hindsight, it becomes apparent that with the data available
to Charles Hays when he made decisions, his willful extravagance,
exaggerations, and outright lies all contributed to the GTP's downfall.
There were three major mistakes directly attributed to Charles Hays
that resulted in the quick failure of the GTP and the stagnation of
development in Prince Rupert only a few short years after his death.

1. *Hays failed to control high construction costs.* The rail line between
Prince Rupert and Hazelton has been described as the most difficult
section of railway ever to be built in North America. Almost 2,000
kilometes of trial lines and surveys were required before three hundred kilometres of track were finally laid on the Skeena River.[17] It
took two million blasts of dynamite and ten million pounds of high
explosives over twenty-six months to clear a single rock cut of more
than 2,000 metres (6,600 feet) at a single estuary on the edge of Kaien

Island.[18] Charles Hays told the GTP board chair that construction of the BC portion of the railway line could be done for the government subsidy of $30,000 per mile, despite the fact that internal assessments forecasted a cost of $50,000 per mile for just the section between Prince Rupert and Hazelton. A government inspector later certified the cost of the mountain section of the GTP across BC at more than $112,000 per mile[19]—more than double the GTP's internal forecast and nearly quadruple what Hays had claimed to his board of directors.

The original 1903 budget for the rail line from Prince Rupert to Edmonton was less than $40 million. Already facing overruns in 1909, Hays hired an appraiser, who concluded that without his cost-saving recommendations, the new estimated cost of the project was on track for $51 million. Ultimately, the western section of rail cost a total of $93.3 million, more than double the original budget. By the time the *Titanic* was getting ready for launch in 1912, the GTP had already accumulated a debt of nearly $100 million on Hays's watch.[20] Despite the enormous size of the company's debts, "Hays's solution—which smacks of blind obstinacy or unreasonable pride—was to spend more money."[21]

Many historians and railway analysts have attributed the construction overruns to Hays's obsession with achieving the lowest possible rail gradient. His stated hope was to keep the mountain section gradient at Prairie-low levels to give locomotives up to seven times the hauling capacity of its competitor to the south, the Canadian Pacific Railway. But Hays's own words in 1909 contradict this claim and betray a major flaw in his negotiated deal with the federal government: "the high standard of perfection, with attendant high rate of expenditure, was imposed upon us... by the Canadian government."[22] A 1921 inspection was even more blunt: "the standard was too high for that time and place and population and traffic."[23] In other words, Hays knew the ballooning costs and failed to manage the GTP's debt effectively.

2. *Hays grossly overestimated traffic and income on the railway.* To convince the skeptical GTP board to continue funding his increasingly expensive enterprise, Charles Hays made several outlandish forecasts and projections. Without any realistic basis, he claimed that immediately after completion, the rail line would see fourteen trains per day running in and out of Prince Rupert, a number that was 40 percent higher than the already well-established CPR line to Vancouver.[24] The GTP made astounding public predictions that the

land within a one hundred mile radius around Prince Rupert could produce enough timber to keep twenty-five modern sawmills busy for twenty-five years[25] and that they would soon be shipping 100 million bushels of wheat annually to Europe through the Panama Canal, somehow for the same cost and in the same amount of time as Atlantic ports.[26] They also bragged extensively that halibut and salmon returns would secure the rail's future forever.[27]

These far-out public promises are particularly perplexing given that Hays was privy to private information that indicated much smaller prospects for the GTP line. Two surveys done by the CPR in 1877 and 1879 of the Skeena, Bulkley, and Nechako Rivers concluded that "for the development of revenue... there can scarcely be any doubt that this route... would be found inferior to "a more southerly route.[28] The GTP general manager warned Hays as early as 1905 that the huge expenditures on the west end of the transcontinental railway had no prospect of earning sufficient returns from traffic. In 1907, a GTP vice-president stated that "there was no likelihood of the Mountain Section paying its fixed charges for a long time to come... it is on a very different footing to the Prairie section where revenue would be derived immediately."[29]

After the rail line opened a few months after Hays's death, the underwhelming reality of eight trains per week paled in comparison to the prediction of fourteen trains per day. The following year, a federal government commission revealed that the GTP liabilities were more than five times its income from the rail line, concluding "that it will need... a good many years' development to create a business that will make it profitable."[30] Based on these facts, one must conclude that Charles Hays was either an eternal optimist, a seasoned swindler, or both.

3. *Hays's building plan was rushed and flawed.* Unlike most other nineteenth century railways, the GTP did not secure a land grant from Canada or BC to finance construction. Securing land grants first was the very strategy Hays used with his previous railway experience in the US, yet he was unable to emulate it with the GTP in Canada. Instead, he demanded immediate, high returns on townsite lot sales in Prince Rupert to "establish a very strong basis for our issue of bonds which should then sell at a good price and furnish us the capital for additional development purchases."[31] But once lot sales

were completed in Prince Rupert, GTP publicity basically came to a standstill. Combining this fact with the bleeding of money on grand hotels suggested that Hays wanted to maximize profits from townsite development before investors realized that lacklustre traffic would not adequately support the operating costs of the rail line.[32]

A 1914 appraisal had already concluded that the numerous land-slides and washouts in remote areas meant maintenance costs would be incredibly higher than anticipated. It was no surprise, then, that findings in a 1922–23 customs data traffic report showed that Vancouver exported 625,000 tons compared to only 5,000 tons from Prince Rupert. Despite all the grand pronouncements about proximity, actual trans-Pacific trade was virtually non-existent in Prince Rupert because the high operating costs of the rail line effectively eliminated the advantage of having a shorter shipping route. As a result, the cost for goods to reach the US industrial heartland was higher from Prince Rupert than Vancouver, leaving the Prince Rupert rail line to be described as "a road from nowhere, to nowhere, passing nowhere."[33]

Hays's single most damaging decision that all but ensured the GTP's bankruptcy was to build the railway west and east concurrently instead of focusing on the money-making Prairie routes to start generating positive cash flow to service debts.[34] It is no small irony that Hays was legally compelled to begin rail construction from Prince Rupert to settle a dispute with the provincial government that stemmed from his company's illicit land acquisition tactics on Kaien Island. Had the GTP taken a more conservative and longer-term approach, the transcontinental railway may have taken a few more years to complete but could likely have avoided bankruptcy. As the former GTP chairperson put it, "Hays was in too much of a hurry... he constituted a danger for the Company."[35]

COLOURFUL CHARACTER: CHARLES MELVILLE HAYS

Born in Illinois, Charles Hays seemed destined for a life working on the railway, having graduated school at the age of seventeen and immediately joined the Missouri Pacific Railway as a clerk. When the general manager was looking for a secretary, he found Hays was the only young clerk preoccupied with work, not wasting time chatting or watching the clock. Hays allegedly said to the general

Charles Hays, the "Father of Prince Rupert."
CITY OF PRINCE RUPERT FONDS. PRINCE
RUPERT CITY & REGIONAL ARCHIVES

manager that the only two stations on the line that clockwatchers know are sundown and payday.[36] His career saw steady growth from there: by the age of twenty-six, he was the confidential secretary to the general manager; by twenty-eight, he was promoted to assistant manager; at thirty-three, he was appointed as general manager of the entire system; and at thirty-eight, he was elected vice-president of the company before being recruited to Canada to complete his meteoric rise in charge of the Grand Trunk Pacific Railway.[37]

Dubbed "the Little American" for his stocky stature, the *Railway Age Gazette* described Hays as "very self-possessed, seldom showing irritation or anger, and his capacity for work seemed unlimited."[38] His intense management style and penchant for centralized decision-making was described by Rivers Wilson, the chairperson of the GTP, as being "disinclined to delegate any portion of his authority, or even to encourage initiative in his subordinates."[39] One of Wilfrid Laurier's cabinet ministers went so far as to call Hays "heartless, cruel and tyrannical."[40] Hays may not have possessed the self-awareness necessary to admit to those accusations, given a notion he expressed in some of his personal correspondence that "they always say I bring the sunshine and the facts seem to prove it."[41]

A staunch member of the American Presbyterian Church in Montreal, Hays was already firmly entrenched in the elite aristocracy when he first reached Canada. In addition to having a direct line of communication with his friend Prime Minister Wilfrid Laurier, he had also served as governor of McGill University, Montreal General Hospital, and the Royal Victoria Hospital as well as vice-president of the St. John Ambulance Association.[42] Hays's high status was also the partial cause of his eventual demise when his family and colleagues secured four first-class cabins on the *Titanic* as invited guests of the White Star Line's managing director.[43]

For his varied contributions to Canadian railway development, he was offered a British knighthood, but declined in order to retain his American citizenship. For his efforts in building the closest port to Asia, he was recognized by Prince Fushimi Sadanaru in 1907, on behalf of the Japanese emperor, with the Order of the Rising Sun.[44] Upon the official confirmation of his death, "sanctified by this tragic end and by his high social standing," Canadian newspapers mourned "a national loss" and the entire Grand Trunk system halted in tribute while simultaneous services were held in Montreal, London, Prince Rupert, and elsewhere.[45] Said his obituary: "exactly how much good he wrought for the land of his adoption will very likely not be fully realized until his deeds are viewed in the perspective which only distance of time can give to a contemplation of the gigantic schemes which he fathered."[46]

Now that we have the distance of time—indeed, the benefit of a century of hindsight—it is reasonable to ask: how much good did Hays do for Prince Rupert? Can it truly be said that "Charles Hays is beyond question the greatest railroad genius in Canada"[47] as Sir Wilfred Laurier once proclaimed?

When it comes to how Hays built the GTP's Pacific terminus at Prince Rupert, it was said by a government appraiser in 1921 that the railway was built "about one hundred years too soon."[48] Hays's failure to control or reduce expenditures, his acquiescence to BC's and Canada's requirements to build eastward from Prince Rupert at a strict gradient, and his unfounded promises of huge traffic volumes spelled quick financial ruin for the railway. And yet, more than a century after his death, the railway line is now being marketed as having "the gentlest grade through the Rocky Mountains compared to any West Coast port," and reaching the Midwest a full day or two faster than any other port on North America's Pacific coast. Now the third largest port in Canada, Prince Rupert is handling approximately $60 billion in trade value every year and over 32 million tons of cargo.[49]

While he may have been ahead of his time in regard to the railway, Charles Hays was certainly a man of his time when it came to the prejudices of the white upper class. He appointed his own brother as the sole GTP land agent and awarded the Prince Rupert townsite plan to his daughter's husband.[50] He was less generous in his relationship with organized labour, however. When GTP workers in Prince Rupert went on strike in demanding wage parity with their local labourer counterparts, Hays almost immediately fired all the leaders of the movement. Even after a protracted settlement was agreed upon, he reneged on his promise to reinstate 250 men and denied many of his workers their pensions.[51] Much of Hays's railroad career is defined by his "implacable disdain" for organized labour.[52]

Hays's prejudice was not limited to social class. While he may not have been as openly racist as the provincial government of the day, his multicultural motivations were primarily based on finding cheap labour and land. He sought to encourage the immigration of up to 5,000 Japanese and Chinese labourers to build the railway, yet subjected them to poor wages and deplorable living conditions. And his heavy-handed tactics with Indigenous groups saw him pay a pittances for land and forced relocation. This was only slightly more than can be said for Richard McBride's provincial government, which neglected to even negotiate with Indigenous Peoples, choosing rather to completely ignore them while appropriating their territories and the resources that came with them.

Charles Hays may well be considered the "father of Prince Rupert," albeit an absent and problematic parent with racist, elitist, and ruthless tendencies. He did expend an intense amount of energy within a short timeframe to plant the necessary seeds for the city to be born. However, the claim that Prince Rupert is today somehow his "orphan" is wrong on numerous counts. Only a child who has lost both parents is considered an orphan. If Prince Rupert lost its father, we cannot forget the importance of Mother Nature. Without the safe deepwater harbour and proximity to Asia, Kaien Island would simply not have been able to play host to an Asia–Pacific port city. Being labelled an orphan also suggests that Prince Rupert was in some way deprived or disadvantaged by Hays's absence after 1912. Given his anti-worker elitism, refusal to pay local taxes, proclivity for unsustainable debt, and fantasy forecasts, this claim is dubious. Lastly, long before Charles Hays was born, Kaien Island had served as a multicultural trade and gathering hub for thousands of years. The Ts'msyen and their neighbours set the table for multicultural exchange, and thousands of their descendants have since helped nurture the city into what it has become today. The major irony is that Hays's divide-and-conquer strategy is what managed to connect Prince Rupert with the rest of the continent. Perhaps Hays is most deserving of the nickname bestowed upon his own railway company: "the Grand Trafficker of Promises."

RIP VAN RUPERT

It would not take long before whispers began that the tragic death of Charles Hays was a bad omen for the city of Prince Rupert. Sir George Foster, the federal minister of trade and commerce in the Borden government is recorded to have said that "Prince Rupert appears to be struggling under a curse."[53] This quip later inspired the character of Rip Van Rupert.[54]

The life of the ss *Prince Rupert* quickly validated the theory of a curse. One of Charles Hays's many dreams was to build a first-class passenger steamship line. This was to compete with the Princess ships of the Canadian Pacific Railway, so he decided to call his new ships the Princes. Commissioned by the GTP in 1910, just two years before the *Titanic* set sail, the ss *Prince Rupert* was built to provide passenger and freight service between Vancouver, Victoria, Prince Rupert, Stewart, Haida Gwaii, and Seattle. For the early years of the ship's service, it served the GTP fleet well. However, after the death of Charles Hays, the ship experienced a string of misfortune.

In December 1916, the ss *Prince Rupert* collided with a tugboat in Vancouver Harbour before running aground only three months later, requiring two months of repairs in the dry dock. Soon after, someone accidentally stripped the ship's screws, and it was forced to dock in Victoria for repairs. After the First World War, in 1919, the ship was struck by lightning that split the mast in two, and later that year suffered a fire in the cargo hold. Then, in 1920, the vessel struck a reef in the Inside Passage, tearing a hole in the bottom of its hull and getting beached until being completely submerged at high tide. After salvaging and reconstructions, in 1923, the ship again ran aground during a snowstorm before being freed by a passing Princess steamship liner without any damage. Four years later, the *Prince Rupert* ran aground yet again, but this time on Ripple Rock in the Seymour Narrows, in tides so strong they pulled the vessel back over the rock again. It was back to dry dock for more repairs. In August 1927, a broken rudder that saw the ship swept out into the Seymour Narrows by the tide before another ship came to the rescue, affixed a tow line, and transferred all passengers to safety. Four years later, during an annual refit, a leak caused the vessel to keel over and sink, resulting in an additional month of repairs. The cause of this particular mishap: a window was left open by a painter during low tide to air out the smell. Another four years after that, the *Prince Rupert* rammed into and sank a halibut vessel. Finally, it rammed a Princess cruise liner just north of Prince Rupert, cutting a twenty-eight-foot hole in the bow. While both ships were deemed at fault, the ss *Prince Rupert* was ultimately taken out of service and sold for scrap to a Japanese iron company in Osaka.

Despite enduring this series of both serious and minor accidents, not a single person was ever killed during the ship's forty-four years of service, which covered more than 150,000 miles and carried more than 300,000 passengers.[55] The life of the ss *Prince Rupert* can be interpreted much in the same way as the early life of the city of Prince Rupert: for the pessimists, the ship was cursed and pre-destined to fail; but for the eternal optimists, the series of unlikely near-misses and close calls was really good luck after all.

DERAILED PLANS

Similar to how the arrival of steamships on the Skeena River ended the centuries-old Indigenous canoe freighting industry seemingly overnight in 1891, the last spike of the Grand Trunk Pacific railway saw the final steamship on the Skeena bow out.[56] A new era had officially begun for Prince Rupert as Kaien Island was finally connected to the rest of the North American continent.

Almost exactly two years to the day from the sinking of the *Titanic*, the first GTP train arrived in Prince Rupert from Winnipeg in April 1914. Welcomed with huge fanfare, the train was a watershed moment that must have given local residents a sense of renewed optimism and hope that Prince Rupert's plans were back on track. But if the death of Charles Hays really was the start of a Prince Rupert curse, that curse materialised as bad timing. The railway was completed just a few months before the outbreak of the First World War, just in time to carry many residents away to Europe.

CHAPTER 9

HALIBUT CAPITAL OF THE WORLD

1914–38

> "All the fish you ever heard or dreamed of, appear to
> be found at or near Prince Rupert. Fish are referred to
> by the ton. Any other term would be inadequate."
>
> SUE ROWSE, *BIRTH OF A CITY*

THE FIRST WORLD WAR IN PRINCE RUPERT

From the beginning to the end of the First World War, not a lot changed in Prince Rupert, but the city did experience its fair share of local scares. "Prince Rumours" abounded, such as that of a German destroyer apparently arriving to commandeer coal deposits. Two local dry dock workers were charged with spying for Germany, and there were reports of German cruisers sailing north from the Vancouver area eager for a fight. The world was gripped by war and Rupertites were obviously invested in the outcome. When "Victory Loan" war bonds went for sale, Rupertites offered five times more than the average Canadian.[1]

While generally uneventful, the war years did heighten local tensions and differences based on race. Local sports leagues segregated Indigenous players and local theatres separated Indigenous people to their own seating. Anti-Asian sentiment was growing more rampant; Prince Rupert hotels advertised that "no Orientals of any kind have ever been employed."[2] Even the ever-popular politician Duff Pattullo had to justify during the 1916 election that, despite his last name, he was not of "Italian extraction."[3]

Although the fighting did not spread to the west coast of North America, the influenza pandemic did reach Kaien Island. In October 1918, with twenty-five cases overcrowding the local hospital, the mayor and city council decided to close schools, poolrooms, and theatres in an attempt to slow the spread of the virus. Large gatherings and public meetings were strongly discouraged. Churches, stores, and the library were ordered to close. Two to four Rupertites died every day for a week, including a city councillor. A school was converted into an emergency hospital and citizens were encouraged to donate beds and volunteer as nurse aids.[4] The pandemic had a tremendous impact on the local economy, which was evident in the total fish catch being halved from over one million pounds in November 1917 to just over 600,000 pounds the following November.

PRINCE RUPERT IN THE FIRST WORLD WAR

The outbreak of war found Prince Rupert without any military organization. So little organization, in fact, that the mayor requested that the authorities in Ottawa send two hundred soldiers, which they quickly did.[5] Luckily, a former Vancouver military instructor named Cyrus Peck had recently arrived to the Prince Rupert area. After first serving as the sergeant of the local militia, Peck took command of a 225-man, ad hoc volunteer unit dubbed the "Prince Rupert Company." After a few months of training, Prince Rupert sent off their company by closing all businesses and having thousands of people attend the wharf to honour the men.[6]

Up until the First World War, Indigenous military service was not used by any imperialist European state because the so-called "science"—that is, racist social biases and public opinion—believed it dangerous for domestic security to train and arm Indigenous people. Nevertheless, after Britain's declaration of war on Germany in August 1914, many Indigenous communities and leaders openly declared who they were siding with. In Prince Rupert, public praise was given to the people of Metlakatla, who donated $1,000 to the Allies.[7] They were so invested in the outcome of the war that they offered to purchase war bonds but were refused by the Indian agent because "war profiteering was unbecoming."[8] Most of the volunteers from Prince Rupert were of British heritage, but there were a handful of Indigenous soldiers as well. Although no official policy forbade the enlistment of Indigenous Peoples, the Ministry of Militia and the Department of Indian Affairs actively discouraged enlistment; thus, few were accepted for service.[9]

COLOURFUL CHARACTER: CYRUS PECK

Lieutenant Colonel Cyrus Peck, Victoria Cross
recipient. DR. R. GEDDES LARGE FONDS.
PRINCE RUPERT CITY & REGIONAL ARCHIVES

The Prince Rupert unit stayed together on the front lines in Europe
with the 16th Battalion (Canadian Scottish) of the Canadian Expe-
ditionary Force, led by Major Cyrus Wesley Peck. Born on Canada's
east coast to American parents, Peck had taken military training
but was not accepted for service. After a failed stint as one of the
thousands of Klondike gold rushers, he arrived in Prince Rupert to
help start a salmon cannery.

Less than a year after being sent overseas with a rank of captain,
Peck was promoted to lieutenant colonel for his efforts in the Battle
of the Somme.[10] After the capture of Vimy Ridge, he won the Distin-
guished Service Order (DSO).[11] His command came to be defined by
the fact that he had his own personal Highland bagpiper on the battle-
field, despite not being Scottish himself. During one intense skirmish
with the Germans, despite being shot in the leg and wounded on the
other, Peck was reported by a member of the Prince Rupert company
as "walking along unconcernedly and not ducking, waving his cane
and shouting: come on boys, come on!"[12] After the commander of
the 16th Battalion was wounded, it was Peck who led the regiment
into a dark, rainy-night attack that was so successful it eventually
resulted in his promotion for the battle of Vimy Ridge.

In the fall of 1917, Peck was asked to run in the federal election for Prime Minister Robert Borden's Conservative party in the Skeena riding. Peck accepted on the condition that he would remain in the trenches. After Peck was claimed the winner, he refused to return to sit in the House of Commons until the war was over, staying at the front with his troops. As one of his officers put it, Peck "was forever marching in the shadow of death. How he survived is one of the great mysteries of the war."[13]

In 1918, Peck was awarded with the Victoria Cross for his coura-geous leadership and bravery. He is reputedly the only member of Parliament in the British Commonwealth to have been awarded the Victoria Cross while in office.[14] Upon his return to Prince Rupert in 1919, as he walked the boardwalks along the muddy streets, Peck declared "I love you better than any spot in the world."[15]

It is unfortunate that even the most conspicuous of Prince Rupert's war heroes harboured the same racist and prejudiced sentiments of his era. During his time in elected office, Peck showed a public disdain towards Asian immigrants, going as far to say "for 30 years politicians have talked white B.C., but it was getting more yellow all the time."[16] He viewed fishing as a "means of colonization," saying to the House of Commons that "what we want in this country is a great white fishing population, men of our own brawn and breed."[17] In addition, he whitewashed the experience of Indigenous peoples, saying their history on BC's North Coast was a "strange and grand romance which does the utmost credit to the Indian department and the missionaries of the various churches."[18] Peck was in equal measure a celebrated war hero fighting for freedom abroad and an embodiment of Prince Rupert's prejudices of the time, a colourful contradiction.

POSTWAR RECOVERY

By the time Cyrus Peck and the Prince Rupert Company made it home from war, the circumstances of life in Canada, British Colum-bia and Prince Rupert had changed. Countless lives had been lost, including nearly one hundred men from the Prince Rupert area. Unemployment was high and inflation was rampant. Working con-ditions and wages were incredibly poor. The city was forced to rely on banks for financing and slashed its workforce.

Only a few months after the war had ended, Prince Rupert's population was approximately 5,000. Prohibition had been rescinded. The General Strike of 1919 solidified Prince Rupert's standing as one of the strongest Labour cities on the Pacific Coast, as nine local unions walked off the job in solidarity with the Winnipeg General Strike. Without the longshoremen, machinists, pipe-fitters, railway checks, freight handlers, and fish packers, railway freight and steamships stopped running and fish boats went elsewhere to unload. After the GTP threatened to terminate all of the participants, the Prince Rupert strikers held out an extra week longer than Winnipeg to ensure everyone was reinstated.[19]

While the city had survived the stresses of the First World War, the GTP did not. Just a few months before the November 1918 Armistice, the railway defaulted on its federal construction loans. The company's once-famed dry dock had sat idle through the conflict, labelled as the "the greatest slacker in Canada." Quite ironically, while the use of cheap Chinese labour is what got the GTP dry dock built, it is one of the reasons that Canadian ships were being sent to China to be dry docked.[20] Furthermore, the high cost to transport steel to Prince Rupert, combined with a shortage of steel plates meant that the local dry dock was entirely left out of Ottawa's contracts.[21]

GTP stock was worthless, so the federal Department of Railways and Canals took over control and created the Canadian National Railways from the remnants of the GTP. The GTP was quickly relegated to a branch instead of a mainline because of the low traffic. Still deep in debt, the railway convinced the Prince Rupert city council to reduce its taxes by nearly half in 1922, before defaulting on over $300,000 in taxes the following year. This resulted in the termination of all top-salaried staff at City Hall and a 10 percent wage cut for all remaining staff.[22]

But there was some good news for the local troops to return to. Within five days of war being declared over, the dry dock finally got a contract to build two government ships, the *Canadian Scottish* and the *Canadian Britisher,* and then a lot more. Hundreds of jobs were created for steel and wooden boat-building. Of particular significance, during the war, women in BC (not including those who were Asian or Indigenous) had earned the right to vote and hold public office. Prince Rupert had elected its first female councillor, Elizabeth Kirkpatrick, who also served as a school board trustee in

1918. Additionally, although construction had been halted due to the onset of war, the provincial courthouse was finally under construction, built directly in front of the foundation that had been previously abandoned at the start of war.[23] Thousands of tourists were arriving on cruise liners,[24] and mainly as a result of significant halibut fishing activity, the city's finances had returned to good shape by the 1920s.

HALIBUT BE THY NAME

With close proximity to the salmon runs at the mouth of the Skeena and the Nass Rivers, plus the plentiful halibut, Prince Rupert was quickly becoming the home port for one of the largest fisheries in the world, sustaining thirty-eight canneries and processing facilities in the immediate area.[25] Without international fishing boundaries at the time, Americans fished on common grounds with Canadians and gained port privileges to land halibut at Prince Rupert. Millions of pounds and dozens of varying species were being unloaded and shipped out every month. Having landed over 90 percent of all the halibut in BC, the local industry of halibut fishing was so consequential that a young boy was reported to have said his prayers in front of his mother one night as "Our Father, which are in Heaven, Halibut be Thy Name."[26]

Unsurprisingly, Prince Rupert earned the titles of Halibut Capital of the World and the World's Halibutropolis. Word was quickly spreading around the world about the abundance of seafood surrounding Kaien Island:

> The arrival of fishing boats each with a catch averaging 100,000 pounds of Halibut excites no particular comment in Prince Rupert. People are getting used to it. A man toiling up town from under the weight of a salmon almost as long as himself, may not be given a second glance. Herring, cod, flounder—all the fish you ever heard or dreamed of, appear to be found at or near Prince Rupert. Fish are referred to by the ton. Any other term would be inadequate.[27]

This was all made possible by the "mosquito fleet," coined because the boats it comprised were small and very plentiful. The success of the fishing industry created success for the local boat shops. The era of fish boat building was unprecedented. At one point, at least one new boat was being reported every week, built wherever someone could find a spot to lay out a keel. Across the harbour at Dodge Cove, then known as the "Norwegian Village," Ed Wahl began a legendary boat-building career, eventually launching over 1100 boats before his death and earning the nickname "Henry Ford of wooden boat-building."[28]

Heightened race tensions exacerbated during the war were acutely demonstrated by the growing fishing industry. Significant white resentment was growing, particularly against Chinese and Japanese immigrant fishermen. Local white fishermen demanded that the federal government forbid Japanese fishermen from having gas boat licenses, so that a "great step would be taken in ridding the fisheries of them."[29] Ottawa obliged and further reduced fishing licenses issued to non-British subjects by 15 percent.[30] Prince Rupert's ethnic makeup may have been diverse, but it was hardly a place of equal opportunity.

THE NOT-SO-ROARING TWENTIES

By 1920, it was obvious that the original grandiose vision for the city may have been misleading. The *Prince Rupert Daily News* editorial reported:

> The attitude of dissatisfaction that prevails in some quarters is due to a well defined reason. In 1910 a brilliant, too brilliant, future was painted for Prince Rupert, one that probably would not have been attained had conditions continued as indications at that time promised. Everybody predicted 50,000 population in 1920, with skyscrapers and ocean steam routes and pretentious institutions. There was a boom and following it came the reaction with stagnation. Then following the great war, when the world was straining every nerve to increase its powers of destruction. Progress could not be expected at that time. Now again, however, the city is on the upgrade and the future looks rosy.[31]

For Prince Rupert residents, it seemed that the veil had been partially lifted on the truth that Charles Hays's and the GTP's predictions were self-promotion, not prophecy. The prosperity of the Roaring Twenties did not quite reach Kaien Island's shores. A critical shortage of refrigerated rail cars took its toll on the seafood industry; halibut, salmon, and cod that could not be kept cool began to rot and become odorous on its journey eastward.[32] The local shipyard remained entangled in various legal disputes. Predictions of economic growth blazoned in countless front-page headlines, such as the building of pulp and sawmills, a smelter, a cattle market, energy utilities, hotels, a butter factory, and even an Alaskan free trade zone, never came to fruition.[33]

Yet, while there were plenty of broken promises, there were also some bright spots. Salmon runs and halibut prices reached record highs. The provincial courthouse, which had been abandoned during the war, finally celebrated its grand opening, with Duff Pattullo receiving a golden key as thanks for his work in the provincial cabinet. The first ship sailed directly from Prince Rupert to Asia in 1923.[34]

But the most notable and symbolic form of progress was the construction of a grain elevator. When the first grain ship arrived from Japan in 1927, it was considered important enough to be greeted by the Canadian governor-general. The new elevator was seen as the realization of the original dream for Prince Rupert to be a hub for trans-Pacific trade, earning the city the nickname "Prince of Pacific Ports." By the end of its first season of operation, almost eight million bushels of wheat were processed—a far cry from the 100 million predicted by Charles Hays and the GTP, but a respectable number nonetheless.

THE GREAT DEPRESSION

If people doubted that Prince Rupert was truly cursed by bad timing, then the Great Depression could not have come at a better time to convince the skeptics. The new president of the Canadian National Railways (CN), which had absorbed the GTP in 1919, had just launched an ambitious plan to build three luxury steamships to call on Prince Rupert. On the exact same day as the Black Thursday stock market crash on October 24, 1929, the CN president one-upped his promise to Prince Rupert, stating his intention to also build a hotel that would bring passengers from Vancouver in time for the 1930 tourist season.[35]

Less than three weeks later, the New York stock exchange was in the midst of its historic and dramatic fall. On November 10, Canadian prime minister William Lyon Mackenzie King arrived on Kaien Island to deliver an incredibly positive but ill-timed message:

The vision of the late Sir Wilfrid Laurier would soon be realized and that Prince Rupert would come ere long to share more fully in

that prosperity . . . it is true that you may have had your discourage-
ments and disappointments but I can assure you that as I see this
city and compare it year after year I feel the greatest possible success is in store.[36]

King then echoed Laurier's belief that Prince Rupert was still
destined to become one of the great cities of Canada and the world,
and that the time was not far distant when the railway would fulfill
the prophecies that had been made. Only three days later, the stock
market hit rock bottom. King would go on to lose the 1930 federal
election after his critics accused him of being out of touch and slow
to respond to the growing crisis.

Despite raising and levying new taxes, firing numerous staff, and
reducing salaries, the city was unable to afford interest payments
on its debt and was forced into provincial receivership in 1933.[37]
Luckily for Prince Rupert, another change in government closer to
home saw MLA Duff Pattullo lead the Liberals into provincial office.
The newly minted Premier Pattullo would not forget who sent him
to Victoria. His provincial relief program funded the construction
of a bridge off Kaien Island to Prudhomme Lake, the repurposing
of the abandoned courthouse foundation into the Sunken Gardens,
and the building of Totem Park. All of these public works projects
remain as landmarks in Prince Rupert today.

The onset of the Great Depression in Prince Rupert took a little
longer than elsewhere. Rupertites never quite felt the same pain as
the Dust Bowl prairies thanks to the abundance of fish and seafood,
which offered a stable food supply and employment. Nonetheless,
the economic turmoil still took its toll: the anticipated CN steamships
arrived but did not set sail, hotel foundations were outlined but not
built, and the new grain elevator was nicknamed the "White Ele-
phant" as it lay idle for most of the 1930s.[38] It was said that "about
the only growth industry in Prince Rupert from the late 1920s to
the mid 1930s was bootlegging, which carried on a steady business
with the 'dry' communities to the north in Alaska."[39]

The extended period of economic challenge even seems to have
dampened the Prince Rupert boosters' unbridled optimism, best
evidenced by the evolution of the annual New Year's prognostications
in the *Daily News*:

- *1929:* "It looks as if we are over the brow of the hill and from this time on there will be easier going. There should be much greater progress made in 1930 than in 1929."
- *1930:* "Prince Rupert is closing one of the most prosperous years in her life... while many have suffered from stringency, Prince Rupert has been busy and money has been plentiful. Only during the past few weeks has there been felt any sign or reflected bad times... but happily the future is shrouded in mist."
- *1931:* "In the year just closing there have been many disappointments. Financial conditions have gradually become worse but the consensus of opinion is that the worst has passed and that the future is full of hope."
- *1932:* "1931 brought a desire to agitate for a change that would make another such a year as 1932 impossible. The new year is full of hope for betterment."
- *1933:* "Prince Rupert has had a difficult time during this year... at least [it] has not been as bad as in 1932... It seems as if Prince Rupert conditions generally would be likely to improve. The year 1934 should be much better than 1933."
- *1934:* "The future of Prince Rupert is very much in the lap of the gods."

And after a visit from federal officials in October 1935, the local headline read "Frenzied Fancy and Fiery Froth Feature Final Phase of Federal Fantasy". After hearing from numerous politicians making big speeches, a local chief quietly remarked, "High wind, big thunder—no rain."[40] In other words, after the initial fervour of city building had set expectations incredibly high, Rupertites had internalized a new story of unrealized potential that has been perpetuated to the present.

COLOURFUL CHARACTER: DUFF PATTULLO

Born to Scottish immigrants in Ontario, Thomas Dufferin ("Duff") Pattullo was raised in a middle-class family steeped in the Canadian Liberal tradition. At the age of twenty-four, his father's political connections got him on the staff of the new Yukon territorial government as it as attempted to establish control over the Klondike. After a few years in the Dawson City gold commissioner's office, Pattullo attempted to strike it rich by becoming a realtor, just as the boom was

Thomas Dufferin Pattullo, third mayor and first Prince
Rupert-based Premier of BC. DR. R. GEDDES LARGE
FONDS, PRINCE RUPERT CITY & REGIONAL ARCHIVES

busting. Undeterred by bad timing, he successfully ran for Dawson
City Council in 1903. Thus began a nearly forty-year career in the
public service.

Pattullo was attracted to Prince Rupert for a second chance at
striking it rich in a politically Liberal boom town. He knew that Prince
Rupert was not a place for the faint-hearted, saying, "It behooves us
not to be discouraged by the doubters... this town is going to be a
wonder. There are no pessimists in heaven, it could not be heaven if
there were. It follows therefore that all pessimists go to hell."[41]

Duff put money where his mouth was, purchasing twenty-three
lots when they first became available, selling insurance policies, and
partnering on a construction company. A prominent advocate for
publicly owned utilities, he helped build the local telephone system
and sold it back to the city at cost. He also invested one thousand
dollars in the *Prince Rupert Optimist*, the predecessor to the *Daily
News*. He even imported the first motor vehicle into Prince Rupert,
despite there being almost no roads to drive on at the time.

Little did anyone know that Duff maintained his appearances with
borrowed money. He accumulated over $270,000 in paper-value
land holdings in anticipation of a railway-fuelled boom that did not
materialize. His lavish lifestyle earned him the nickname "cock of the

North," but he racked up over $40,000 in debt (nearly $1 million in 2024 dollars). Similar to when he was in Dawson City, politics was his means to find steady income in Prince Rupert, which he achieved by getting elected first as a city councillor and then as mayor.

After failing to secure municipal debt financing, Duff lost his mayoral re-election but was again undeterred by the setback. He was elected MLA of Prince Rupert in 1916 and subsequently appointed Minister of Lands, moving himself full-time from Prince Rupert to Victoria. But having spent his political apprenticeship on Kaien Island, he was successful at bringing in large sums of money for Prince Rupert in the form of government buildings, bridges, roads, a hospital, and economic development projects.[42] The provincial courthouse remains a testimonial to the extent of his influence.

When Pattullo was elected as premier, the 1933 economy in BC was half of what it was in 1929. The unemployment rate was 25 percent. In response, he oversaw some of the most ambitious government reform in Canada. As part of a program of the "Little New Deal," a nod to Franklin Roosevelt's initiative in the US, Pattullo oversaw the launch of health insurance, a higher minimum wage, the first minimum wage for women, more money for schools and teachers, mortgage assistance for homeowners, and tax relief for those with low income. He also directed the establishment of the Department of Municipal Affairs. The *Hours of Work Act* of 1934 introduced the maximum eight-hour workday in all major industries. He brought in regulations on public utilities and allowed for the establishment of credit unions.

Pattullo also led the first government in Canada to limit the price of gasoline, likely motivated by his experience in Prince Rupert when "strolling down the wharf one day, he had climbed on the scale used for coal; it showed that he weighed 250 pounds when . . . he weighed only 175 . . . At the next Council meeting, he introduced a bylaw to regulate the measuring and weight of coal."[43] All of these actions are consistent with one of Pattullo's oft-stated philosophies: "Every man for himself and the devil take the hindmost simply means that the devil is going to get everybody."[44]

Despite being ahead of his time in many respects, like many white British Columbians at the time, Duff Pattullo held incredibly discriminatory views. His perspective of Indigenous people was no different than any government official since the 1860s: they were to be moved aside to enable Europeans to develop resources.[45] He opposed extending the right to vote or serve in the armed forces to "Orientals" because doing so would make it easier for them to obtain citizenship, and he was in favour of an outright ban on all immigration from Asia.[46] He promoted the exclusion of Japanese people from the fishing industry. He tried to prevent BC from welcoming Jewish refugees. While he was a vocal supporter of the benefits of increased immigration, he stated that Canada should only "admit every mentally sound and healthy individual of white extraction."[47] He even toyed with the notion of eugenics, saying "for its own protection, society might someday require laws that will prevent the propagation of unfit human species."[48] As historian Robin Fisher explains in his book *Duff Pattullo of British Columbia*, "in British Columbia, developmental optimism has always had its racist dark side, and Pattullo, as much as he epitomized the one element of the provincial psyche, was not immune from the other."

Due to his many failures in business, Duff Pattullo was an improbable leader to run the province through the Great Depression, but his experience in Prince Rupert honed his political intuition. As a realtor, he had experienced the downturns caused by uncontrolled speculation. As a city councillor, he stood up to one of the most powerful companies on the continent and reached a compromise. As mayor, he saw his inability to secure financing spell failure to get re-elected. And as MLA for Prince Rupert, his experience with the post–First World War recovery helped prepare him for governing the province during the Great Depression.

Today, Pattullo is probably best known as the namesake of a Metro Vancouver bridge rather than a Premier. Likewise, his name may be more recognizable in Prince Rupert as a sports field than a founding council member, former mayor and MLA of three decades. His career was defined by audacious plans, relentless optimism in the face of steep odds, and bad timing for investment, all tempered by racism and prejudice. For all of these reasons, he serves as a sort of emblem for Prince Rupert's formative experiences from the First World War through the Great Depression until the outbreak of the Second World War.

CHAPTER 10

THE SECOND WORLD WAR
1939–45

"If it had not been for the co-operation of the Canadian ports
of Prince Rupert and Halifax, war operations might have gone
conversely for the American efforts, instead of running so
successfully as they had during those months of anxiety
and unrest so widespread throughout all the world."

US PRESIDENT DWIGHT D. EISENHOWER

OUT OF DEPRESSION

After declaring bankruptcy in 1933, Prince Rupert's governance was
placed under a provincially appointed commissioner who held sole
decision-making authority for the rest of the decade.[1] For the better
part of the 1930s, local front-page headlines were devoid of content
more exciting than the arrival of a single grain ship or the colour
chosen for a new building. To get a sense of just how bad the Great
Depression was, the construction of the new federal building in
Prince Rupert saw the city's building permit value jump to the fifth
highest of all Canadian cities, even more than four other provinces.[2]

As the prospects of war loomed large on the international psyche,
the so-called sleepy fishing village of Prince Rupert was set to be
jarred awake by the arrival of thousands of troops, ships, and the
infrastructure of a twentieth-century global war. British military
officers toured Prince Rupert as early as 1937 to lay out sites for
forts and guard camps, including at Barrett Point on Kaien Island
and Frederick Point on Digby Island. Within a few days of war being
declared in 1939, approximately sixty men were mustered to Prince
Rupert for signalling defences. The first few years of the war were
relatively uneventful as the world's focus was on Europe and not the

Pacific—but that's not to say it was boring. Within days of war being declared, a German U-boat was believed to be sighted lurking off the coast near Prince Rupert. It turned out to be a whale.[3]

Without proper guns and ammunition yet delivered, the local troops felt vulnerable enough to fill empty cans with pebbles from the beach and hang trip wires across the tops of bluffs.[4] As small groups of locals departed for the frontlines in Europe, over one hundred men from the B Company Canadian Scottish and Irish Fusiliers arrived. But the local newspaper reported that by the end of 1939, "we have so far felt the stress of war not at all."[5]

In 1940, many serious international developments happened: Winston Churchill ascended to the British prime minister's seat; Franklin D. Roosevelt was re-elected as US President; Adolf Hitler invaded France; Italy and Japan joined the Axis powers; and the Battle of Britain and the Blitz raged on. But for Prince Rupert, beyond a few defence encampments being constructed, the early days of the war were defined by two primary wartime industries: shipbuilding and canned herring in tomato sauce for export to Great Britain.

With everyone's attention directed to Europe, BC premier and Prince Rupert MLA Duff Pattullo felt confident enough to call an early election in October 1941. While his government was narrowly re-elected, it was reduced to a minority. And on December 3, 1941, members of the Liberal party passed a motion in favour of a wartime coalition with the Conservatives, the first coalition government in BC's existence.[6] The next day, Pattullo officially tendered his resignation effective for the following week, saying, "I am accepting the verdict in the best spirit... and as I do not agree with it, I cannot allow my name to be submitted in any form."[7]

Three days later, the Japanese bombed Pearl Harbour and the pace of the Pacific war effort drastically increased.[8] Prince Rupert was put on high alert that an attack by Japanese forces in the area was imminent. One of Duff Pattullo's last official acts on his final day in the Premier's office was to order a complete blackout for the entire coast of BC. Lights and radios were required to be shut off from dawn until dusk.[9] Guards were dispatched to Prince Rupert and ordered to remain on alert for four days afterward.[10]

JAPANESE INTERNMENT

One week after the Pearl Harbour bombing, the Canadian government approved the forced extraction and internment of all Japanese civilians. With so many Japanese fishermen having travelled the Skeena River, there was fear that the Imperial Japanese Navy would attempt to take over the railway along the Skeena as they might have already been familiar with the maps and charts.[11] The federal government prohibited Japanese fishing operations and forced the transfer of their fishing assets to "Canadian" operators. And for the duration of the Second World War, Japanese Canadians were forbidden from possessing or using radios or cameras, or even buying gasoline without RCMP approval.[12]

One of the Japanese fishermen recalled his experiences of the seizures at the time:

The morning of December 14, 1941, as we were preparing for the high tide, we received an order from the military. All 26 floating boats from the Inverness Cannery were to be confiscated... 20 boats belonging to other Japanese fishermen had already been taken into custody... even after repeated negotiations, we did not receive permission to go ashore. We couldn't buy anything in the stores... because we had been planning to go ashore, all of our clothing, bedding, and food was left at home... Under the watchful eye of three minesweepers, and pulled by a tugboat, our chained boats began a frightening sea voyage. On Dec 15th, 26 boats chained together and six of their owners left Prince Rupert for Vancouver guarded by the minesweepers... the marines threatened us by saying that sooner or later we would be shot. These young men, who had never even seen Japanese people or the ocean, treated us like animals... Three of the boats, with no one riding on them, overturned and filled with water. Even though we tried to negotiate piloting our own boats, it was not permitted.[13]

Contrary to this firsthand account, the *Prince Rupert Daily News* reported that "the seizure of boats was done on a friendly basis."[14] The general attitude and opinion of the local population was best described in numerous editorials, in which the writers opined that "while there is no desire to be hard on the Japanese in this country, we cannot afford to take chances," or that "many of these Japanese citizens... may be friendly... but it is difficult to know who may be trusted... seems to be that it is not safe to trust any."[15]

One month after the Pearl Harbour bombings, an official order was issued that "all enemy aliens except those holding RCMP permits will be required to move from 'protected areas' on the Pacific Coast and accommodation will be provided by the federal government where necessary."[16] At the time, Prince Rupert had a large Japanese population, a large portion of which was old and respected citizens and business owners. Without exception, all Japanese Rupertites would soon be detained before being transported to an internment camp. Their possessions were seized and disposed of with little or no compensation.[17] Hundreds of fishing boats, cars, businesses, and homes were left behind to deteriorate and were eventually sold for a fraction of their actual value. To add salt to the wound, the funds from these sales were used to cover some of the costs of the internment.[18]

The explicit goal of the government was made clear by the federal minister of immigration: to "get these people out of B.C. as fast as possible. It is my personal intention, as long as I remain in public life, to see they never come back here. Let our slogan be for British Columbia: No Japs from the Rockies to the seas."[19] The local attitude in Prince Rupert was equally as hostile. The local youth committee and Gyro Club requested the prime minister go further than internment, asking for the immediate deportation and permanent removal of those of Japanese origin from Canada.[20] The Prince Rupert branch of the Canadian Legion went as far asking the federal government to exhume Japanese bodies from the local Fairview cemetery and rebury them elsewhere.[21] Even the local Native Brotherhood passed a motion in favour of deporting all Japanese people after the war.[22] The local paper went to the extent of suggesting that Japanese Rupertites should actually be thankful for the opportunity to be interned instead of killed: "We understand that some of the Japanese residents feel rather badly at having to move away... if they are really loyal Canadians it should not be so... in the case of invasion the local Japanese are either traitors to their own people or to us. Any really Canadian Japanese who hopes to live following an invasion should be glad to move away until the war is over."[23]

On March 22, 1942, less than four months after Pearl Harbour, the local headline read "Jap Train Off Today," which was followed up the next day with "Most Japs Have Left." In total, more than five hundred Japanese residents from Prince Rupert and the surrounding area were forced aboard the train and sent off to an internment camp near Valemount, coincidentally known as Rainbow. Only thirteen Japanese locals were given an exemption because of personal or family illness.[24] Quite depressingly, only forty to fifty Japanese families returned to the area afterwards. It is a mostly unspoken local tragedy that the majority of Japanese Rupertites chose to rebuild their lives elsewhere.

1942–43: THE FORGOTTEN BATTLE

Several years before entering the war, the United States had been eyeing Prince Rupert as a base of supply for operations in Alaska because it could offer a supply route that cut off hundreds of sea miles on the so-called Road to Tokyo. Nearly a third shorter than the other transportation routes in Seattle or Anchorage, the route from the Prince Rupert port would allow ships to carry 50 percent more cargo.[25] Thirty-five days after the Pearl Harbour incident, the first US army transport sailed from Prince Rupert with men and supplies to bolster the continent's slim northwestern defences. Less than two months later, at a meeting of the Joint Chiefs of Staff in Washington, DC, Prince Rupert was designated by the United States Army as a sub-port of embarkation for troops, supplies, and equipment.[26]

In June 1942, the Japanese navy launched aircraft carrier raids on Dutch Harbor, Alaska, located more than halfway from Japan to Prince Rupert. This marked the first aerial attack by a foreign enemy on the continental United States. The Battle of Dutch Harbour was a wake up call for Canadians: the war was no longer a distant concept, but rather a stark reality fast approaching our doorstep.[27] Soon after, almost simultaneously with the Battle of Midway, the Japanese landed unopposed on the unoccupied Aleutian Islands of Attu & Kiska. While the Aleutian Islands campaign has come to be known as the "Forgotten Battle" because of so many other events overshadowing it,[28] the invasion by the Japanese resulted in an American invasion of Prince Rupert that would forever alter the city.

Thousands of us troops, ships, workers, and all kinds of machines flooded Kaien Island, opening up new lands in the forest. All of the latest electronic, electrical, and mechanical equipment was brought in, with highly trained personnel alongside. New buildings, businesses, and homes shot up like mushrooms. Nine anti-aircraft gun forts were erected. Dock space doubled. The federal building was set up as military headquarters. Artillery camps, ammunition and fuel bunkers, observation posts, searchlights, and many more installations were quickly put up.[29] As the gateway to a shorter route to Alaska than any other American port on the west coast, Prince Rupert helped the Americans build a massive supply chain. A four storey, 400,000-square-foot warehouse was built to store enough rations to feed 125,000 troops for two months and clothe them for three months.[30] By the time the us Army Corps of Engineers completed construction of the port facilities in 1942, Prince Rupert's population had swelled from 6,000 to approximately 25,000.[31]

Meanwhile, Japanese forces in the Aleutians were busy building runways for fighter jets as their forces exceeded 10,000. The strategic value of holding Alaska was not lost on the Americans, who had been building airfields in there since 1935. Despite the Americans having received testimony from General Billy Mitchell that "he who holds Alaska will hold the world,"[32] it was generally believed by military forces that the Allies did not posses enough defence capabilities to stop the Japanese from reaching Vancouver as it was "a wilderness that could not be defended."[33]

The Japanese occupation of Kiska and Attu obviously caused high anxiety amongst Rupertites and there were worries of further invasions somewhere along the mainland coast.[34] The two-hundred-bed Miller Bay hospital was built in preparation for the casualties from an Aleutian counterstrike. Rumours of Japanese air attacks abounded. A Japanese atlas was found with red ink marking routes down the Pacific coast and circles around Dutch Harbour, Sitka, Prince Rupert, Vancouver, Victoria, Seattle, and San Francisco.[35] After an alleged sighting of submarines, submarine nets were installed at the mouth of the harbour, the deepest such defensive fortification in the British Empire.[36] And when two Japanese cruisers and transport vessels were spotted four- to six-hundred miles off the coast, the crisis prompted almost one thousand men into active service.[37] In just a single month that year, the one-track railroad sent more ammunition tonnage through Prince Rupert than any year prior.

As the only shipyard in Canada operated by a railway, with two thousand full-time workers on its payroll doing three- to eight-hour shifts, the Prince Rupert Dry Dock was extremely busy.[38] Over 2,400 crafts docked during the war, of which nine hundred were dry-docked. Guarded round the clock by over one hundred soldiers, the dry dock and shipyard built a 10,000-ton cargo ship from keel to delivery in only fifty-eight days, an achievement which "at the time... broke all previous records in Canada and probably Britain."[39] By the end of the war, over nine hundred ships were repaired, thirteen freighters built, and four minesweepers launched in Prince Rupert.[40]

Fearing that Japan would attempt to take over the rail line along the Skeena, patrols were doubled and completion of a road to the town of Terrace became a top priority. A top-secret train was even purpose-built to guard the river. One of the best-kept secrets of the war, the No. 1 Armoured Train weighed 650,000 pounds and travelled the Skeena between Prince Rupert and Terrace once per day throughout 1942. Armed with light machine guns, 75-millimetre guns, and anti-aircraft cannons, it was the only armoured train to run in Canada and the only such train to run in North America since 1865.[41]

After months of relentless bombing by the Americans on Attu and Kiska, the effort to retake the islands was intense, but relatively short-lived. In May 1943, Attu Island was taken back by the Americans at the cost of nearly four thousand lives.[42] Kiska was retaken shortly thereafter in August with the help of 5,300 Canadian troops, the Royal Canadian Air Force, and bombs shipped through Prince Rupert,[43] although the Japanese had stealthily removed their troops and abandoned the island a few weeks earlier. Unfortunately, there were more than three hundred Allied casualties as the result of friendly fire, Japanese mines, timed bombs, "accidental ammunition detonations, vehicle accidents; unexploded bombs in the tundra; and insidious booby trap explosions."[44]

The Forgotten Battle of the Aleutian Islands is notable as the only foreign invasion on North American soil in the Second World War, and the first occupation of US territory since the War of 1812.[45] The Japanese expulsion from the Aleutians was one of the first times that Canadian conscripts were sent to a combat zone in the Second World War, with most of the men going through Prince Rupert.[46]

At the peak, there were more than 3,500 American troops stationed in the Prince Rupert.[47] As the threat of further provocations by the Japanese sharply diminished, the level of defences required on the West Coast was also greatly reduced. The armoured train was no longer needed. Like so many soldiers, its passing went unremarked, and it has no memorial.[48] The number of supply trains in and out of Prince Rupert dropped from six a day to five per week.[49]

COLLATERAL DAMAGE

At the end of 1943, Prince Rupert had become the fourth most populous city in BC. This dramatic expansion, however, did not come without costs. After a decade of bankruptcy, the city's commissioner had restricted school attendance to children aged seven to sixteen due to insufficient funds to run the schools.[50] Only 5 percent of children in Prince Rupert had a diet without deficiencies, and the provincial school inspector declared Prince Rupert's facilities to be the worst in the province.[51] To respond to such an abrupt influx of people, temporary wartime housing had to be quickly constructed from the muskeg marshes to accommodate the newcomers who were arriving to assist with the war efforts. Under urgent pressure and completely neglecting long range planning, the city commissioner obtained special permission from the provincial government in January 1942 to sell and lease hundreds of vacant parcels to the federal crown corporation Wartime Housing Ltd. By April, a three-year lease was signed with the corporation for an annual cost of $10 for the dozens of lots, plus $122 for the sale of over one hundred lots. The corporation built the subdivisions, and in exchange for not levying taxes, the city was reimbursed $24 to $31 per house per year for street maintenance, lighting, fire and police protection, and school costs.[52]

The rapid swelling of the population did inspire some morale-boosting stories: the Irish Fusiliers showed up with a brass band and offered public performances; the Rocky Mountain Rangers formed their own motorcycle unit and routinely toured the city; and the Canadian Women's Army Corps arrived in 1943 and made Canadian history as the country's first women posted to a first line of defence.[53] Prince Rupert also had the distinction of being "the only

City in Canada with an all-woman sales force" for the Victory Loan canvas.[54] When the B Company of the Canadian Scottish Regiment was stationed in Prince Rupert in 1939, the corner of downtown was blocked off every evening for a colourful sunset bagpipe ceremony.[55] However, their departure from town in 1941 was less entertaining. The night before the regiment was shipped out to the United Kingdom, a local totem pole mysteriously disappeared, and a couple years later appeared in Edinburgh, Scotland. A local Ts'msyen artist named Charlie Dudoward had sold a carved totem pole to the owner of a local fur store in Prince Rupert. Police discovered that "a group of Canadian Scottish soldiers had been spotted in the vicinity that night and were reported to have been 'in a festive mood.'"[56] Today, the totem pole remains at the Royal Scots Club in Edinburgh.

Morale in Prince Rupert was decidedly higher than its neighbours. For a remote city, the social life was quite active. But more importantly, while the Americans had impressive food and amenities to share, Rupertites had "beer in every canteen and wine and spirits in the sergeants and officers' messes, something forbidden on the dry American facilities."[57] The large American encampment on Acropolis Hill was dubbed "Little America" before being renamed after US president Franklin D. Roosevelt. Rupertites seemed to welcome the US troops into both their homes and hearts.

Meanwhile, only 150 kilometres away in Terrace, a group of conscripted soldiers mutinied and seized command of two thousand troops while senior officers were away. They took over ammunition dumps and machine guns, closed the canteens, and threatened any who were going to march in parade. Armed with rifles, gas masks, and grenades, the mutineers patrolled the camps in their jeeps. After multiple failed attempts by the Prince Rupert officers to rescue their fellow officers, one soldier braved the mutineers by facing a machine gun and lied that planes loaded with bombs were ready at the airport to break the uprising.[58] The four-day insurrection is an important event that has been described as "the worst crisis—outside of actual combat—ever faced by the Canadian armed forces to that date."[59]

END OF WAR

From 1943 to 1945, the energy of war was once again focused on retaking Europe. As Operation Overlord advanced through France, the Skeena River highway was officially opened, connecting Kaien Island to the rest of North America by road. With Hitler's death and Germany's surrender, the focus shifted once more to the Pacific theatre. BC ports began "tropicalization" of ships to switch from Atlantic to Pacific service, including the HMCS *Prince Rupert*.[60] While the city of Prince Rupert look poised to serve as a critical supply line to Japan, Canadian troops reached the Pacific just as the US dropped the atomic bombs on Hiroshima and Nagasaki.

Within three days of the formal Japanese surrender, the American army began rapidly leaving Prince Rupert. Over $17 million in improvements were left behind and 40,000 tons of supplies were removed within weeks. While Canada had lost its European and Pacific trading partners throughout the war, the amount of traffic generated at the Prince Rupert port was quite significant. It is estimated that between 1942 and 1945, over 75,000 American military and civilian personnel and over 100,000 tons of high-explosive incendiary ammunition travelled through Prince Rupert. More than 1.6 million tons of supplies were shipped through a single Prince Rupert warehouse to American theatres of war,[61] and almost 20,000 freight cars were unloaded in Prince Rupert or on Watson Island.[62] The final munitions ship to depart Watson Island carried two hundred cars, including a considerable number of eleven-ton "blockbuster bombs," which had been destined for Japan if they had not surrendered. The CN superintendent commented, "Lucky folks couldn't see inside those cars. They'd have been sorta nervous! If Watson Island had ever exploded, it would have sounded like repeat performance of the eruption of Krakatoa."[63]

Dwight Eisenhower, US president and supreme commander of the Allied forces, paid tribute to Prince Rupert in a press release after the war's end, in which he stated, "If it had not been for the co-operation of the Canadian ports of Prince Rupert and Halifax, war operations might have gone conversely for the American efforts, instead of running so successfully as they had during those months of anxiety and unrest so widespread throughout all the world."[64] This commendation was echoed by the locally stationed US brigadier general Robert Wylie: "We appreciate very greatly the way we have been received at Prince Rupert since the very beginning... it has been a matter of much satisfaction to use of the United States Army... the installation at Prince Rupert was really of considerable more importance than its size might have indicated. It played a very important part, indeed, in our war against Japan."[65]

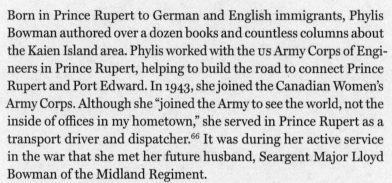

COLOURFUL CHARACTER:
PHYLIS BOWMAN (NÉE HAMBLIN)

Born in Prince Rupert to German and English immigrants, Phylis Bowman authored over a dozen books and countless columns about the Kaien Island area. Phylis worked with the US Army Corps of Engineers in Prince Rupert, helping to build the road to connect Prince Rupert and Port Edward. In 1943, she joined the Canadian Women's Army Corps. Although she "joined the Army to see the world, not the inside of offices in my hometown," she served in Prince Rupert as a transport driver and dispatcher.[66] It was during her active service in the war that she met her future husband, Seargent Major Lloyd Bowman of the Midland Regiment.

After the war, Phylis took a job at the *Prince Rupert Daily News*, working her way up to becoming the editor before taking over the tourist bureau. She initiated the first iteration of the local Cruise Ambassador program and co-created the Prince Rupert Archive Society.[67] For all her varied works documenting the goings-on of Kaien Island, she was the recipient of the Alec Hunter Award for acts of good citizenship. Upon her death in 2012, a quote was attributed to her describing both the weather and the attitude of Prince Rupert: "It's going to clear up, wet, dull and foggy—you gotta love this country."[68]

Thanks to her pride of place and avid notetaking, Phylis Bowman is unrivalled at chronicling Prince Rupert's development through the Second World War. Her works remain crucial to the remembrance of the nearly six hundred Rupertites who, like her, volunteered to join the army, navy, or air force. Phylis Bowman's own words remain the most succinct description of the impact of the Second World War on Prince Rupert: "Although it was a busy, hectic, perturbing span in Prince Rupert's history, World War Two left a lasting mark and memory in the lives of thousands, and changed both the face and future of the city."[69]

CHAPTER 11

HERE COMES THE BOOM

1946–59

"Britain experienced her greatest periods of expansion and wealth under two queens—Elizabeth and Victoria. Who knows the analogy may hold good and that, now you have a woman mayor, Prince Rupert will begin to have its golden years."

NORA ARNOLD, APRIL 3, 1947

RESETTLEMENT

While the First World War was defined by local stagnation, the Second World War transformed Prince Rupert from a village into a city. In the new peacetime, the city struggled to return to a new normal. After thirty years as MLA, Duff Pattullo lost his seat in legislature in 1945. Hundreds of barracks, mess halls, and gyms were quickly demolished. Forty thousand tons of supplies were shipped back to the US while large amounts of ammunition were sent to Japan.[1] Equipment, linens, dishes, supplies, tools, and furniture were either burned, thrown into dump yards, or towed out to sea and thrown overboard.[2] A few government buildings were converted into apartments and retail stores while most other wooden structures were left vacant and boarded up. The population contracted in half as rapidly as it had grown.

Overseeing this time of upheaval was Prince Rupert's first female mayor, Nora Arnold. Unsympathetic to the union movement and cozy with the centre-right provincial coalition government, Arnold began her term with a tenuous relationship with the Prince Rupert Trades & Labour Council, who had lost their majority on the city council to a majority group of independents, including Arnold herself. Facing early questions about her leadership, the new Mayor Arnold quipped that "Britain experienced her greatest periods of expansion and wealth under two queens—Elizabeth and Victoria. Who knows the analogy may hold good and that, now you have a woman mayor, Prince Rupert will begin to have its golden years?"[3]

This statement would prove prophetic for Prince Rupert. First elected just two years after the end of the war, Nora Arnold was in office during a powerful time of global human development. On a national level, federal war-time rations were ending, income taxes were being reduced, and wages were increasing after years of austerity. On the international stage, the United Nations adopted the Universal Declaration of Human Rights and the Genocide Convention in December 1948. NATO was established. While numerous smaller conflicts raged elsewhere, global war was now in the rear-view mirror, unleashing new hopes, dreams, and a feeling of emancipation for humanity. For locals in Prince Rupert, the most important development was that in 1948, a few years after the city emerged from its thirteen-year bankruptcy, the provincial government announced that negotiations had been completed to repurpose the former US Army dock on Watson Island into a fifteen-million-dollar pulp mill.[4]

A pulp mill was not a new idea for Prince Rupert. The idea had been publicly promised as early as 1935 but suffered setbacks due to years of delays, a six-year global war, followed by a six-year period of post-war resettlement. Nearly six thousand days after first being promised, the construction of the Skeena Cellulose pulp mill on Watson Island was finally underway. Some might say better late than never. Construction of the mill was a prerequisite for the city to be granted the first provincial tree farm license.[5] It was one of the greatest—if not *the* greatest—peacetime conversions within the city.[6]

COLOURFUL CHARACTER:
NORA ARNOLD (NÉE RIVETT)

Growing up in Wellingsborough, Northamptonshire, England, Nora Arnold had first come to Prince Rupert only to visit her brother for six months, but she remained to become a teacher and got married to a local real estate and insurance agent.[7] When her husband died in 1936, she took over his business, joined the library board, and was first elected to the Prince Rupert city council in 1942, just as the city was reinstated from receivership.[8] She was the founder and

Nora Arnold, 1946. DR. R. GEDDES LARGE FONDS.
PRINCE RUPERT CITY & REGIONAL ARCHIVES

first president of the Prince Rupert Business & Professional Women's Club. And when the Prince Rupert Chamber of Commerce finally allowed women in their ranks in 1947, she was unanimously elected as their first female member.[9]

After topping the polls for the city council in 1943 and 1945 as part of the local Ratepayers Association, Arnold opposed the leadership of the incumbent mayor, saying, "From 1932 to 1942, we were ruled with a pretty rigid hand. We needed it and it got us out of the hole. But ah, by 1942 we began to get pretty restive about it. We were fighting wars against dictators and we figured we had one right here in Prince Rupert."[10] When she ran for mayor as an independent in 1946, she won by only four votes, becoming the first woman elected as mayor in Prince Rupert, the first female mayor in the Province of BC, and only the third in the entire country.

When asked if women should even be in politics, Nora Arnold responded, "I certainly think so . . . most of them are not jockeying for political power. They're there to do a job and I have always found that women are impatient and [are in office] to get things done. Things started and finished."[11] Many things certainly were started and finished during her first year in office. One of her first acts was to cut the mayor's salary by 40 percent.[12] She oversaw a bylaw for the quick sale of war houses to veterans at a deep discount of $500 to $2,000, with monthly payments as little as $25.[13] She negotiated hundreds of thousands of dollars in compensation from the federal government for damages done to the city's streets during wartime by the military, as well as the purchase of the Seal Cove Airbase for only $1. And she also instituted the five-day work week at city hall.[14]

At the next election, running again against the man she had previously ousted as mayor, Arnold was still facing questions about being a female mayor. Her simple retort: "We can't make a worse job of the world than the men anyway, can we?" She went on to increase her margin of victory from 4 to 142 votes. Soon after her re-election, she was awarded as Canada's Woman of the Year by the Business and Professional Women's Club. During her awards speech in Regina, with Saskatchewan Premier Tommy Douglas in the audience, the conservative-leaning mayor called out the trade unionism movement, saying, "The whole trend is towards less work."[15]

Despite being ahead of the times in many ways, she was also undoubtedly a product of her time. She promoted more rigorous religious instruction to reduce juvenile delinquency. Using crusade-like language, she endorsed the idea of "the family that prays together, stays together" as the cure for what she perceived as the breakdown of society's morality. The most illustrative example of her social conservatism in public office is an episode where she voted to cancel the trade licenses of taxi drivers for selling liquor to Indigenous people, even going as far as trying to get the provincial government to limit taxi licenses across BC because "they seem to do a lot of bootlegging."[16] Despite her decision being overturned months later by the city council in the appeal process, Arnold remained steadfast in her views, even going as far as using one of her last days in office to stage a public protest.[17]

If not for some health-related challenges in her final year in office, coupled with her desire to see someone younger get elected, there is no telling how much more positive change Nora Arnold could have had on Prince Rupert. She won four elections in a row, twice as councillor and twice as mayor. Her political influence was obviously sustained through the next election as both the mayoral and council candidate she endorsed won handily.

Her obituary read: "It was the destiny of... Mrs. Nora Arnold to become Prince Rupert's first woman mayor. For one who had come here as a young teacher and lost her husband after five brief years of marriage, it was a courageous undertaking. But courage was a fundamental quality of Mrs. Arnold... she transferred his business responsibilities to herself and still had sufficient strength to carry far more than her share of civic duties. Her selection in 1950 as Canada's Woman of the Year was a great honour. But it did not tell the full story. Her achievements could not be compressed within such fixed limits of time. Her whole life was remarkable, and the memory she leaves is equally so."[18]

Even though Prince Rupert's streets and parks have been named for past mayors, political figures, or GTP employees who had never stepped foot in the City, there has been nothing in Prince Rupert named after Nora Arnold.[19] Her legacy, while generally uncelebrated, is that of efficiently steering the city through a consequential period immediately following the end of the Second World War.

NIFTY '50S

When Nora Arnold's reign came to a close at the end of 1949, the construction of the pulp mill on Watson Island was only a few months away from completion. The first census conducted after the Second World War showed a 1951 the population of 8,500. While this was a far cry from the wartime peak of 25,000, it was a notable increase from the pre-war population of 6,500.[20] Mayor Arnold said that Prince Rupert was like the orphaned child of Charles Hays, but one that was now fast approaching adulthood: like a troubled youth who could now finally stand on their own two feet.

After construction was completed on the Skeena Cellulose pulp mill in 1951, Prince Rupert certainly was hoisted back on its feet. The facility quickly became the largest employer in the city and its highest tax contributor, offering employment to many locals, Canadians moving west from Ontario and the Prairies, and immigrants alike. Its near instantaneous growth quickly created both a local housing and labour shortage, competing with the likes of the world's largest fresh halibut business and fish cold storage plant.[21] Prince Rupert's unemployment rate went down by 25 percent year-over-year from 1952 to '53 while the population jumped by 30 percent to over 10,000 people.[22] So important was the grand opening of the new facility that it garnered a visit from Prime Minster Louis St. Laurent, with Governor-General Vincent Massey, marking the third visit by a sitting prime minister to Prince Rupert.[23]

Buoyed by the establishment of the new pulp mill, the 1950s in Prince Rupert were defined by the rapid expansion of civic amenities. The Totem Theatre celebrated its grand opening as the "most modern theatre in the Province" because it was the first floating screen in BC. The city's first indoor swimming pool opened its doors. The Museum of Northern BC building and the Friendship House were built.[24] Three new schools were opened after the 1951 Indian Act amendment finally allowed Indigenous students to attend public school.[25]

However, along with this growth, there were also some liabilities: debts from the city's bankruptcy were not fully retired until 1953[26]; the Prince Rupert General Hospital had the worst ratio of staff to beds in the entire province[27]; the highway into the community was deemed to the "worst access in BC"[28]; one in every three houses was deemed to be sub-standard while most of the streets and buildings built fifty years prior had become obsolete; and the race-based tensions built up over years of wartime propaganda made for tenuous intercultural interactions. The combination of rapid community expansion with underlying social, cultural, and economic structural problems soon came to a dramatic crescendo.

RACE RIOTS

During fishing season in Prince Rupert in the early 1950s, the local Indigenous population grew to six thousand poeple, which was claimed to be the "largest congregation of natives in Canada."[29] Proportionately, this was the largest population of Indigenous people of any city in BC.[30] Despite this growth, inequality between Indigenous and non-Indigenous people was still widespread in the decade following the Second World War. Not until 1951 was the ban on the Potlatch rescinded. Indigenous people still did not have the right to vote, and health care was kept separated by race at the Miller Bay Indian Hospital, sometimes by coercion and by police force.[31] Indigenous people were even forced to sit in their own designated section at local theatres.

The segregation of Indigenous Peoples in northern BC was being publicly compared to the segregation of Black people in the southern US. Prince Rupert's Social Credit MLA W.H. Murray even raised the troubling issue in the legislature, questioning how his colleagues "glibly criticized the segregation prevalent in the US when we ourselves tolerate a similar practice here on our own doorstep."[32] The most pertinent example of the time had to do with liquor restrictions.

From 1884 to 1951, Indigenous Peoples in Canada were legally prohibited from buying alcohol, entering a liquor establishment, or being intoxicated, all punishable by fines and jail time. Although they were legally allowed to consume alcohol after 1951, Indigenous Peoples still could not legally be intoxicated off their reserves,[33] and the BC liquor control board stringently interpreted the reform such that hotel beer parlours were the only establishments that Indigenous people could legally drink in public.[34]

For Prince Rupert, alcohol was a particularly relevant issue. Even though the city made up only 1.2 percent of the province's population, it accounted for 2.6 percent of all liquor sales in 1952. Per person, Rupertites were spending twice as much money on alcohol as the provincial average. Policing also presented a unique challenge, which was described as having "no parallel in British Columbia to the situation that exists on that one block of Third Avenue after the beer parlours close... there are three hotels and about five restaurants and at 11:30 at night there are between 300 to 400 people dumped in one small area."[35]

The dense strip of bars and hotels was known by locals as the "Apache Pass," a vague reference to a historic mountain pass in Arizona known in Spanish as Puerto del Dado. Literally translated as "Pass of the Die," this name alluded to the notion that it was a risky crossing or a path on which one would be taking a chance with their own life, with a not-so-subtle reference to the Indigenous people of Arizona. In the case of Prince Rupert, the risk was bar fights, public drunkenness, and a multitude of other potential transgressions. It was such a popular spot for fishermen and shore workers that "payday Fridays were like Mardi-Gras."[36]

On July 27, 1953, allegedly in response to police brutality during the arrest of an Indigenous person, a truck was flipped on its side, which sparked a melee of chaos by seemingly opportunistic troublemakers. Not long after, a four-hundred-person mob marched up Third Avenue to throw rocks and eggs at city hall and the RCMP barracks. Every officer of the Prince Rupert RCMP and reserves from the regional sub-division was called up to confront them. Only after tear gas bombs were dispersed did the crowd leave. Police arrested fifty-nine people for intoxication or for obstruction of police officers.

Five white people and two Indigenous people were charged of unlawful assembly. Seventeen more were charged with intoxication under the Indian Act for their role in the riot, despite numerous reports that Indigenous people were not the ringleaders in the affair.[37]

While the mob consisted mainly of white people, the news quickly played up the stereotype of the "drunken Indian." As a result of the charges being made public, many drew the faulty conclusion that the riot had been sparked by an influx of Indigenous people for the fishing season. But the wider public conversation became about aggressive police tactics. The local chamber of commerce had received multiple reports from the Native Brotherhood of RCMP discrimination and unfair persecution, unlawful searches, and the entering of homes without warrants. The use of analogy to Black Americans in the American south and to the Nazi Third Reich signalled that the moral-political landscape was shifting.[38]

Despite the comparison, there were no major acts of public resistance, violence, marches, or sit-ins used in Prince Rupert like in the American south. But there was one very notable public objector who helped shape local public opinion. Jane Adams, the daughter of the Native Brotherhood's former president Alfred Adams, challenged the local theatre's policies after she accidentally sat outside the segregated section. When the projectionist refused to start the film and sent a young usher to move her, Jane adamantly refused to move—a standoff that Jane later recalled as embarrassing for both her and the young man. Jane's persistence paid off, however, as the projectionist soon relented, and the movie began shortly thereafter.[39]

By the mid-1950s, it was clear that there was growing unrest related to racial stigma and the discrimination of Indigenous Peoples under the law. An Indigenous Rupertite named Ivan Adams foreshadowed the growing resentment in 1953, predicting that "if the police continue to use methods too closely allied to the former Nazi S.S. methods, we may have an Indian riot."[40] Five years later, on August 2, 1958, Prince Rupert's centennial celebration fulfilled that prophecy.

THE CENTENNIAL RIOT

In the year leading up the BC's hundredth anniversary celebration, despite organizers billing the local event as "Potlatch week," many Indigenous leaders announced a boycott of festivities. "We are not citizens in our own country... we are still waiting for freedoms that we helped fight for in two world wars" said one Ts'msyen Chief.[41] Said another, "Skeena River Indians will join the other BC Indians in boycotting the Centennial celebrations because the federal and provincial governments are guilty of the biggest land steal in the history of North America."[42]

At 11:30 PM on the last day of Centennial Week celebrations, seven liquor establishments on the "Apache Pass" strip closed their doors and hundreds of people spilled into the street in various states of drunkenness. A half hour later, the RCMP allegedly beat two drunk Indigenous women with flashlights, provoking a violent response from bystanders who, in the words of the *Native Voice* magazine at the time, "fanned what should have been a smouldering cigarette... into a forest fire."[43]

Before long, one thousand rioters swarmed the police station and the city hall in Prince Rupert's downtown. For nearly two hours, waves of stone-throwing demonstrators fought against the town's police regiment, reinforced by military reserve units with bayonetted rifles, local firefighters, and members of the US Coast Guard with billysticks. Additionally, several onlooking civilians were unexpectedly equipped with helmets and pressed into service to restore the peace.[44]

Only a few months into his new job as mayor, the recently elected Peter Lester climbed on top of a fire engine amongst the chaos to read the Riot Act twice through a loudspeaker as bottles and rocks were thrown. This marked only the third time in Canadian history that the Riot Act had been read since Confederation, the only other time being the Winnipeg General Strike of 1919. The Riot Act established a maximum penalty of life imprisonment for those refusing to break up the crowd. Despite the very public and real threat of punishment, it wasn't until the deployment of three-hundred-pound pressurized fire hoses and twenty-five tear gas bombs that the crowd finally dispersed. About eighty people were detained and thirty-nine arrested, of which twenty-four were Indigenous. Fifteen civilians and five police officers were injured.[45]

News of the riot was allegedly broadcast from Moscow throughout the Eastern Bloc on Soviet short radio wavelengths as an example of the horrors caused by "capitalist decadence."[46] Much like the preceding 1953 fracas, the local news claimed that "the complexion of those who seemed to be getting the most kick out of things ... was predominantly white."[47] Less than twenty hours after the riot, the city council "pledged a merciless crackdown" and gave a vote of confidence to the RCMP's suppression tactics. Mayor Lester then appointed himself, a councillor, and the city manager to a special committee to investigate.[48]

While local Indigenous leaders called for an investigation into police brutality, the mayor's committee instead prepared its report within a week with recommendations for more severe penalties and tough enforcement of existing liquor laws, finding no evidence of police brutality.[49] In the face of accusations of bias, Mayor Lester was unequivocal: "Law and order must come first."[50] He then attempted to create a committee of Indigenous village representatives, but was initially rebuffed by all the local Indigenous Nations.[51] It had become apparent that interracial relationships in Prince Rupert were shaky and required collaboration.

A few days after the riot, the *Vancouver Sun* editorialized that "the stupidity of BC's liquor restrictions against Indians got frightening proof in Prince Rupert."[52] The Centennial Riot, as it came to be known, quickly came to be seen as both a local and provincial rally against the paternalistic Indian Act and the RCMP, who were responsible for enforcing it.[53] Provincially, the incident proved to be a seminal moment that sparked the necessary changes for achieving legal liquor equality in 1962 for all Indigenous people in BC.[54]

Locally, the most positive outcome was the start of a productive cross-cultural conversation between the City of Prince Rupert and its Indigenous population[55]. Thanks to a motion by two city councillors, the city took up the cause of advocating alongside the Native Brotherhood for changes to the Indian Act's liquor laws.[56] A subsequent report to the city council confirmed that there was "a certain element, small in number, in the White population, willing and anxious to capitalize on this Native feeling of discrimination. This same element on occasion insidiously incites the Natives to acts of defiance."[57] Additionally, city-commissioned statistics showed that the RCMP was prosecuting Indigenous people at a 25 percent higher rate than white people for liquor-related offences.[58] Mayor Lester eventually came around from his rigid "law and order" stance. Nearly two years after the riot, he went as far as saying, "This form of apartheid has no place in Canada."[59] He was later recognized as the third white man to receive honorary membership to the Native Brotherhood.[60]

BOOM GOES THE TOWN

If the end of the 1940s was to be considered Prince Rupert's adolescence as Mayor Nora Arnold stated, then the end of the 1950s are best described as a growth spurt with the associated growing pains. By 1956, Prince Rupert's population exceeded 10,000 for the first time since the Second World War, comparable to major BC cities like Kelowna and Nanaimo at the time.[61] Construction values were setting new record highs. In the latter half of the 1950s, new housing, new schools, new sewer and water systems, and a new fire hall, museum, and indoor swimming pool were all built.[62] The local paper even claimed that "Prince Rupert now has more paved streets on a per capita basis than any other City in Canada."[63]

Some of Prince Rupert's newfound growth was thanks to the re-opening of the grain elevator, which had practically been forgotten by Canadian grain officials for two decades. The late 1950s saw 9–10 million bushels of barley shipped[64]—still a long way off from Charles Hays's prediction of 100 million, but better than the zeroes it had piled up through the 1930s and '40s. The former dry dock property had been repurposed into a sawmill in 1958.[65] Fishing continued to be a major economic driver; in 1959, 80 million pounds of fish landed in Prince Rupert, which translated to $4.6 million in local wages.[66]

But the primary fuel for Prince Rupert's expansion was the Watson Island pulp mill. After eight years in operation, even though they accrued a cumulative operating loss of $14 million, the facility had doubled its average daily production, supporting $4 million in wages for more than seven hundred employees and paying hundreds of thousands in local taxes.[67] The mill had such a large footprint as an employer that in 1958, when pulp workers went on a short-lived strike, the city's unemployment rate jumped overnight to 20 percent.[68]

And it wasn't just pulp workers who took strike actions. A multiplicity of local and provincial unionized strikes dominated 1950s news coverage from the sheer volume: longshore workers, city workers, bar staff, waiters, railway workers, firefighters, carpenters, nurses, civil servants, halibut fishermen, salmon fishermen, herring fishermen, and fish plant workers. All either walked off the job, threatened to strike, got an injunction, or reached an impasse over wages, hours of work, or working conditions at some point between 1955 and 1960.[69] The 1950s further solidified Prince Rupert's standing as "one of the strongest labour cities on the Pacific Coast."[70] Likely in part for this reason, by 1960, Prince Rupert's average income was 13 percent higher than the Canadian average, and nearly 20 percent higher than the BC average.[71]

It's difficult to pinpoint exactly when Prince Rupert's boom times officially started, but a strong case can be made for the time between 1959 and 1960:

1. Symbolically, Watson Island turned its first net profit since beginning production nearly a decade prior. By 1960, the wages being paid by the single facility were comparable to those of the entire local fishing industry combined.[72]

2. Metaphorically, the completion of the Digby Island airport signalled a community ready for takeoff. After 1.1 million cubic meters of rock was required to replace seventeen feet of muskeg, the project was nicknamed Rupert's "Battle of the Bulge." With a runway long enough to handle the largest passenger aircrafts in service, a federal engineer estimated that more rock had to be moved than at any other airport in BC.[73] The initial cost estimates were described as "slightly shocking" by the federal transportation minister,[74] but after flying over the muskeg he understood why. In the end, the $7.6 million price tag, which included building the access road, made Prince Rupert the most expensive airport project ever undertaken in Canada when it broke ground.[75]

3. Culturally, the first All Native Basketball Tournament tipped off, marking the start to what is now one of the largest Indigenous cultural events in Canada.[76] Soon after the first tournament was held, the federal government finally gave Indigenous Peoples the right to vote, and Indigenous youth were integrated into local public schools.[77]

4. Internationally, after Alaska officially became part of the US, the state pronounced Prince Rupert as the southern terminus of its marine highway system. New ferries were being commissioned. CN reserved the local site for their dock and the BC government committed to extending the highway to reach it.

5. Coincidentally, 1960 was the fiftieth anniversary of Prince Rupert's official incorporation. Beyond being a round number

and the start of a new decade, the Golden Jubilee Year ushered
in a new golden era of economic prosperity, much like Mayor
Nora Arnold had predicted.

If Nora Arnold's 1940s Prince Rupert was a troubled youth getting back on its feet, then 1950s Prince Rupert had become a young
adult with a new sense of freedom and independence. With economic stability courtesy of the pulp mill, the city in the 1950s were
a far cry from the bankrupt community of the '30s and '40s. Rather
than being the city of fabulous fortunes as predicted by Charles Hays,
it could be said that Prince Rupert had become a city of fluctuating
fortunes; it was a community that had weathered many storms yet
maintained its "unquenchable optimism."[78]

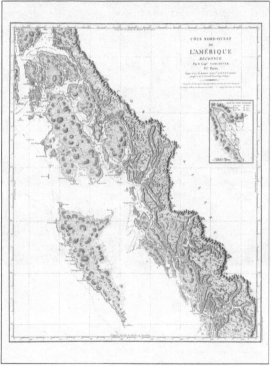

TOP Captain James Colnett and his crew were taken prisoner at Nootka Sound in 1789, after first contact with the Gitxaała. LC-DIG-PGA-01050

BOTTOM Captain George Vancouver missed the Skeena and Nass Rivers, as well as Kaien Island's protected inner harbour. RAREMAPS.COM

TOP, LEFT An early painting of the stockades of the HBC Fort Simpson by Sir Henry Wellcome. NAID 297310

TOP, RIGHT Close view of Metlakatla Church between 1874 and 1901, allegedly the largest north of San Fransisco and west of Chicago at the time. NORTHERN BC ARCHIVES & SPECIAL COLLECTIONS/2009.7.1.036

BOTTOM Brass band, men, women, and children pose with Bishop Ridley the year before Metlakatla's church burned down in 1901. NORTHERN BC ARCHIVES & SPECIAL COLLECTIONS/2009.7.1.037

TOP, LEFT Bishop Ridley residence and mission house in Metlakatla.
NORTHERN BC ARCHIVES & SPECIAL COLLECTIONS/2009.7.1.059

TOP, RIGHT Oolichan, the "saviour fish," on drying racks at Port Essington.
HARRIS FAMILY FONDS. PRINCE RUPERT CITY & REGIONAL ARCHIVES

BOTTOM The first hotel in BC's North Coast region at Port Essington.
PRINCE RUPERT CITY & REGIONAL ARCHIVES

TOP An aerial view of Port Essington in 1905, then the largest community in the region just prior to the coming of the railway. OLSON FAMILY FONDS. PRINCE RUPERT CITY & REGIONAL ARCHIVES

BOTTOM A view of the first salmon cannery in Port Essington and boats in the foreground. PAM CHAMBERS COLLECTION. PRINCE RUPERT CITY & REGIONAL ARCHIVES

TOP The Hazelton river boat enroute from Port Essington up the Skeena River to Hazelton. WRATHALL PHOTO FINISHING LTD. FONDS. PRINCE RUPERT CITY & REGIONAL ARCHIVES

MIDDLE Boardwalk on Centre Street, Prince Rupert, circa 1908. J.D. ALLEN PHOTOGRAPHIC COMPANY FONDS. PRINCE RUPERT CITY & REGIONAL ARCHIVES

BOTTOM Knoxville, the first tent settlement built on a mineral land claim to avert the GTP. J.D. ALLEN PHOTOGRAPHIC COMPANY FONDS. PRINCE RUPERT CITY & REGIONAL ARCHIVES

TOP 1909 Dominion Day celebration arch above main thoroughfare in Prince Rupert. J.D. ALLEN PHOTOGRAPHIC COMPANY FONDS. PRINCE RUPERT CITY & REGIONAL ARCHIVES

MIDDLE Charles Hays's brother was appointed as the sole GTP agent auctioning off lots in 1909. WRATHALL PHOTO FINISHING LTD. FONDS. PRINCE RUPERT CITY & REGIONAL ARCHIVES

BOTTOM Trees cleared but stump and muskeg farms remain while boardwalks are built in 1909. DR. R. GEDDES LARGE FONDS. PRINCE RUPERT CITY & REGIONAL ARCHIVES

2nd Ave. looking East

First Train Leaving Prince Rupert June 14 1911

TOP 2nd Avenue West, downtown Prince Rupert, 1910.
J.D. ALLEN PHOTOGRAPHIC COMPANY FONDS. PRINCE
RUPERT CITY & REGIONAL ARCHIVES

BOTTOM First train to leave Prince Rupert, June 1911.
GEORGE A. MCNICHOLL FONDS. PRINCE RUPERT CITY
& REGIONAL ARCHIVES

TOP, LEFT Prince Rupert's supposed "curse" after the death of Charles Hays, Rip Van Rupert.

TOP, RIGHT Another ship hit by the ss *Prince Rupert*. Five men stand and look out the hole. WRATHALL PHOTO FINISHING LTD. FONDS. PRINCE RUPERT CITY & REGIONAL ARCHIVES

BOTTOM ss *Prince Rupert*, September 28, 1920. One of many mishaps in the ship's long but unlucky career. MCRAE BROS., LTD. FONDS. PRINCE RUPERT CITY & REGIONAL ARCHIVES

TOP A man stands at the Prince Rupert docks beside his catch—a 350-pound halibut and 85-pound salmon. WRATHALL PHOTO FINISHING LTD. FONDS. PRINCE RUPERT CITY & REGIONAL ARCHIVES

BOTTOM The largest landing of halibut in September 1937: 677,000 pounds. Truly the Halibut Capital of the World. WRATHALL PHOTO FINISHING LTD. FONDS. PRINCE RUPERT CITY & REGIONAL ARCHIVES

A Company of 11ᵗʰ Irish Fusiliers of Canada leaving Prince Rupert, B.C 1914.

3RD OVERSEAS CONTINGENT LEAVING PRINCE RUPERT BC JULY 8ᵀᴴ 1915

TOP Company of the 11th Irish Fusiliers of Canada leaving Prince Rupert for the First World War. PRINCE RUPERT CITY & REGIONAL ARCHIVES

BOTTOM The third overseas contingent leaving Prince Rupert, July 8, 1915. MCRAE BROS., LTD. FONDS. PRINCE RUPERT CITY & REGIONAL ARCHIVES

TOP Arrival of the first train from Winnipeg, April 1914. MITCHELL FAMILY FONDS. PRINCE RUPERT CITY & REGIONAL ARCHIVES

BOTTOM One of the largest steel submarine nets installed during the Second World War at the mouth of the Prince Rupert harbour. PHYLIS BOWMAN COLLECTION. PRINCE RUPERT CITY & REGIONAL ARCHIVES

TOP, LEFT American encampment during the Second World War on Acropolis Hill, Prince Rupert. DR. R. GEDDES LARGE FONDS. PRINCE RUPERT CITY & REGIONAL ARCHIVES

TOP, RIGHT Bombs being loaded at Watson Island, destined for war in the Pacific. DR. R. GEDDES LARGE FONDS. PRINCE RUPERT CITY & REGIONAL ARCHIVES

BOTTOM, LEFT A view of Watson Island in the early 1950s. DR. R. GEDDES LARGE FONDS. PRINCE RUPERT CITY & REGIONAL ARCHIVES

BOTTOM, RIGHT The first arrival of the BC Ferries ship *Queen of Prince Rupert*, 1966. WRATHALL PHOTO FINISHING LTD. FONDS. PRINCE RUPERT CITY & REGIONAL ARCHIVES

TOP The Royal Family attends the grand opening of the Prince Rupert Regional Hospital, 1971. PHYLIS BOWMAN COLLECTION. PRINCE RUPERT CITY & REGIONAL ARCHIVES

BOTTOM The city of Prince Rupert today, with container terminal at right and a cruise ship docked at top, left. CHELSEY ELLIS PHOTOGRAPHY

CHAPTER 12

BOOM
1960–82

"Prince Rupert is probably one of the
most booming cities in Canada."
CITY PROPERTY ASSESSOR, 1966

THE SPECTACULAR SIXTIES

The 1960s in Prince Rupert have been described as "the most spectacular period of industrial expansion in [the city's] history." Almost every data point backs up the claim: with a 40 percent increase in population since the 1950s, 13,600 people were living in the city by 1964. Building permit value went up ten times from 1953 to 1963. Exports soared by 70 percent between 1957 and 1962. The fishing industry employed nearly 5,000 people, and the Halibut Capital of the World was landing 15–17 million pounds, more than double the amount of Vancouver.[1] The local sawmill was awarded the largest timber contract in BC since 1927.[2] The local grain elevator was at full capacity to help send 40 million bushels of wheat to China, the largest commercial transaction in Canada since the Second World War.[3] By the mid 1960s, Prince Rupert had jumped into the third spot for average personal income across Canada, higher than Vancouver or Toronto.[4] As a result of the phenomenal economic growth, the total assessed value of Prince Rupert's real estate more than tripled between 1956 and 1966. The city assessor, who was the person responsible for providing local property value assessments for tax purposes, said: "If the sale, re-sale and estimated value of future sales means anything, then Prince Rupert is probably one of the most booming cities in Canada."[5]

There were also plenty of symbolic signs of progress in the early 1960s, such as the arrival of BC Hydro, the first televisions, and a daily scheduled flight to Vancouver. The new federal government building opened with six departments and hundreds of civil servants working in it, a new high school and two new elementary schools were built, multiple apartment complexes began rising, and the Alaska Ferry terminal opened its doors.[6] The Watson Island pulp mill continued to be the city's single largest economic driver.

PULP CITY OF CANADA

For the early part of the 1960s, every year set a new record for both profits and production on Watson Island. Skeena Cellulose was able to start paying out dividends and announced an expansion through the building of a new kraft pulp mill in 1964. The $80 million investment saw Watson Island become home to the world's largest single-line pulp mill and pulp dryer, increasing the capacity to make Prince Rupert the largest pulp producer in Canada, and one of the largest in North America.

To house the hundreds of new people required for their growing operation, the company offered $1 million to the municipality to guarantee the purchase of hundreds of homes whereby they paid for installation of water, sewer, and street services, and the cost of servicing was charged back to the new homeowners. This building scheme is responsible for the majority of the neighbourhoods of Crestview Circle, Overlook Street, and Rushbrook Heights, all of which are home to hundreds of Rupertites today.[7]

The new kraft industrial complex was so expansive that it required raising two nearby dammed lakes, Diana and Rainbow, by almost thirty feet each to supply enough water for the operation. To supply the energy required to fuel the facility, Skeena Cellulose partnered with Pacific Northern Gas to build a 430-mile natural gas pipeline from the Interior.[8] To this day, the pipeline is the sole natural gas provider for the Prince Rupert. By the late 1960s, the combined employment numbers between the two mill facilities was nearly 1,400 direct jobs,[9] more than one in ten residents.

QUEEN OF PRINCE RUPERT: MISSED THE BOAT

By the mid-1960s, the recently established BC Ferries had the goal to link to the new Alaska Marine Highway system, of which Prince Rupert would serve as its southern terminus. Having long recognized the strategic value of Prince Rupert's location, Alaskan authorities saw the Inside Passage route from Prince Rupert to Vancouver Island as necessary to connect Alaska with the rest of the continental United States. But to accomplish this shared objective, a new vessel had to be constructed.

Perhaps the cursed life of the ss *Prince Rupert* should have served as caution not to name another vessel after the city. In the marine community, an improper christening is considered a bad omen. When it came time for the traditional smashing of champagne against the hull, a youngster tripped over the restraint, sending the *Queen of Prince Rupert* prematurely towards the water. The rushed first try of the champagne bottle missed the boat, so the shipyard president grabbed the bottle and flung it towards the quickly disappearing hull. It failed to connect and the bottle landed unbroken before a workman, who was barely able to smash it against the bow just as it entered the water. The ship was then caught by a gust of wind and pushed towards the rocks before two tugboats were able to steer her into berth.[10]

This sort of launch meant trouble ahead. In only its second year of operation, the *Queen of Prince Rupert* was grounded on a reef in August 1967 and was sent for repairs. The event appears to have created strife between the Alaskan and bc governments. The Alaskan governor spent months asking bc premier W.A.C. Bennett when service would be resumed but said the only communication his office received was a Christmas card. Bennett responded by saying he would not phone, write, visit, or even acknowledge the governor's requests because he had gone to the media. To make matters worse, the Bennett government had delayed upgrading the forty unpaved miles of Highway 16 into Prince Rupert, which had been drawing the ire of Alaskan officials for years. Ultimately, the Alaskan governor acquired funding to build additional ferries and launched a Seattle-to-Ketchikan service, bypassing Prince Rupert and removing its designation as the Alaska Marine Highway's southern terminus.[11]

The new route and ferry were initially temporary, but quickly became profitable for the Alaskans, so they continued permanently even after the *Queen of Prince Rupert* was returned to service.[12] The local *Daily News* editorial wrote that the Bennett had "shot off his mouth to the advantage of someone else ... the fact is he got a slap in the face and so did we."[13]

GETTING HEADLINES

The early 1970s saw Prince Rupert jump into the Canadian conscious-ness with a string of high-profile visits and developments, solidi-fying the city's reputation as a boom town. Trudeaumania swept through the city briefly in 1970 in the same week that Premier Bill Bennett and his entire cabinet met in Prince Rupert, kicking off a series of good news events. One of the main topics of discussion was Prince Rupert's port facilities, the first such time that all three levels of government had met on the issue. The talks culminated in an announcement by the federal government of a study for a bulk cargo terminal in Prince Rupert.[14]

Through 1970–71 alone, the city opened its first and only 18-hole golf course, launched a new, custom-built airport ferry dubbed the "mini aircraft carrier," opened multiple seniors housing developments, celebrated the new Civic Centre complex, built a new public library, and installed a seaplane base.[15] All of these public assets have since surpassed the 50-year mark and are still in active use in 2024.

The crowning achievement of the early 1970s was the opening of the 150-bed Prince Rupert Regional Hospital. The city had donated the site donated for $1. At its grand opening in 1971, it was the most modern hospital in the province and substantially larger than the Miller Bay Indian Hospital,[16] which had closed in ther previous year. Marking the occasion were Queen Elizabeth II, Prince Philip, and Princess Anne. When the royal tour was being organized at Buck-ingham Palace, the Queen expressed a wish to ride a fishing boat while visiting the BC coast.[17] So, she was shuttled across the harbour to Digby Island aboard the fifty-five-foot fishing vessel *Signal*, and was presented with a halibut.[18] What a fitting way for the Halibut Capital of the World to share its crown jewel on the global stage.

PORT POTENTIAL PINPOINTED

In 1972, nearly a decade after Mayor Peter J. Lester first appointed a committee advocate for instituting a harbour commission, Prince Rupert was declared a national harbour and allocated $5 million for terminal development.[19] Ownership of Ridley Island was trans-ferred by the provincial government to the newly created National

Harbours Board.[20] In 1973, the federal government committed to the construction of the Fairview bulk terminal at a cost of $23 million.[21]

Just a few years prior, the first-ever archeological study of the Prince Rupert harbour had gotten underway. In 1971, the first Ts'msyen cedar plank house had been uncovered.[22] Richard Inglis, a researcher with the Archaeological Survey of Canada, said, "On Sept 07, 1972 the lead article in the *Prince Rupert Daily News* heralded plans for construction of a deep-sea shipping terminal in Prince Rupert. I immediately noted that two of the last remaining middens on Kaien Island would be destroyed by the development."[23] It was clear that the Fairview site had been occupied by the Ts'msyen people, that people of all ages lived there, and that they had left "some of the most extraordinary artifacts ever found on the northern Northwest coast."[24] Unfortunately for the Ts'msyen, the same features that made the site so strategically important for them for thousands of years were the same reasons that the area was being primed for industrial development.[25]

With the flagship port project underway despite the protests of the Ts'msyen and archaeologists, port-related growth continued in earnest through the remainder of the 1970s. In 1975, the Prince Rupert Port Corporation was created, and Mayor Lester himself was appointed to the board.[26] In 1976, a coal export terminal was announced for Ridley Island. 1977 saw the Fairview terminal welcome its first ship, a Japanese vessel loaded with six hundred tons of frozen herring. And in 1979, a new, $125-million grain elevator was announced, also on Ridley Island.[27]

THE GOOD & THE BAD

For decades, Prince Rupert's hope of port development had cycled from anticipation to agony. Sixty years after the sinking of the *Titanic*, the dream of Charles Hays suddenly seemed within reach. Amid rapid growth, and with a population exceeding 17,000 by the early 1980s, it finally seemed possible that Prince Rupert was on its way to becoming a world-class port city. Bill Vander Zalm, who at the time was the provincial minister for municipal affairs and would later become premier, went as far as claiming a "relatively conservative" projection that Prince Rupert was set to reach a population of 50,000 within ten years. Mayor Lester did not go quite as far, although he did concede that doubling to 34,000 was entirely possible.[28]

But as with any economic boom, there were costs to this growth. Prince Rupert was recognized with the dubious distinction of having among the worst staffed schools in the province.[29] According to the Skeena Health Unit director, Prince Rupert also had the "world's worst death rate in Indian babies," almost 3.5 times higher than the Canadian average.[30] And at the height of the city's housing shortage, a report concluded that the crisis "appears to be a lack of planning at the community level ... what appears to be the answer is to give housing the priority over some of the other government expenditures."[31]

Consistent with the city's reputation after two alcohol-fuelled downtown riots, by this time the average Rupertite was spending 58 percent more than the average British Columbian on alcohol, the second highest rate in the province.[32] Prince Rupert's crime rate leapt 70 percent between 1975 and 1980, and perhaps correlated to alcohol spending, the crime rate was also the second highest in BC.[33] Vandalism was rampant in the downtown area as people made their way from the bars that closed at 1 AM to the cabarets that were open until 2 AM and then the restaurants that closed at 4 AM before spilling out into the streets to drink further.[34]

Drunk with rekindled optimism, Prince Rupert's boom-time building spree in the 1970s changed the entire complexion of the city. A 2,600-acre (1,052-hectare) industrial site was carved out of the rainforest on the outskirts of town. New subdivisions on both sides of town not only expanded the urban footprint, but also necessitated the building of new schools and parks. Multiple hotels, motels, and shopping malls built in the downtown area fundamentally altered the community's physical form and aesthetic. With more commercial activity came more foot traffic; more people meant a changing demographic, more events, more entertainment, and more tourism. There was an apparent cultural shift in the city. No longer was Prince Rupert considered "the town that sunk with the Titanic." Instead, a growing cosmopolitan city had emerged. Beyond the physical and economic expansion, the social networks, sense of belonging, and community identity grew as well.

COLOURFUL CHARACTER: IONA CAMPAGNOLO

Iona Campagnolo, October 1982. NORTHERN BC
ARCHIVES AND SPECIAL COLLECTIONS

Iona Campagnolo grew up at the North Pacific Cannery ("a sacred place for me"), where she attended a one-room school as one of only four white students in a majority Indigenous and Japanese classroom. It was while living here that she learned the Ts'msyen and Nisga'a oral histories, the importance of treaties, and traditional land acknowledgements.[35] After graduating high school in Prince Rupert in 1951, Iona started work as a private broadcaster before launching her political career as the chairperson of the local school board from 1966 to 1972. She was then elected to the city council from 1972 to 1974, saying that she was motivated because "I sometimes feel Prince Rupert is a spiritual island, as well as a physical one. I hope to help reach out and let other people know of the good life we have here."[36]

In 1973, she was made a member of the Order of Canada for her "wide-ranging services in organizing, promoting and conducting community projects in Prince Rupert."[37] Those dynamic volunteer services included being the coordinator of the Queen's visit in 1971 and the Governor General's visit in 1974, and being the coordinator of Folkfest, the first ever cultural celebration to "embrace, promote and celebrate diversity" in Prince Rupert.[38]

Campagnolo was elected as an MP in 1974 for Pierre Trudeau's Liberal Party, extending her poll-topping streak to five elections over eight years and ending the NDP's seventeen-year local winning streak.[39] As an MP, she was first appointed as the parliamentary secretary for the minister of Indian Affairs and Northern Development (1974–76) before being appointed to the newly created position of Minister of State for Fitness and Amateur Sport. She held this position from 1976 to 1979, and was the country's first-ever female and northern voice to be included in the federal cabinet.[40] She was an early advocate for immigration equity, saying policy "must not be discriminatory and must not be prejudiced against any race, sex, colour or creed."[41] Even in the face of significant protest,[42] she was one of the first Canadian MPs to openly call for the removal of abortion from the Criminal Code.[43]

Closer to home, Campagnolo helped secure money for the Prince Rupert SPCA to build a shelter, for the Civic Centre to install a new rock-climbing wall, and for the construction of the Mount Hays gondola.[44] Her philosophy was that, much like the building of the railway, "the social and cultural and recreational facilities [are] part of the price of shaping the Canada of tomorrow."[45] She was also the government's representative for celebrating plenty of federally-funded local initiatives, including the ribbon-cutting for the Fairview terminal and the investment announcements for the new coal and grain terminals.

In 1979, Trudeau and his Liberals lost the general election Joe Clark and the Conservatives, who formed a short-lived minority government. Campagnolo went on to become the first female president of the Liberal Party in 1982 and the founding chancellor of the University of Northern BC in 1992. She was awarded the Order of BC in 1998 before being appointed as the province's first female lieutenant-governor, holding the position from 2001 until 2007.[46] She has received six honorary degrees, was made a lifetime member of the Liberal Party of Canada and the Union of BC Municipalities, and even has two varieties of BC rhododendrons named after her.[47]

Campagnolo credits Prince Rupert mayor Nora Arnold as being an inspiration for her own career. Seeing a woman in an influential position was a powerful formative experience for her:

[Nora Arnold] had a big impact on me... I went down with my friends from high school to see her getting off the train from the far away place [where] she had been named "Woman of the Year"... she was in her black suit and her black hat and her silver fox and everybody was saying, "Your Worship this" and "Your Worship that," and my friends and I said to ourselves, "we can do that." And we did.[48]

A 2017 article in the *Vancouver Sun* mischaracterized Campagnolo as being "best remembered for the bum that brought down a prime minister" after John Turner patted her bottom on TV, setting off a feminist uproar ending in his decisive defeat.[49] But for Rupertites, she is proudly remembered for being something far more important: a champion for human rights, women's rights, Indigenous rights, environmental protection, and international democracy. She was adopted into the Gitksan community and gifted two Indigenous names: Notz-whe-Neah (Mother of the Big Fin), from the Ts'msyen Nation, and Saan-naag-Kaawaass (Person who Sits High), from the Haida Nation.[50] She has acknowledged and credits her upbringing on BC's North Coast as being profoundly impactful on both her attitude in life and her career.[51] At her swearing-in as Lieutenant Governor, Iona Campagnolo concluded her remarks with a sentiment very obviously forged by her years in boom-time Prince Rupert: "konoway tillicums klatawa kunamokst klaska mamook okoke huloima chee illahie." Translated from the Chinook language: "Everyone was thrown together to make this strange new country."[52]

EVERYONE THROWN TOGETHER

With new industries came new jobs and amenities, and with more work and more play came more people. As the city's population increased through the 1960s and '70s, so too did the multicultural tapestry of its residents. The Canadian government had passed the

1948 Family Reunion Act just as construction of the pulp mill on Watson Island was announced. Racist immigration laws were finally turfed after 1967. Then a larger influx of immigrants came to Canada during the Trudeau era in the 1970s thanks to the introduction of the family reunification program, points-based immigrant system, and recognition for the first time of refugees as a distinct class of immigrants, with a new path through private sponsorship.[53] A new generation of immigrants arrived to Kaien Island during the boom.

A strong Chinese-Canadian presence had already been well established in Prince Rupert by immigrants who had arrived to work in the first canneries or to build the Grand Trunk Railway. By the early 1950s, Prince Rupert already had an informal Chinatown with multiple Chinese restaurants, grocery stores, and businesses clustered in two city blocks. There was even a short-lived Chinese Heritage School. By 1968, there were eleven Chinese restaurants listed in the local directory. The Chinese Freemasons Society (Hongmen Minzhidang), and Prince Rupert Chinese Association were formed in the early 1950s. When the local RCMP demanded that every Chinese resident's information be given out to check immigration status in 1960, the association hired a lawyer and stood firm against the infringement on their rights as Canadians. In 1977, Earl Mah, the son of a grocer who was one of the first Chinese immigrants to Prince Rupert, became the first member of the Chinese community to be elected to the city council.[54]

While a few prominent Italian families had arrived in Prince Rupert before the symbolic last spike of the railway in 1914, an influx of Italian immigrants flocked to the city in the 1950s to work in the pulp mill. When the city celebrated its golden jubilee in 1960, the local Italo-Canadian club had grown large enough to gift the city a new downtown plaza and fountain, which still stands beside City Hall today.[55]

The Sons of Norway Vinland Lodge was one of the four sponsoring organizations to build the first civic centre. The organization also purchased a hall that was used for social gatherings from 1948 until the 1980s before being converted into the Dance Academy of Prince Rupert.[56] One notable member of the Norwegian community, a young immigrant fisherman named Ed Wahl, started his working life building one wooden boat per year in the 1920s and eventually went on to build the "most successful commercial fish-boat building enterprise on British Columbia's north coast."[57]

While there were a few early Ukrainian immigrant families in the early 1900s, there were approximately two hundred Ukrainian Catholics who arrived after the Second World War. A "Ukrayinsky Klyub" was started in 1963 and later built and donated Ukrainian Park to the community. They also helped finance a wing of the hospital, participated in the annual Seafest parade, and prepared traditional Ukrainian meals at the city hall for Christmas and Easter.[58]

Through the 1960s and '70s, a wave of Punjabi migration occurred thanks to the establishment of Prince Rupert Sawmills. Started by a Punjabi industrialist on the old dry dock site, the sawmill bunkhouse housed the first thirty to forty Punjabi men. The first Punjabi child born in Prince Rupert arrived in 1961. Prince Rupert was recognized as having hired the first turbaned postman in Canada. And by the late 1970s, dozens of Punjabis were employed in the pulp mill or fish processing plant. In 1972, the local Indo-Canadian Sikh Association was established to acquire its own gurdwara (place of worship), and within three years had a weekly attendance of over one hundred people.[59]

In 1973, the Filipino-Canadian Association of Prince Rupert was established to promote local Filipino culture and participate in civic activities. In addition to hosting an annual Filipino Night, they also became well known being prolific fundraisers for various non-profit causes as well as for selling their famous Filipino shish-kebobs at Seafest.[60]

In the late 1970s, Canada had taken in more Vietnamese refugees than any other country per capita.[61] In Prince Rupert, many Vietnamese newcomers were sponsored by the local Catholic Church. Most created new lives for themselves as their own bosses, particularly in the restaurant and crab fishing industries, reclaiming the meaning of the term "Boat People."

From the 1960s to the 1980s, the rate of Indigenous urbanization increased substantially,[62] and their positive presence was increasingly felt. The Friendship House was built in 1963 and quickly expanded services to include a child milk program, nursery school, youth street works, alcohol rehabilitation, and a hostel.[63] Metlakatla began sending their students into Prince Rupert for school, later resulting in a Sm'algyax language curriculum being launched in the local school district.[64] Lax Kw'alaams began operating a regular passenger service into Prince Rupert.[65] A Nisga'a Tribal Council was formed to represent the hundreds of Nisga'a citizens living in Prince Rupert and Port Edward.[66] The Council of the Haida Nation began electing a Prince Rupert representative to serve as liaisons for its hundreds of members.[67]

Compared to most homogenous rural and remote communities, the local experience of immigrants in Prince Rupert must have been complicated. Arriving in an already ethnically diverse city with their own socio-cultural norms, immigrants not only had to adapt to the "white mainstream," but also had to engage in intercultural inter-actions with Indigenous Peoples and the diasporic communities of other countries. There are many documented racial tensions expe-rienced by immigrants from every origin during Prince Rupert's boom times. But to paraphrase the words of Asian studies researcher Kamala E. Nayar, immigrants were greatly aided in their efforts to acclimatize themselves to their new home thanks to their values of prioritizing family bonds and hard work.[68]

As the wider Canadian society was shifting from policies of assim-ilation to ones of integration and pluralism, Prince Rupert's growing immigrant communities were all becoming collaborative members of a new social fabric. The spirit of the time was captured by mayor Peter Lester, who said, "Prince Rupert is an example for other communities in the province because we take the approach that people do not have to lose their ethnic backgrounds simply because they have moved to another country. We try to mould it all into one community."[69]

CHAPTER 13

BUBBLE

1982–93

> "You've got to feel sorry for the people of Prince Rupert,
> a remote town up the BC coast that seems in a perpetual
> struggle to keep its head above water."
>
> DAVID PARKINSON, *GLOBE & MAIL*, AUGUST 4, 2001

INFLATED '80S

If the 1960s in Prince Rupert were defined as an era of economic expansion and the 1970s the era of amenities, then the 1980s were the decade of decadence. Despite a brief recession in 1981–82, Prince Rupert was relatively insulated from it compared to the rest of Canada. Even though it is sometimes called the "Reagan Recession," Canada experienced higher inflation, interest rates, and unemployment than the US.

Prince Rupert was spared the worst results of the recession courtesy of the gumboot millionaire fishermen, high-paid union members at the pulp mill, and the growing wages at the longshore hall thanks to an expanding port. But the city was by no means immune. Numerous grandiose proposals fizzled and died: a $7-billion LNG facility on Ridley Island, plus another twelve LNG and petrochemical proposals around Prince Rupert and Port Edward,[1] a $1.8-billion tank farm for Albertan bulk chemicals and fuels, an oil refinery, and a steel mill. But the two most prominent and illustrative examples of the economic boom becoming more like a bubble are the Mount Hays Gondola and the Highliner Hotel.

MOUNT HAYS GONDOLA

In the mid-1970s, a local ski committee raised $400,000 from government sources and an additional $295,000 in donations to build a gondola and ski lodge on Mount Hays.[2] Unfortunately, the cost overruns quickly escalated to $1.1 million, and within one year, the committee required a "life and death" guarantee from the city government on loans they had taken out.[3] The grand opening was celebrated in March 1976 to great fanfare, with audacious claims that the hill had the same type of snow as Whistler Mountain[4] and that Prince Rupert's newest tourist attraction would bring thousands of ski visitors throughout the winter and cruise tourists all summer.

By 1980, despite the provincial ski facilities coordinator saying the project should never have been built, the city council guaranteed a ten-year operating subsidy and paid off the equipment debts to prevent foreclosure.[5] But it was still not enough to avoid receivership. In a strange twist of logic, the city council took the position that the ski club was a good investment because bankruptcy was inevitable. Seventy-five percent of unpaid taxes were written off, $382,000 in mortgages held by the banks were bought for $150,000, and more city cash was allocated to overhaul the gondola and take over operations of the facility, aiming to attract the Northern Winter Games skiing competitions. Mayor Peter Lester said at the time, "It is true the money could be spent elsewhere ... but if a facility worth more than $1 million can be purchased for $150K it would be a shame to let it go."[6]

The city government thought it could operate the facility at a small annual deficit of only $12,000 per year. But over the next five years, despite controversy and public objection, the annual operating subsidy increased from $50,000 to $95,000. During that time, the city had lost over half of its cruise passenger traffic during the summer and saw only enough snow to operate for ten days during the winter of 1983–84 and just two days in 1984–85. By 1986, the city had sunk over half a million dollars into the Mount Hays Ski Hill when Shames Mountain received approval to build only 130 kilometres away.[7]

After a $275,000 operating budget was presented in 1991, the city council ruled against providing money to open for the winter season. The city gave just enough funds to get the gondola running for the 1992 summer season before closing the hill for good in 1993 due to budget cutbacks.[8] What an inglorious end to an extravagant amenity that ultimately cost local taxpayers $1.5 million without ever coming close to turning a profit.[9]

SKYSCRAPERS

If Prince Rupert could have chosen an official bird in 1980, it should have been the construction crane. Between 1970 and 1980, the annual value of construction undertaken in the city had skyrocketed from $7.5 million to $18.6 million.[10] As BC saw a province-wide drop in property values of 23.5 percent in the early 1980s, Prince Rupert's went up 7 percent.[11] Beyond the hotels, motels, and malls, a long line of high-rises were proposed for the downtown area, including: an eleven-storey apartment complex overlooking the harbour, a twenty-two-storey, 144-unit condo building near Moresby Park, another high-rise facing the Crest Hotel, a twin-tower, sixteen-storey apartment complex overlooking the golf course, a thirteen-storey seniors housing downtown high-rise, and even a $9-million First Nations cultural centre fit with an eight-storey, 112-room hotel, and six-storey office tower.[12] But the first in line was the Highliner Hotel.[13]

At seventeen storeys tall, the Highliner was designed to be the tallest building outside of the Lower Mainland at that time, the same height as the Hotel Vancouver, which had itself been the tallest building in BC until 1972.[14] Built by a group of local residents, the city's sole skyscraper was given the go-ahead primarily because the city council felt an obligation to the developers who had applied for a building permit under old guidelines, which did not specify a height restriction. However, their approval decision was subject to the formation of a new zoning committee, which ultimately created a new downtown height restriction of five storeys.[15] That decision, paired with record high interest rates, all but ensured the city's skyline would not be dominated by skyscrapers, with the one biggest exception.

The $12.9-million Highliner project broke ground in 1981 with interest rates at 12 percent. But much like the Mount Hays Gondola, things would go quickly downhill. By the time the hotel was ready for occupancy in 1982, Canadian interest rates had reached an all-time record above 20 percent and the building's occupancy levels were 15 percent below the developer's projections.[16] The hotel was forced into receivership the same year, but it still dominates the skyline of Kaien Island today and stands as an emblem for the boom times.

1982: THE BUBBLE BEGINS

It's difficult to recognize a bubble forming in the midst of a boom, but the local impacts from the brief 1982 recession provided a few clear signals that a new chapter was about to turn in the city's fortunes.

First, even as Prince Rupert was being advertised as the fastest growing city in Canada, the federal census showed the city's population had contracted slightly from its peak in 1976. Prince Rupert's school enrolment shrank by the hundreds for the first time in years.[17] Additionally, the gulf quadrupled between how many residents the city claimed it had (20,000) and how many the federal and provincial statisticians documented (15,000).

Second, there was an increase in labour disruptions and unemployment. The pulp mill on Watson Island was shuttered for seven of twelve months, putting eight hundred people on unemployment.[18] Multiple fish filleting lines were temporarily suspended, putting over 350 out of work.[19] Dozens were laid off at the grain elevator.[20] For eight straight quarters in the early 1980s, Prince Rupert's vacancy rate went from 0.6 percent to over 17 percent. The local unemployment doubled to more than two thousand people.[21]

Third, on a larger scale, a macroeconomic downturn was taking effect. CN issued an embargo on export traffic, stopping the flow of two hundred rail cars per week into Prince Rupert. The Fairview terminal saw sulphur shipments decline by over 30 percent and fish shipments evaporate from 22,000 tons to only 1,200.[22] Provincial government cost-cutting resulted in the loss of the company departments for human resources and mining and natural resources, meaning more than 120 government employees were relocated.[23]

Fourth, at the city level, the municipality slashed capital spending and delayed maintenance on critical infrastructure improvements, including the water supply dam. On the recommendation of Mayor Lester and his finance committee, the civic centre was closed for twenty-six days of the year, a half-hour shorter working day was instituted, dozens of staff were laid off, and a furlough of ten days in 1982 and two days per month in the following year was forced. The city council also re-opened the union agreement and reduced the expected 13-percent annual pay increase to only 3 percent. Both the police and fire hall also saw staffing reduced.[24] And the entire budget surplus was utilized to blunt tax increases that stemmed from the drop in tax revenue.[25]

Fifth, and finally, the fishing industry was falling due to increasing costs, currency fluctuations, labour strikes, the loss of catches to Alaskans, the collapse of the Japanese herring roe market, and significant government intervention.[26] Due to depleting fishing stocks, the federal government instituted new taxes and quotas, ended hundreds of fishing licences through transfer restrictions and buyback programs. This ultimately amounted to a loss of 10 percent of BC's fishing fleet.[27]

HALI-BUST

Arguably the most consequential symbol of economic decline was the closure of the Seal Cove Cold Storage Plant in 1982. Built in 1912 to hold 20 million pounds of fish, the plant could handle up to 1 million pounds of fish per day. After seventy years of continuous operation, the world's largest fish processing plant closed its doors for good. The loss of three hundred full-time jobs for some of the highest-paid shore workers in North America amounted to a $5–7 million annual hit to the local economy.[28] The facility was demolished two years later.[29]

To make matters worse, that same year, Prince Rupert lost its title of Halibut Capital of the World to Homer, Alaska. The commercial fishing industry had been the city's economic backbone since its inception, with the bold boasts of "assured growth" and "illimitable wealth" finally proven wrong. Just one year prior, Prince Rupert landed 40 percent of BC's entire fish catch and obviously relied on fishing more than any other community on the west coast of North America.[30] So, there is a tremendous irony that the decline in local fishing activity necessitated the first official instance of the slogan "City of Rainbows." Prince Rupert had unofficially been dubbed with the moniker for years, but in the spring of 1982, the Prince Rupert Tourist Bureau unveiled the new "City of Rainbows" slogan in a Seafest poster as a symbolic hand-off from the former mascot Herbie the Halibut holding a rainbow flag.[31] Not long after, the mayor and city council made it official in a split 4–3 vote.[32] Little could they have known then that the time following the change of moniker to a potent symbol like the rainbow would not be a return to calm after the storm, but rather that there were more storm clouds on the horizon.

RIP VAN RIDLEY

For the first time in more than fifty years, the Rip Van Rupert curse was re-publicized in the local paper with the comment, "The sentiments sound familiar."[33] After decades of uninterrupted rapid growth and expansion, many Rupertites believed their city had overcome the local curse of bad timing. The impacts stemming from the 1982 recession gave plenty of reasons for doubt, and "the only thing propping up the sagging economy... [was] construction at Ridley Island."[34]

With $280 million in industrial activity underway on Ridley Island, the city requested a boundary expansion, which the primary taxpayer strenuously objected to before the province negotiated a compromise. Port Edward argued that they were the closest to the impacts of industry and should be compensated. Prince Rupert argued that they were the primary service centre and that Port Edward residents didn't contribute. And the National Harbours Board argued against any boundary extension and in favour of a moratorium on taxation during development.[35]

In 1980, Municipal Affairs minister and future premier Bill Vander Zalm approved Prince Rupert's boundary extension, with one major caveat: 20 percent of the tax revenue had to be shared with Port Edward.[36] Port Edward then applied for their own boundary extension to capture the entire outlying areas out to the Skeena River, to which Lester accused them of being "about to emulate Hitler."[37] Thus began a four-decade fight between two neighbouring communities.

While 1982 was a challenge for virtually every other sector of the local economy, it was the first year since the creation of the National Harbour that the port's books ended the year with a profit.[38] Even though construction was not yet complete in 1983, the local tax revenue from Ridley Island alone made up for all the losses elsewhere. However, the coal terminal operator, Ridley Terminals Inc. (RTI), took an aggressive stance against paying local business taxes, much like the Grand Trunk Pacific had done seventy-five years prior. First, they appealed their assessment before launching a court case based on a typo within the city's business tax bylaw which mistakenly read "or" instead of "on" property. On this technicality, the company saved

$550,000 in annual taxes. But that was not enough. The company wanted the levy cut in half again. Even after the City rolled back industrial taxes by 21 percent, RTI sued the city and asked the province for a five-year tax holiday.[39] The CEO argued if the company had the money, "we will go out and build our own subdivision and our own swimming pool."[40] Unsurprisingly, the company built neither.

The following year, in 1984, Ridley Terminals Inc. loaded its first vessel. With Northeastern BC coal destined for Asian markets, the day was billed as the "single biggest lift of dry bulk cargo from a North American port" packed into the largest coal carrier afloat.[41] Less than a year later, the grain elevator next door was opened by Alberta premier Peter Lougheed to celebrate their $220 million investment, which increased BC's export capabilities of Prairie wheat products to Asia by 20 percent. CN Rail regained some of the remnants of the GTP's original optimism about Prince Rupert's prospects, publishing a pamphlet trumpeting the emerging "port at the end of the rainbow."[42] Perhaps it was a coincidence, or maybe it was fate: the same day the first grain ship was loaded was also the city's seventy-fifth anniversary of incorporation.[43] After decades of its port being underdeveloped, Prince Rupert finally seemed to have come of age.

And yet, the doubters and pessimists were still able to point to the presumed resurrection of the Rip Van Rupert curse. Shortly after the coal terminal was commissioned, the main customers in the Japanese steel industry entered a dramatic tailspin as prices and shipments declined by double digit percentages. Closer to home, 1985 was being regarded as the year of a "Superdrought in the West"; the Prairies were experiencing sharply diminished crop yields and prices, drawing comparisons to the severity of the Dust Bowl era of the 1930s.[44] Luckily for Prince Rupert, both of these events proved to be temporary blights that were quickly forgotten. But with the benefit of hindsight, each served as a foreboding reminder of the fickle and unpredictable nature of the globalized economy with which Prince Rupert was increasingly intertwining its fate.

With all the new port terminals helping sidestep the worst of the recession, the city was equally as optimistic thanks to a surge in industrial tax revenue. Flush with cash from Ridley Island, in 1984 the city gave a 21 percent tax break to other industries and a 14 percent tax decrease to homeowners and small businesses and was still able to run a multi-million dollar surplus.[45] When the city council voted to use a portion of the surplus to temporarily bolster the recently slashed capital works program, Mayor Lester tried to veto their decision, arguing that the money would be better spent on reducing taxes in future years, or towards a new theatre.[46]

PERFORMING ARTS CENTRE

After nearly a decade of advocacy by community arts groups, Mayor Lester acquiesced to demands for a referendum on a new performing arts centre. He had previously thought that a theatre in a city the size of Prince Rupert was "completely unnecessary unless it is connected with a school" and that a referendum on the topic was a waste of money.[47] Nonetheless, residents were first asked if they approved of borrowing $3.1 million to renovate and expand the Capitol Theatre. The answer was a decisive no by almost a 2:1 margin. But once the city's surplus was known, a rushed one-month design launched a second referendum, asking for $3.7 million to build a brand-new 18,000-square-foot, 690-seat theatre. It was to be the largest theatre in the province outside of the Lower Mainland. With a turnout of only 33 percent, the vote narrowly passed with just a five-hundred-vote differential. Mayor Lester got his wish as almost 90 percent of the city's surplus went towards the new theatre. As costs soared to $4.3 million when the bids came in higher than budgeted, Lester was forced to cast the tie-breaking vote to award the construction contract.[48]

Residents and councillors were rightly skeptical of such a large public project having a meagre $10,000 contingency fund and an aggressive thirty-five-week construction timeframe after seeing hundreds of thousands of dollars go downhill on the Mount Hays Gondola. Plus, the Earl Mah Aquatic Centre had just been completed at more than 50 percent over budget; it was dubbed "Poolgate." As a result, the city administrator resigned after failing to show a memo about cost overruns, citing the "lack of cooperative relationship that has existed between myself and Mayor Peter Lester."[49] After a councillor questioned the PAC cost overruns and accounting procedures in an open meeting, Mayor Lester suggested by motion to prohibit staff from preparing reports on the matter for the council before the tie-breaking vote was cast once again to borrow $2.3 million.[50]

The construction of the PAC demonstrates on multiple levels how supremely confident Mayor Lester and the entire community were in Prince Rupert's future prospects, despite the storm clouds on the horizon. For one, the council felt comfortable borrowing the funds at 12.5 percent financing. Additionally, the loan was taken out for ten years instead of twenty, and taxpayers were on the hook for the projected operating deficit of $60,000 per year.[51] Luckily, the provincial government provided a $500,000 grant from the Expo 86 legacy fund to slightly reduce the debt load, just as the theatre was about to celebrate its grand opening.[52] Today, it seems fitting that the facility bears the Lester name, both for Peter Lester's support with which it was critical to be built, but also in honour of his wife Mary, who contributed much to the local arts scene.

COLOURFUL CHARACTER:
PETER LESTER ("MAYOR PETE")

It is impossible to tell the history of Prince Rupert without the story of Peter Lester. Born and raised in New York, as a teenager he did one year at Ohio State University before crossing the border at Montreal in 1939 to enlist in the Canadian Armed Forces after the Battle of Dunkirk (since the us had not yet entered Second World War).[53] After serving four years overseas, Lester applied for Canadian citizenship and made Prince Rupert his adopted home after discharge in 1946.[54] One of his first jobs was as an instrument mechanic at the Watson Island pulp mill.[55] After serving two years on the city council, Lester went up against a popular incumbent mayor, George Hills, a former MLA with the public support of every sitting councillor. In the 1958 election, Lester won the mayoral seat by only forty votes.[56] Thus began a stretch of seventeen elections over thirty-six years, reversing the digits of his age from thirty-seven during his first term to seventy-three at his retirement, making him one of the longest-serving mayors in Canadian history.[57]

Lester's lengthy unbroken streak in the mayor's chair suggests a sustained commitment and political popularity, but the truth is much more complicated. In 1965, Lester was presented a plaque to commemorate his retirement after making multiple pronouncements before reversing his decision at the last minute. In 1975, Lester announced he would run for council instead of mayor because his time spent on city affairs meant sacrificing personal income, saying "my decision

Mayor Peter J. Lester. DR. R. GEDDES LARGE FONDS.
PRINCE RUPERT CITY & REGIONAL ARCHIVES

is definite and final."[58] Except it wasn't. He won four more elections, but also saw his winning margin shrink down to only 194 votes. With the new municipal record secured in 1981, Lester vowed it was his last term. But again, it wasn't. In 1983, council incumbent Dan Miller announced he was running for mayor Lester had said he was getting out of office.[59] Nonetheless, Lester won for a fourteenth consecutive time and followed that with two more victories against incumbent councillors in 1985 and 1987. Municipal terms were extended from two years to three, and Lester polished off his campaigning career with one more victory in 1990 before finally stepping away in 1993. His extended winning streak was explained by the local paper as a simple equation that he was always the "Lester of Two Evils."

If Peter Lester's reign had one trademark, it would be governing by committee. His goal was explicit: get more people involved in the day-to-day operations of city hall. For his first seven years in office, every councillor sat on every standing committee. Then Lester began creating new community committees and task forces, up to twenty-eight at once,[60] with their focus ranging from big issues (industrial development, social services, housing) to the minutia (tourism slogans, flag design, traffic congestion) to topics completely outside of city hall's control (dentistry, commercial fishing, provincial government centralization). He also favoured using referenda for anything from a new civic centre to whether shopping should be allowed on Sundays (he argued against it due to "moral pollution"), or even nuclear disarmament and "the retention of the family unit." When questioned on his approach, Lester responded: "Whether or not it is within the city's jurisdiction shouldn't concern Council... the legal approach is that it should not be done, but that doesn't stop us from doing it."[61]

Peter Lester was a long-time survivor in municipal politics who did things his own way, which meant a fair share of bruising partisanship. Many tend to forget or overlook that Lester ran provincially as a BC Liberal in 1969.[62] He must have thought he could resurrect the third-party Liberals by becoming Prince Rupert's second mayor-turned-MLA, just as Duff Pattullo had done fifty-three years earlier. But Lester and the Liberals both came in a distant third place with only 19 percent of the vote.[63] This marked the first and only electoral loss in Lester's nearly forty-year political career. Lester had opinions about the other provincial parties. He considered the SoCreds "arrogant, dictatorial, [and] egocentric," and accused them of being conmen, hypocrites, and propagandists. He categorized the NDP as "mentally bankrupt and worn out," and an "old-line party which hasn't had a new idea in 30 years."[64] When the MLA was a SoCred, Lester accused him of selling out Prince Rupert[65]; when the seat was held by an NDP representative, Lester accused him of selling out Northern BC.[66] As the only two provincial political parties to form governments during Lester's tenure, perhaps it is not a coincidence that the longer Peter Lester was in office, the more provincial government services were moved elsewhere in the region.

In his own unique way, Lester always found creative ways to overcome tenuous provincial relations. For example, after repeated unsuccessful attempts to get an answer on an issue from a government minister, Lester placed an ad in the local paper reading, "Anyone knowing the whereabouts of David Zirnhelt, believed to be working in the Victoria area, please contact Mayor Lester." This apparently prompted Minister Zirnhelt to travel to Prince Rupert to meet personally with the mayor.[67] About his unorthodox approach, Lester said: "Sometimes you have to hit them on the head to attract their attention."[68]

Lester won almost all his mayoral elections on a simple platform of long-range planning. His belief in it can be demonstrated through statements he made that "essential for the orderly growth of this city,"[69] and that it "brings results"[70]; that "long range planning pays" and that "the best council is one that plans ahead."[71] His original campaign promise in 1958 was to create a ten-year capital works plan. Despite this, the city was never able to adopt a long-term capital infrastructure plan during Lester's tenure, likely because during his first twenty-five years in office, the only plans ever required were focused on how to react and respond to rapid growth.

The brief 1982 recession altered Lester's governing approach for the remainder of his time in office. One of his signature policies was maintaining a surplus, saying it was "a bulwark against major expenditures and poor times ... I believe in collecting revenue when times are good, so that if times change money is available to carry on city work."[72] When times were good during the boom, the surplus nearly quadrupled from $300,000 to $1.1 million between 1965 and 1982.[73] But when economic circumstances changed, so too did Lester and his council.

From 1982 onwards, Prince Rupert city hall adopted the Reagan-era strategy of tax breaks and spending cuts. Where Lester previously claimed he would fight any reduction in business taxes because it was "robbing the city purse,"[74] by the mid-1980s he was voting to use the surplus to reduce taxes by double digits.[75] No longer budgeting for his promised long-term capital program, Lester committed that "the tax rate will be set first and expenses reduced accordingly."[76] The city's annual capital works budget was slashed by 62 percent through the 1980s.[77] Lester even personally asked the BC Pollution Control Board to defer $2 million in legally-mandated improvements to the city's sewage outfall system with the explicit goal to cut taxes,[78] even though this would mean losing out on an extra $1 million provincial contribution.[79]

During his last election campaign, Peter Lester said that "a mayor's job is to write the music, not direct the orchestra."[80] While he certainly marched to his own rhythm, Lester set the tone and tempo for Prince Rupert's boom-time performance. He claimed his secret to success was that he "represent[ed] the type of thinking of the average person in town."[81] As the only singular political force in town to last for over five decades, Peter Lester's leadership was clearly in tune with the desires of the community; even his bitter rivals were known to occasionally speak well of him. After retirement, he was awarded with the Order of British Columbia and Queen's Golden Jubilee Medal in recognition for his many years of public service.[82] Lester's longevity assured that he helped author many of Prince Rupert's most iconic and enduring developments. It is a shame that his time in office ended on a sour note, with the city left to face the music of the inevitable consequences of the boom–bust economy.

CHAPTER 14

BUST

1993–2006

"The dream of a never-ending boom
has turned into a nightmare"
ANGLICAN BISHOP JOHN HANNEN[1]

By the early 1990s, Prince Rupert had some of the lowest residential taxes in the entire province thanks to nearly a decade of severe spending cuts and increased debt.[3] Confidence was still high, and money still ample. Downtown streets were rebuilt in 1992, going 80 percent over budget. The Digby Island Ferry was running twelve times per day trying to attract more flights. The city even found $2.5 million to put towards the Alaska Ferry Terminal.[4] But much like the early 1980s, a recession hit at the start of the decade. The recession of the early '90s was longer and deeper, and has since been dubbed the "Great Canadian Slump of 1990–92."[5] Even though it was technically over by mid-1992, the worst was yet to come for Prince Rupert.

NO MORE STATUS QUO

Politically, the status quo was shattered in 1993. Federally, the governing Conservatives catastrophically imploded under Kim Campbell, giving Prince Rupert its first Reform Party MP and handing the local NDP only their second loss in thirty-two years. Provincially, the NDP was governing again after a gap of nearly two decades. The new opposition BC Liberals dumped Gordon Wilson for future premier Gordon Campbell. And locally, mayor Peter Lester finally chose to retire after thirty-seven years at the city's helm. He clearly saw that things were changing quickly, saying at his last meeting that "the new council will be faced with difficult financial decisions to a greater extent than any other council in the past 30 years... times are not good, money is short."[6]

THE WATSON ISLAND SAGA

One major player in Prince Rupert's story of boom and bust is on Watson Island. From its origins as the site of a Second World War munitions facility to its peacetime conversion to a pulp mill under many ownership groups, from a contaminated brownfield to now a municipally-owned industrial export and logistics park, as goes the fate of Watson Island so goes Prince Rupert.

For the first fifteen years of the its existence, the pulp mill on Watson Island was operated by the Columbia Cellulose Corporation (ColCel) just outside the City of Prince Rupert's municipal boundary. This meant the company was paying a lower rural tax rate directly to the Province of BC instead of the community where it was based. MLA and Speaker of the House Bill Murray brought forward a proposal in mid-1964 to expand Prince Rupert into a district municipality to bring Watson Island into its tax base. This proposal was quickly supported by the Municipal Affairs minister and by Mayor Peter Lester.[7] However, in the resulting application to the provincial government, Lester chose a different path, instead requesting a boundary extension that excluded Port Edward. Lester claimed that rumours of Port Edward's incorporation were being spread by the pulp mill as a negotiating tactic to scare them into accepting a lower tax rate. But the day after the city's application was made public, Skeena Cellulose filed an objection and Port Edward moved for incorporation,[8] making a bid to have the pulp mill included in their application with the argument that they had "the proximity and the odour, why not a share of the taxes?"[9] With a population of approximately 1,000, Port Edward incorporated in 1966 with only forty votes in favour and eight against.[10] Thus began a cascade of decades-long disputes that have shaped Prince Rupert's development to the modern day.

The boundary expansion was far from the biggest problem at Watson Island, but it had arguably one of the longest-lasting and farthest-reaching outcomes. The failure to amalgamate Prince Rupert and Port Edward into a district municipality in the 1960s resulted in decades-long feuds about taxes, major projects, and shared services. Subsequently, the District of Port Edward expanded its own boundaries to become twice as large as Kaien Island in terms of land mass. Instead of becoming one united body growing in unison, Prince Rupert's decision to cut Port Edward out of the Watson Island boundary later cost the city a great deal. When the province gave Prince Rupert another boundary extension for Ridley Island in the 1980s, they mandated an 80/20 tax share split with Port Edward, despite the population difference being more than 20:1.

After nearly a year of boundary extension negotiations and deferrals, the provincial cabinet announced the approval of Prince Rupert's request, but with a gigantic caveat: the pulp mill was exempted from municipal taxation on sewer, water, telephone, garbage, fire protection, parking, curbs, gutters, and sidewalks. Adding salt to the wound, after the city finalized its new business tax and budget bylaws, ColCel challenged them in the BC Supreme Court. Both bylaws were quashed by the judge on a technicality of the timing of the province's order-in-council, and the city's budget was suddenly left with a $250,000 hole. A negotiated settlement between the city, province, and ColCel resulted in a five-year progressive tax rate increase with exemptions expiring in 1971.[11] But just as the exemptions were about to terminate in December 1970, ColCel requested to renegotiate, asking for another $250,000 tax decrease. By then, the company was paying 40 percent of the entire municipal tax bill.[12] Within just a few months, the company's tone in its communications changed drastically, saying "any increase in costs by taxes or otherwise will further aggravate an already serious situation which could adversely affect the stability of Prince Rupert... our economic problems are many and they are serious."[13]

While Prince Rupert seemed to be prospering through the 1960s and early 1970s, its biggest employer and tax contributor was becoming increasingly unhealthy. After setting record profits and production levels in the early 1960s, between 1966 and 1972, ColCel had only one year of small profit, a large, accumulated earnings deficit, a negative net worth, and a heavy load of short- and long-term debt. The accumulated loss was about $120 million.[14] The year 1972 saw ColCel post a record loss, so the company announced they wanted to sell as soon as possible. After years of losses while privately searching for a buyer, ColCel finally received a takeover offer from a major American timber firm. But in 1972, local and provincial politics were turned upside down as the two-decade reign of W.A.C. Bennett and his SoCred Party came to an end. This included the sixteen-year tenure of the speaker of the house and Prince Rupert MLA Bill Murray. This unexpected defeat was likely because the NDP guaranteed that they would maintain jobs at the Watson Island pulp mill if ColCel decided to shut it down completely. Unfortunately for ColCel, their proposed sale required consent from the new provincial government to transfer the timber rights.

_ce&o_

The new provincial NDP government was worried that the less profit-able and more remote Prince Rupert operations would be reduced or closed in favour of more lucrative opportunities in the south. Unable to find a suitable alternative buyer, the NDP government decided to take a 79 percent stake in the company in 1973, re-assuming control of the 3.71 million hectares (9.17 million acres) of tree farm licenses issued to ColCel, equal to 4 percent of the area of BC.[15] The NDP went to great lengths to assert that it was not nationalization. No payment was made to the corporation. Instead, the provincial government created a public corporation to inherit $78 million in debt.[16] Newly elected Prince Rupert MLA Graham Lea explained, "It's like putting the company on the operating table, opening its chest and applying heart massage to bring Prince Rupert and the whole northern area back to life. And at a cleaning out, bargain basement price."[17]

But the surgery was not without pain. The province took pos-session of Watson Island on July 1, 1973, heralding the "beginning of a new era" for the once foundering company. Watson Island was rebranded as Canada Cellulose (CanCel). One of the first orders of business was a $130 million conversion of the sulphite mill to kraft pulp.[18] The conversion resulted in the loss of three hundred full-time jobs in a city already facing 11 percent unemployment.[19] Despite the NDP's controlling interest, Watson Island experienced multiple strikes, furloughs, and shutdowns in its first few years of government own-ership, with up to 1,100 people affected at a time.[20] A later analysis showed the conversion and resulting strike actions cost $5.4 million per year in lost local incomes and 724 spin-off jobs gone.[21] Real estate values dropped. Local businesses suffered. The city lost hundreds of thousands of dollars in tax revenue. The number of welfare recipients increased. Emigration went up. And yet, mostly due to a 2.5-times increase in the global price per ton of kraft pulp, the operation turned a profit from 1973 to 1977. A 1977 _Financial Post_ headline proclaimed, "David Barrett's CanCel Deal Was A Good Buy."[22]

Converting the former sulphite mill was the single largest industrial development in BC at the time, with a price tag of $135 million.
The project required 350 labourers and a timeframe of almost six
years,[23] temporarily masking the impending decline of operational
jobs, which plummeted down to seventy.[24] But it was legally necessary to reduce pollution levels below federal standards. The sulphite
mill had been documented as one of the worst polluters in the entire
province. Approximately 26 million gallons (98.8 million litres) of
effluent were being discharged per day. The spent sulphite liquor
discharge was so sterile that dead bivalves did not decompose in
it and an orange slime coated the nearby area. Lab tests on coho
salmon fry with mill leachate saw them die within five to ten minutes
due to extremely high toxicity.[25] A 1962 study showed a three-metre
thick field of pulp sludge in Wainwright Basin.[26] Numerous studies
documented large volumes of organochlorine compounds and pulp
fibres smothering other organisms on the nearby beaches as well
as the loss of intertidal algae, contaminated sediments, and higher
toxicity in nearby crabs.[27] In adjacent ocean inlets, drastic decreases
in biological productivity were found to be the result of the waters
becoming anoxic (greatly deficient in oxygen).[28] The company had
also been charged dozens of times with illegal hazardous effluent
discharge, liquor spills, and line ruptures, which had resulted in
extensive fish kills.[29]

Beyond the ongoing environmental damage, the company was
also in the process of inflicting financial damage on the city before
it was acquired by the provincial government. ColCel had launched
a tax appeal in early 1973, asking the court for an $800,000 refund.
The company president reasoned that just because the province owns
the pulp mill does not make it a "financial plum ripe for the picking...
We will do our part... but we are not the vehicle to underwrite
any relatively excessive or absolutely unwarranted part of municipal expenditures."[30] Within a few months of the NDP taking power,
the appeal was withdrawn. When asked about the implications for
the municipality, Mayor Lester simply responded that "the city can
carry on with a normal budget for 1974."[31] But unfortunately for him
and the community, nothing was ever going to be normal about the
Watson Island pulp mill. During the conversion process, the NDP
lost the 1975 provincial election to the reincarnated SoCreds under
W.A.C. Bennett's son, Bill. CanCel re-engaged the taxation appeal,

eventually getting a reduction of $230,000 per year, equivalent to 4 percent of the city's budget.

Once the mill conversion was complete in 1979, the power required for Watson Island was so immense that the combined mills utilized over 33 percent more energy than the entire city of Prince Rupert.[32] The first year's tax bill amounted to 52 percent of municipal financing thanks to a jump in assessed value. Eight hundred people were on the annual payroll of $18 million. And yet, only four months after re-opening, a month-long strike was initiated.[33] The only certainty at the revamped pulp mill was its interdependency with the community. The labour, financial, environmental, political, and operational uncertainty at Watson Island all now threatened the decades of stability that the facility had brought to the city.

Since the NDP had purchased a majority stake in the pulp mill in the early 1970s, the SoCreds bought all the outstanding shares in 1981, restructured the timber rights and facility under a crown corporation, and re-branded the company to BC Timber. While the reorganization clarified that the Watson Island mill was now a public entity, it did not improve its financial performance. Between 1979 and 1984, the company lost an average of almost $17 million per year.[34] Its environmental performance also remained problematic. In 1981, there was a spill of 2.2 tons of sodium hypochlorite into the adjacent Porpoise Harbour, and in 1985, an effluent link break spilled 45 million litres of waste into the ocean, which provincial officials claimed wiped out the last twelve years of ecosystem recovery since the sulphate mill conversion.[35]

A strike and shutdown saw the mill sit idle for seven of twelve months in 1982–83, with the company president saying, "In today's poor market, we can no longer afford to incur any additional losses by continuing to operate."[36] The Watson Island pulp mill shutdown was the most severe out of the province's eighteen mills at the time. Pulp prices in 1982 were close to what they were in 1975, but costs in the north had more than doubled in the same period.[37] Every day that the mill remained shuttered, approximately $100,000 in local wages were lost. The labour force shrank to 420, down from seven hundred only a few years earlier.[38]

In 1983, the mill had contributed 42 percent of Prince Rupert's total tax bill. Valued at $24 million, the facility made up 75 percent of the city's industrial assessment.[39] The company claimed they were paying the highest "astronomical" taxation level of any pulp mill in the province, if not the world, and that municipal taxes had climbed by 66 percent in only four years.[40] When the company appealed to the city for a significant tax break, one city councillor said at budget time, "If we're not careful it could be a case of killing the golden goose." Mayor Lester responded, "It's a big goose."[41]

In a classic case of what's good for the goose is good for the gander, the city dropped the pulp mill taxation by 21 percent "out of concern for industry in general and BC Timber in particular."[42] Once the mill restarted in 1984, a new daily production record was set, and it must have seemed like everything was back to normal. But far from it; the facility's problems were far more complicated than property taxes.

After a complaint was lodged by the Nisga'a Tribal Council, a 1985 ombudperson's report found seven instances of the Ministry of Forests either acting improperly or contrary to the law with respect to the timber rights originally granted to the pulp mill in the late 1940s, TFL 1, which were now owned by the province. These indiscretions included: reforestation requirements being eight years behind schedule, substantial amounts of timber being left to rot on the ground, and the annual allowable cut being manipulated. The ombudperson's recommendation was clear: suspend or cancel the crown corporation's timber rights or launch an independent royal commission of inquiry. His conclusion was even more damning:

> The Ministry had embarked upon a program of trading the forest resources of TFL 1 for only the tenuous expectation of continuing employment for some... I am afraid that in the not too distant future the forests of TFL 1 will have no economic value at all. When that happens, not only will [the company] cease operations but no other forest company will be interested in operating in the area. In turn, there may be no employment for local communities.[43]

The province took the opposite position, claiming that stricter enforcement would force mill closures, not their own forest mismanagement.[44] Unbeknownst to the public, BC Timber had begun searching for buyers. Despite having invested $130 million in the mill, plus assuming almost $80 million in private debt, in June 1986, the province sold the assets and timber rights to Repap Enterprises Inc. for only $69 million[45] and extended the company a $75 million loan to avoid any further layoffs and assure re-opening.[46] With taxpayers absorbing the significant loss, new ownership also meant the third new name for the facility in as many decades: Skeena Cellulose.

ᴇᴄ

An entire book could be written about the labour history of the Watson Island pulp mill given the frequency of strikes, threats of job action, wildcat walkouts, solidarity strikes, intense negotiations, and lively picket lines over the years. But one thing was markedly different by the 1990s: the entire pulp industry was in trouble.

In 1991, as softwood lumber tensions mounted with the US, the demand for pulp weakened, and prices dropped from $840 to $400 per ton, nineteen of twenty BC pulp mills reached labour agreements. The lone holdout was Prince Rupert. The local union characterized the dispute as a Mexican standoff, and true to form, neither party would win. After seven hundred people were locked out of their jobs on and off for the next two years, Repap announced its worst ever year on record in 1992. The following year, despite setting new daily production highs, the Watson Island pulp mill was still losing $50 for every ton of pulp it produced.[47]

In 1993, 250 people were laid off for three months. Then a three-week Christmas shutdown was extended to three months.[48] The relationship between company and employees soured to the point that eventually a 108-day strike took place in 1995, which required famed mediator Vince Ready to be brought in.[49] According to former pulp employee and now MLA Dan Miller, the pulp mill had an "atrocious history" of labour relations, distrust and animosity, barriers of suspicion between union and management, scrapping and antagonism.[50]

From the perspective of the union, company, and industry as a whole, the gloomy projections about the pulp industry in general would not threaten the survival of Watson Island because of its sheer size. "There seems to be a survival of the fittest situation going on ... [the] small mills seem to be the ones that fall by the wayside," said the company's general manager.[51] But as Prince Rupert had learned from the *Titanic*, that type of hubris quickly attracts disaster.

On March 3, 1997, almost fifty years to the day since the pulp mill's construction was announced, Skeena Cellulose filed for bankruptcy. The announcement was tied directly to the sale of Watson Island's parent company, Repap Enterprises. Avenor Inc. was acquiring them to create Canada's biggest pulp-and-paper producer, but the deal did not include Repap's west coast operations. Therefore, Repap BC was "saddled with $400 million in debt, set adrift on its own."[52] In Repap's eleven-year tenure, the company had incurred a $600 million debt by 1997.[53] Bankruptcy meant that TD and Royal Bank assumed control as the primary debt holders and were stuck with mounting losses of $10 million per month.[54]

The banks stopped advancing funds and operations on Watson Island were shut down on June 27, 1997.[55] After nearly five decades as the city's biggest employer and the largest local taxpayer, supporting 10,000 forestry jobs from Prince Rupert to Burns Lake, the former symbol of Prince Rupert's economic prosperity now required immediate and significant government assistance just to survive.

After months of an impasse between the union, banks, and province on a restructuring deal, in September 1997, union workers agreed to a seven-year, 10 percent wage rollback and the phase-out of 25 percent of the jobs in exchange for a 20 percent stake in the company. The banks agreed to write off $305 million in debt. The province agreed to pay 40 percent of the remaining loans ($116 million in total) and take a 45 percent stake. And operations would restart within weeks. Dan Miller was hailed as a local hero for his role brokering the agreement as deputy premier and minister for employment and investment. A massive celebration party was hosted at the civic centre, attended by NDP premier Glen Clark.

But only eleven days later, the provincial government and banks signed a restructuring deal that added another $26 million in provincial cash and reduced the union's equity share from 20 percent to 15 percent. The union rejected the revised deal.[56] Ultimately, it would take a few more months before the provincial government stepped in to fund $180 million in loans and cash to purchase a majority stake, plus $65 million in low-interest loans to small creditors to secure their support for restructuring.[57]

In the few months between its first closure and the deal being announced, falling pulp prices and currency devaluations caused by the 1997 Asian financial crisis meant that the bailout plan was $30 million short.[58] A total of $329 million was pumped into the company by the provincial government, the largest corporate bailout in BC's history at the time.[59] Despite the substantial investment, the net result was five hundred jobs being only temporarily restored. Within a few months, half of the pulp mill's operations were permanently shut down because of poor markets and high operating losses. By the following year, the province's initial $120-million operating loan had to be increased to $200 million just to keep the doors open for a few extra months.[60]

Many critics contended that the NDP's interventionist efforts were akin to providing life-support for a doomed patient. But in this analogy, the patient at risk was not Watson Island, but rather the political seat of local NDP MLA Dan Miller, who at the time was the minister of energy and mines responsible for northern development, the deputy premier, and the "second-most powerful politician in the province's NDP government, after his close friend Premier Glen Clark."[61]

COLOURFUL CHARACTER: DAN MILLER

Born in Port Alice in 1944, Dan Miller was a millwright and trade unionist before he got his first taste of politics working for Prince Rupert's NDP MLA Graham Lea. He then entered politics himself, topping the polls for the Prince Rupert city council at age thirty-three[82] and going on to serve for three terms. In his capacity with the municipality, Miller also served as the president of the Prince Rupert Housing Commission and the chairperson of the City Planning Commission.[83]

It was probably for the best that Miller lost to Peter J. Lester for mayor in 1983 because he was then elected as the NDP MLA for North Coast in 1986, 1991, and 1996. During these terms, he held positions as minister of Forests (1991–93), minister of Skills, Training & Labour (1993–96), minster of Municipal Affairs (1996–97), minister of Employment and Investment (1997–98), minister of Energy and Mines and minister responsible for Northern Development (1998–2000), and deputy premier (1996–99).

When two of the Prince Ruperts's largest employers, the Fishermen's Cooperative and J.S. McMillan Fisheries, declared bankruptcy

Former BC Premier Dan Miller.
PRINCE RUPERT CITY & REGIONAL ARCHIVES

in the mid 1990s, Miller ensured they received millions in emergency loans to restructure and salvage hundreds of jobs.[84] Shortly thereafter, when the Watson Island pulp mill first closed in 1997, Miller's cabinet role and prior history made him a key figure in the on-again, off-again bailout negotiations with the banks, union, and province. After Glen Clark suddenly resigned under criminal investigation in August 1999, Miller was elected to the premier's post, joining Duff Pattullo as the only other premier from Prince Rupert.

Miller is credited with creating Royal Roads University[85] and was awarded lifetime membership to the Union of BC Municipalities. While many tried to convince him to seek the permanent leadership of the NDP, Miller chose not to run for re-election in 2001, saying that "the only Miller draft that interested him was one he could order in the bar."[86] In a case of life coming full circle, Miller later helped convince his former chief of staff John Horgan to run for the BC NDP leadership[87]; Horgan when on to become premier in 2017 and later appointed Miller as a special forestry consultant in 2018.[88]

Compared to other premiers, Dan Miller might not be as well remembered, given that he only served in a brief six-month interim capacity, sandwiched between the tumult of Glen Clark and the near-decimation of the BC NDP under Ujjal Dosanjh in the 2001 election. However, as a Prince Rupert city councillor, North Coast MLA, provincial cabinet minister, and Prince Rupert's second premier,

Miller's political legacy will be well-remembered locally for his abilities to effectively confront near-constant chaos and controversy. The *Globe and Mail* put it best with their headline on February 15, 2000, that Miller provided an "oasis of calm in stormy BC."[89]

By the year 2000, after the last full year of government-subsidized operations for the Watson Island pulp mill, the entire community was put at risk of bankruptcy. Watson Island had sustained a combined loss of a staggering $750 million since declaring bankruptcy in 1997.[62] No additional provincial funding approvals came before the BC Liberals swept to power in 2001. In Prince Rupert alone, 750 direct jobs plus 1,331 indirect jobs were lost.[63] At the regional level, estimates suggested direct and spinoff job losses exceeded 6,700 in Terrace, Hazelton, Stewart, Smithers, and everywhere in between.[64]

The 2001 election reduced the BC NDP to only two seats in the legislature and saw Bill Belsey win the North Coast riding for the BC Liberals for the first (and still only) time since the 1969 election. Elected on a platform to return the pulp mill to the private sector, the BC Liberal government, creditors, and courts approved the facility's sale to NWBC Timber and Pulp Ltd. in 2002.[65] Despite a new ownership group, name (New Skeena Forest Products Inc.), and strategy, the company never found financing. In fact, they never opened the doors and quickly went bankrupt in 2004, despite the fact that the City of Prince Rupert had voted 70.5 percent in favour of a referendum to approve a $20-million assistance package[66] that would have deferred tax payments for years.[67] As a result of the uncertainty of whether or not each shutdown would be temporary, the final shutdown was so abrupt that the equipment, chemicals, and pulp processing materials were not properly shut down.[68] A later court filing noted that "the mill looks like everyone went for a coffee break and did not come back."[69]

As a result of the company's inability to pay its outstanding municipal taxes, the City of Prince Rupert was forced to "take out the axe" to cut millions of dollars to make up for the lost taxes. Even worse, the municipality had borrowed $13 million against the outstanding tax dollars that would now never be seen.[70] Rather than raise taxes by 60 percent, the city terminated thirty employees, eliminated one out of five police officers, reduced hours at the swimming pool, arena, and library, sold the municipal campground, and reduced the budgets for the museum, visitors centre, Performing Arts Centre, and golf course. The financial trouble was so serious that Prince Rupert was days away from losing its own borrowing power. Less than a decade from the mill's first closure and Prince Rupert had gone from having some of the lowest taxes in the province to almost twice as high as the provincial average.[71] Watson Island's struggles had evolved from an already devastating loss of jobs into a full-blown community crisis.

Through the bankruptcy process in 2005, the timber rights originally granted to the pulp mill in 1946 were separated from the facility and purchased by Lax Kw'alaams for $4.8 million.[72] While their community-owned approach would go on to build a successful forestry company, the same cannot be said for the pulp mill. Sun Wave Forest Products Ltd. purchased 80 percent of the pulping equipment as part of the liquidation process with the intention of dismantling and relocating it to China. However, after lobbying by MLA Bill Belsey, the city, the union, and Lax Kw'alaams, Sun Wave agreed to also buy the land to restart the mill's operation in Prince Rupert.[73]

The signing of memorandums-of-understanding was trumpeted with great fanfare, greeted with feelings ranging from jubilation to cautious optimism to cynicism that the deal had been announced the day before the 2005 provincial election.[74] The cynics must have been right as Bill Belsey was soundly defeated. Soon after, Sun Wave and the City of Prince Rupert entered a thirty-year agreement under which the company was completely exempted from municipal taxes for five years in exchange for restarting the mill operations before the end of 2007. This would be followed by twenty-five years of taxes based on the fluctuation of pulp prices.[75] Unfortunately, the generous tax concessions yielded worse than nothing.

After the deal was signed in 2005, Sun Wave was obligated to re-open by December 2007 or lose their tax breaks. The courts would later state that during this period, "no steps were taken to get the mill up and running."[76] Despite receiving an extension to February 2008, Sun Wave failed to restart operations. The city repealed the tax exemption bylaw and took the position that the $6.1 million in outstanding taxes were now due. By September 2007, the tax bill remained unpaid and the city proceeded with a tax sale.

While Sun Wave eventually paid a small amount of delinquent taxes on a small parcel, there were no takers at the tax sale auction. As a result, the City of Prince Rupert was forced by provincial legislation to become the unwilling owner of Watson Island in 2008.[77] Mayor Herb Pond sarcastically quipped, "I've always wanted to own a pulp mill."[78] Having sat fallow for nearly a decade, the holding costs for the contaminated brownfield were upwards of $90,000 per month for security and environmental monitoring. In addition, there was the opportunity cost of over $1 million a year in taxes that could not be collected.[79] The city's goal became to sell the facility for an asking price of $13 million.[80]

Once news was made public that the city was soliciting purchase offers to Watson Island, Sun Wave responded by commencing three court actions against the city in 2009, challenging the tax sale process and demanding return of the land plus damages.[81] While these legal proceedings were ongoing, the courts awarded Sun Wave a certificate of pending litigation (CPL). This meant the city was legally barred from selling the property until the court case was done.

CATCH-22: AT ROPE'S END

In addition to the Watson Island saga, the 1990s saw the fishing industry experience numerous headwinds that eventually brought a "bust by a thousand cuts." While the number of fish plants across BC fell substantially at the beginning of the decade, the Prince Rupert area actually saw a net increase, reaching a peak of seventeen in 1996.[90] After nearly a century of fishing being the backbone of the local economy, Kaien Island was uniquely vulnerable to the perfect storm of changes in the industry.

From government restructuring to licence buybacks, single-gear restrictions, new quota systems, and unemployment insurance restrictions, some changes were so immediately unpopular when announced that protestors occupied the federal fisheries offices in Prince Rupert until a court injunction was granted.[91] Federal intervention was deemed necessary because of declining fish stock assessments with the overly simplistic slogan that there were "too many boats chasing too few fish."

Fishing competition was also intensifying. After the Supreme Court of Canada confirmed that Indigenous Peoples has the right to fish for "food, social, and ceremonial needs" and were given first priority, a separate First Nation commercial allocation was created in 1992.[92] Recreational fishing allocations were increased in 1999, up to 5 to 12 percent of the total allowable catch by 2005.[93] Steller sea lion populations had been increasing 5 to 7 percent per year since the mid-1980s,[94] and northern resident killer whale populations peaked in the mid-1990s thanks to new protections.[95] Also, low-cost farmed salmon was exploding onto the market, driving salmon prices down.

Lastly, tensions had been brewing between BC and Alaska for years over Pacific salmon fishing. For all these reasons and more, the optimism that had traditionally buoyed the fleet for the better part of a century was quickly replaced with frustration and despair. Those feelings manifested themselves as early as 1981, when hundreds of Prince Rupert fisherman blockaded boats in the harbour in protest of disputed waters, declaring that "a bunch of guys are at their rope's end."[96] Despite a Pacific Salmon Treaty being signed in 1985, tensions continued to simmer.

On July 9, 1995, two hundred fishing boats and one thousand people prevented the Alaska ferry *Taku* from docking for two hours. The goal was to send a message to the Americans, by using one of the few US symbols available, that "salmon can't be treated like the buffalo—harvested into extinction."[97] It was generally regarded as an effective peaceful protest as, within a week, the Alaskan governor agreed to mediation. Union organizers were clear: "This is the first action ... we want the world to know we're frustrated." Alaskan ferry officials were quick to label the protest as an isolated incident, but they made a point to add they "would have to look at changes if this is not a one-time event."[98] Unfortunately, tensions continued to rise before reaching a boiling point two years later that burned Prince Rupert at the most inopportune moment.

PACIFIC SALMON WAR: FISH & SHIPS

By 1997, Canada and the US had stalled renegotiating the Pacific Salmon Treaty. More fishermen in Prince Rupert were collecting unemployment than ever before. It had gotten so bad that the fishermen's union had to raise money to buy Christmas presents for their members' children.[99] BC suffered a bad year of salmon returns while southeast Alaskan numbers near the border were healthy, so the Canadian government demanded they shut down their fishery. But after the Americans refused, a group of about fifty BC fishermen attempted to blockade a full American fish packer steaming into the Prince Rupert harbour. This resulted in the violent ramming of the vessel and a Coast Guard escort back to Alaska.[100] The day after BC premier Glen Clark declared that a "full fledged salmon war" had broken out on the Pacific Coast,[101] the biggest battle arrived at Prince Rupert's shores. Almost two years to the day after the two-hour blockade of the *Taku,* a different blockade of a different Alaskan ferry resulted in a very different outcome, with much more far-reaching and longer-lasting impacts.

On July 19, 1997, only three weeks after the first shutdown of the Watson Island pulp mill, more than two hundred fishing boats tied up hull to hull to surround the docked Alaska ferry *Malaspina* in the Prince Rupert harbour.[102] The initial plan had been to encircle the vessel when it arrived to the Prince Rupert harbour, much like the peaceful 1995 *Taku* protest. But when the *Malaspina* sailed into the harbour three hours ahead of schedule at 6 AM, dozens of surprised fishermen could not get their boats off the dock before the ferry was secured in port. The new plan became to symbolically delay the ferry's departure to later that same afternoon. But when a reporter asked how long the ferry would be held hostage, the response was unequivocal: until the fisheries minister arrived to talk and agree to do something.[103]

The fishermen had organized a steering committee and voted in favour of sticking to their original demands despite the legal implications. But after one fisherman burned an American flag in front of a crowd of reporters, the ensuing media firestorm turned what was an "obscure regional fish flap" into a fast rising tide of international public opinion against the blockaders.[104]

With 385 passengers and crew stranded for three days, news of the blockade was played repeatedly on major US networks, even making the headlines of the *New York Times.* The American anger even prompted the US Senate to vote 81–19 in favour of calling on President Bill Clinton to send the US Navy to "protect Alaskan ferries' right of innocent passage through Canadian waters."[105] The growing public pressure saw local police in Prince Rupert begin to enforce the injunction by arresting blockade leaders.

Unlike the *Taku* blockade, comparisons were being made to a hostage situation. This time around, instead of civic officials joining the protestors in solidarity at the docks, they hung an American flag from city hall as an attempted sign of respect. The Chamber of Commerce protested the losses for local tourism operators. Angry ferry passengers were left scrambling to find accommodations or make other travel arrangements. The Alaskan governor labelled the actions as "terrorism,"[106] secured an injunction in the Canadian Supreme Court, and suspended all ferry service to Prince Rupert from Alaska indefinitely.

At the highest levels of both governments, Prime Minister Jean Chretien and the American State Department agreed that the ferry blockade had worsened the situation.[107] When the fisheries minister arrived to meet in Prince Rupert, virtually all of the fishermen demands were rejected, with only a commitment from the minister to try to persuade the Alaskan governor to drop the lawsuit.[108] One of the blockade organizers summed up the disappointment: "We wanted [the fisheries minister] to come here and he did. He didn't say what we wanted him to say, but we still made our point. We're losing the public now so we've got to let the ferry go."[109]

Later that night in the pouring rain, after three long and intense days, the blockaders voted to let the ferry go.[110] They certainly got America's attention. But instead of getting a new Pacific Salmon Treaty, Canada got sued by the Alaskan government, and Prince Rupert paid the price. First, Alaska launched a court case claiming $2 million in damages on the same day that 674 pulp mill workers applied for employment insurance. Second, Alaskan officials pulled the ferry route from Prince Rupert for the first time in over three decades. The eventual gap of service stretched over five months, with estimates ranging from a hit of $10–12 million and 70,000–170,000 tourist visits lost.[111] Third, a local fish plant laid off one hundred workers after the uncertainty of being able to continue processing Alaskan salmon in Prince Rupert.[112] And lastly, lawsuits filed on both sides were fought in court for another four years before the "Pacific Salmon War" was declared over.[113]

From the Ts'msyen's salmon specialization to industrial canneries to the Halibut Capital of the World, fishing had always been central to the identity of Kaien Island. But, the Alaskan ferry blockade served as a kind of symbolic last stand for the local commercial fishing industry. Against a seemingly unending litany of external pressures, 42 percent of the BC commercial fishing fleet and 54 percent of the salmon fleet disappeared between 1996 and 2000.[114] For Prince Rupert, the long-term loss of hundreds of fishing boats, skippers, crew, their incomes, and the spin-off benefits at docks, shops, stores, and more left an outsized hurt that will probably never be forgotten.

TRADE TROUBLES

Beyond the problems with the fishing and forestry industries, to complete the turmoil trifecta, the port complex was also faced with its darkest days in the late 1990s and early 2000s. The port overall saw a 30 percent drop in cargo at the end of the 1990s, due to many factors. Partly due to the 1997 Asian financial crisis, BC mines experienced a steady decline in exports before some closed altogether between 2001 and 2003. As a result, Ridley Terminals tonnage dropped dramatically.[115] For the grain terminal, tough markets overseas, low prices, and increased transportation costs saw wheat exports drop by 40 percent.[116] For multiple years in a row, closures of three to five months at a time forced layoffs of half the staff. At the Fairview terminal, lumber exports declined because of weak housing construction markets until almost all activity was ceased in 2002. With exports reaching some of the lowest levels in the port's history, the number of longshore jobs shrank from 275 to 108 and forced workers to leave to find consistent work elsewhere.[117] Former Prince Rupert Port Authority CEO Don Krusel recalled that at that time "we were looking death in the eyes ... it got to the point where our auditors were telling us we may have to talk about whether or not this is a going concern."[118]

BRAIN DRAIN

Almost simultaneously over the late 1990s and early 2000s, the states of Prince Rupert's fishing, pulp, and port industries had transformed from promise to peril. Labour disruptions and economic troubles took their toll on the community, tearing at the social fabric. Prince Rupert had proven its ability to weather countless storms, but the resulting damage was the economic disaster equivalent of a getting hit by a tsunami, tornado, and earthquake at the same time.

After 1997, numerous businesses were forced to close. Countless popular local small businesses and restaurants packed it in, as did many major franchises, including Shopper's Drug Mart, KFC, Dairy Queen, Zellers, and Fountain Tire.[119] Even the supposedly recession-proof West Fraser sawmill, built in 1994, closed by 2001.[120] Down-town vacancies skyrocketed to 20 percent. One local small business owner observed, "Downtown looks like a toothless smile with all the empty shops."[121]

Unemployment rates topped 15 percent, more than double the BC and Canadian average at the time. The median income in Prince Rupert dropped by double digits to the point where the average household income in 2006 was $10,000 lower than 1996. Residents left in search of work in Alberta's boom time or to be nearer family down south. Real estate values contracted rapidly, and foreclosures swamped the courthouse.[122] In 2003, only one new house was con-structed in town compared to seventy-four only a few years prior.[123] The BC government withdrew services from Diana Lake and Butze Rapids and moved the provincial highways and land title offices, terminating dozens more government jobs elsewhere in the region. The ladies fastball and men's amateur hockey leagues folded. The Racquet Centre required a bailout to stay open.[124] Alcohol sales and crime statistics saw double-digit increases.[125]

Between 1996 and 2007, Prince Rupert's population dropped approximately 25 percent, making it one of Canada's top ten cit-ies with the fastest population declines[126] and tied for the fastest population decline in BC.[127] Tragically, it was mostly young families that were leaving. In 1996, there were 4.1 kids for every senior, but by 2006, the ratio was less than two. The proportion of the senior population nearly doubled. In 1991, 96 percent of youth remained in Prince Rupert after graduation, but following 2001, only 66 percent stayed.[128] The median age of Rupertites jumped by 7.5 years.[129] By 2008, school enrolment was down 40 percent over a nine-year period, forcing the closure of two of the city's eight elementary schools. Only two years later, the two high schools were consolidated, with one converted to a middle school, resulting in the additional closure of Westview Elementary in 2010.[130]

For a community in desperate search of hope, there were no good omens. A series of symbolic losses added insult to injury. The man who replaced Mayor Lester resigned after improprieties with the city credit card.[131] Former city councillor Jim Ciconne and two of his young children were tragically killed after being struck by a speeding impaired driver.[132] Peter Lester passed away just two days before the renaming ceremony for the Lester Centre of the Arts.[133] The true extent of the Highway of Tears was starting to become known.

A series of blazes must have felt to the community like their spirits were being kicked when they were down: the Mount Hays chalet was set alight in 1995,[134] the former Co-op fish plant burned in 2002, and over one hundred residents were made homeless due to the Elizabeth apartments fire in 2004.[135] Worse still, one of the city's last public waterfront access points was shut down indefinitely due to a lack of funds after landslides knocked out the Rushbrook Trail in 2003. Then, the sinking of the BC Ferries vessel *Queen of the North* in 2006 saw Prince Rupert reach new depths. In addition to the tragic loss of two lives, the sinking occurred when the only other northern BC Ferries vessel was in dry dock, contributing to a 60 percent year-over-year drop in passengers to Prince Rupert. Add literal shipwreck, arson, and landslides to the metaphorical tsunami, tornado, and earthquake that were battering the city.

WEAVING CLOSER TOGETHER

In the rainiest city in Canada, the only option during the depths of the bust was to look for the silver linings in the clouds. They may have been few and far between, but they were worth celebrating. In the mid-2000s, a new Acropolis Manor was opened for seniors care living. A $12-million, 50,000-square-foot campus was built downtown for Northwest Community College (now Coast Mountain College). After five years of money-related delays, the Millennium Waterfront Walkway project was finally finished.

One of the bright sides of population loss was how the complexion of the city changed. One in four Rupertites left during the bust, but by and large, they were not the original Indigenous inhabitants or immigrants. While the population as a whole dropped 25 percent in ten years, the proportion of immigrants in the community only decreased by 9 percent, and people identifying as Indigenous jumped almost 10 percent.[136] By 2006, immigrants made up 13 percent of Prince Rupert's shrunken population and 35 percent of the community identified as Indigenous.[137] With fewer people, businesses, and public amenities and less money, the outcome could have been strife, disenfranchisement, and malaise. Instead, a vibrant arts and culture scene emerged, fuelled by greater diversity and volunteerism.

The Performing Arts Centre was hosting the BC Annual Dance Competition, bi-annual community musicals, acting camps, school plays, magic shows, and author readings. Harbour Theatre launched Udderfest, an annual week-long performance festival. With hundreds of people identifying as a multiplicity of ethnicities, Prince Rupert played host to several annual celebrations, such as Chinese New Year; the Vietnamese lunar new year, Tết; the Nisga'a new year Hobiyee; Filipino Night; and the Sikh and Indian communities' Vaisakhi and Diwali. A Francophone Association and Portuguese Club were formed, hosting the Festival d'Hiver and Vindimas. The annual Seafest became a sort of unofficial multi cultural extravaganza, with Ts'msyen and Nisga'a drummers, Bollywood fusion and bhangra dancers, Chinese Lion Dancers, Filipino shish-kebabs, Vietnamese spring rolls, Métis fiddling, and so much more.[138]

ecs

During such a trying time for Prince Rupert, there were plenty of opportunities to give up hope or give in to despair. But in such a close-knit community, there was no such thing as six degrees of separation. We were all just a handful of interwoven friendship networks. This meant that the bust fostered a newfound sense of identity and belonging, built upon a shared struggle to survive near-simultaneous economic disasters. While the economic pulse had wavered and weakened, the heart of the community did not stop beating. And by the mid-2000s, the general prognosis was that the port offered the best road to recovery.

CHAPTER 15

RECOVERY

2007–23

> "Prince Rupert's had its down times before and even
> though this seems to be one of the worst down
> times we've had, hope springs eternal."
>
> PHYLIS BOWMAN[1]

PROJECT SILK

As early as 1969, a local port company director who also happened to be an optometrist had clear vision when he posited that "if [the Fairview] project is planned properly and proper consideration is given to long-range port development, that it is conceivable that with the development of containerized shipping that the port of Prince Rupert could augment facilities [in Vancouver and Seattle]."[2] But it wasn't until 2004, when the Prince Rupert Port Authority was nearly broke and desperate enough to launch a Hail Mary, that this idea was put into action. Preliminary designs were drawn up to convert the Fairview terminal from a break bulk to a container facility. Code-named Project Silk, the proposal was to offer trans-Pacific shippers a more efficient route for intermodal trade from the Asia-Pacific, using Prince Rupert to reach the us heartland more quickly. The price tag: $170 million.[3]

There were plenty of reasons the so-called experts said it could not be done. Prince Rupert was too small; major ports only existed in big cities with enough of a population and manufacturing base to support them. It was too expensive to build, too remote, too unconventional, too unknown, too risky, too far north, or all of the above. "People literally laughed at us," Port Authority CEO Don Krusel said, "they thought we were on something."[4]

What they were onto was the number one rule of real estate: location, location, location. The provincial and federal governments each put up $30 million, Maher Terminals committed $60 million, CN Rail $15 million, and the Prince Rupert Port Authority borrowed $25 million, risking everything they had.[5] In August 2007, the arrival of three thirty-storey cranes transformed Prince Rupert's harbour,[6] lifting the spirits of the entire community. After decades of ups and downs, people could not contain their excitement as six thousand people attended the grand opening. The facility was hailed as "the most important piece of infrastructure in Northern BC since the railway came through almost a century ago."[7]

Symbolically, the cranes also represented the fulfillment of Charles Hays's vision for Prince Rupert as an Asia-Pacific gateway. And the ill-timing of Fairview's opening only initially looked to be as bad an omen as the Hays's death. In October 2007, as the first containers were offloaded in Prince Rupert,[8] the seeds of global financial turmoil were already sprouting. The Great Recession of 2008–2009 was the most serious financial crisis and the worst global recession since the Great Depression. Yet, as other west-coast ports saw container traffic drop by 15 percent, Prince Rupert's rose 46 percent courtesy of its newfound intermodal efficiency. The city's new flagship development posted double digit year-over-year growth in 2009 and soon after became North America's fastest growing port.[9] After nearly a century, the Rip Van Rupert curse of bad timing finally seemed to be in the rearview mirror.

But much like the work of Charles Hays, many things done in the name of Prince Rupert's progress had flaws. Fairview was already known to be located on a more than 5,000-year-old Ts'msyen village site, and after years of negotiations, Lax Kw'alaams and Metlakatla filed a court application in 2006, stating that "the proposed container terminal violated native land rights."[10] In the words of Metlakatla Chief Councillor Harold Leighton, "Our members are extremely frustrated with the complete lack of interest from the federal government to negotiate as required by the law... we have a 'prima facie' case of aboriginal rights and title to the area of port expansion and the federal government just continually refuses to recognize our rights."[11]

In response, the federal government initially argued that Metlakatla gave up their rights to consultation from the 1906 Kaien

Island surrender agreement, and the Port Authority CEO said that "the consultation and accommodation process that took place was done within what was the best we could do."[12] Once the federal environmental assessment was granted, construction was legally allowed to begin.[13] In early 2008, with the facility already operational, the federal government appointed a special representative to assist in the ongoing discussions.[14] While negotiations were underway, a study reported over 250 artifacts found alongside archeological sites that had been totally destroyed by road and rail development.[15] Archeologist Dr. George MacDonald publicly pronounced that "it would be a national shame to lose what remains of this legacy as we prepare ourselves as a nation for a new role in global trade."[16] Harold Leighton stated that "our people want to be able to support the development of the port" but that "it is important to us that the burial sites and traces of our history that are here are protected and handled with proper care and integrity."[17]

In June 2009, after the Ts'msyen reached a benefits agreement with Ridley Terminals Inc., the delegation marched from the signing ceremony, led by a drumbeat, into the Port Authority's Annual Public Meeting. "Today is a positive step in reclaiming our history as some of the best traders in the world," said Lax Kw'alaams member and legal consultant Calvin Helin, "We are here to send you a message that we are trying to get there with the port. Five years is too long. We are not going anywhere and you have to negotiate with respect and honour."[18] It took another two years of negotiating, but an agreement was finally reached that recognized the Port of Prince Rupert was in Ts'msyen traditional territory and created a protocol for future consultations and accommodations.[19]

After overcoming the concerns, the port-related economy created by the container terminal clearly had made Prince Rupert's economic fortunes resurgent. Prince Rupert was named as Canada's number one next boom town by the *National Post* in 2007. The values of home sales shot up 50 percent. The first new subdivision in over a decade got underway.[20] Hundreds of people were hired, local unemployment dropped, and household wages rose. The Obama-era "hope and change" energy was no longer something far-removed in the news. Unfortunately, there were still some major obstacles the community needed to deal with.

NO SILVER BULLET

By 2013, it was clear to everybody that port growth was not going to be a flash in the pan. In just that year alone, an expansion to Fairview was announced with a fourth container crane, a $90-million rail project broke ground on Ridley Island, and the Westview Wood Pellet terminal was built.[21] Real estate prices were climbing ever higher. But the hundreds of millions of port investment could not be expected to solve every problem facing a community still picking itself up from twenty years of serious socioeconomic challenges.

Between 2011 and 2016, even as the port complex was actively hiring, the local unemployment rate hovered between 12.4 percent to 14.6 percent, nearly double the national and provincial rates.[22] During that same time, hundreds of fish plant jobs were lost, totalling $2.3 million in local annual wages.[23] J.S. McMillan Fisheries closed in 2011,[24] as did Ocean's Fish in 2012.[25] But it was the 2015 closure of Canfisco's Oceanside Plant that hurt the most, in more ways than one.[26] In addition to the loss of up to five hundred jobs, the closure marked the definitive end to the salmon canning industry. The plant had been the largest in North America, and the last in operation in BC. About three quarters of the workforce was Indigenous, most of whom were women.[27]

Even after years of port-related growth, the city's child poverty rate was the second-worst in BC at 30 percent.[28] Homelessness was increasing. The Crime Severity Index showed Prince Rupert in the top ten in Canada, and the second highest in BC.[29] The disparity between Indigenous and non-Indigenous residents was pronounced: the median total income of Indigenous residents was only 56 percent of the median for the entire city, and nearly half of Indigenous residents had not completed high school.[30]

And it was evident that the record-setting port complex was not destined to become the city's next "big golden goose" of taxation. In 2004, the provincial government had enacted a temporary property tax cap for ports to incentivize new investment. Unfortunately, the compensation formula was flawed, and as a result, the city was losing more tax revenue from the port industry every year and was forced to shift the tax burden increasingly onto homeowners and small businesses. While the tax cap was designed to expire in 2009, it was later made permanent,[31] creating an unsustainable budget situation. To make matters worse, the city and Port Authority were locked in a court battle for years, disputing how much the port should pay as a "payment-in-lieu-of-taxes" (PILT). With these multi-million-dollar uncertainties, the city was forced to make deep cuts to the operating budget through the early 2010s, including laying off staff, not back-filling vacant jobs, reducing community enhancement grants, and closing the civic centre an extra two weeks per year.[32]

By 2017–18, in addition to the first physical signs of progress on Watson Island, AltaGas began construction of a $500-million propane export facility on Ridley Island, the first of its kind on Canada's west coast.[33] The Calgary-based company Wolverine Terminals announced a new marine fuelling terminal.[34] The one-millionth container was handled at Fairview.[35] Despite numerous LNG companies cancelling their plans to spend billions in the area, the port continued its steady growth, with the Port Authority generating over $24 million in profit in both 2017 and 2018.[36]

And yet the dichotomy between the health of the port and the wellbeing of the community was becoming increasingly pronounced. The city's former mainstay of fish processing continued to suffer, losing another five hundred jobs and millions of dollars more in local wages.[37] After the 2017 return on the Skeena River was one of the worst on record, the entire Skeena and Nass River watershed was closed for salmon in 2018.[38]As well, commercial fishing was found by a Senate report to be Canada's most dangerous job in 2018 due to death and injury.[39]

Meanwhile, a tent city was erected beside city hall in late 2017, partly as a protest for more housing, and partly as a place for dozens of homeless people to warm up and sleep. Unlike other tent cities across BC that lasted up to a year, the tents at Prince Rupert's city hall were set up only from November 8 to 23. For a small town to see such a big problem, the province and city quickly partnered with the local Transition Society to open a new emergency shelter less than a block away. Mayor Lee Brain went as far as scrubbing the floors with a toothbrush to get the facility ready as quickly as possi-ble. Five months into operating the emergency shelter, the province announced funding for thirty-six units of modular housing on land that the city offered for $1. Sixteen months after tent city was set up, the Crow's Nest Lodge was open.[40]

THE WATSON ISLAND SAGA CONTINUES

After the City of Prince Rupert unwillingly took possession of the pulp mill from Sun Wave through the tax sale in 2008, the city's cumulative operating deficit for Watson Island over the next three years was "well in excess of $1 million" due to environmental monitoring, liability, security, and legal costs.[41] Making matters even more complicated: Prince Rupert's former MLA Bill Belsey had become both the vice-president of the BC Liberal Party and a consultant for Sun Wave Forest Products in 2012. He was quickly implicated in a conflict-of-interest scandal for failing to register as a lobbyist prior to corresponding with three different BC Liberal cabinet members. Jobs minister Pat Bell was found to have been keeping Belsey apprised of the latest news of settlement structure meetings and allegations against Sun Wave.[42]

Motivated by increasingly urgent financial pressures, the Prince Rupert entered into an exclusivity agreement in 2012 to sell Watson Island for $5 million, a far cry from the 2009 asking price of $13 million. The proposed buyer: the newly created Watson Island Development Corporation (Watco), a non-binding MOU partnership of Colonial Coal, Lax Kw'alaams, and Metlakatla. As part of the deal, Watco agreed to pay for the city's legal costs on the condition that the lawsuits with Sun Wave were settled. Just before Christmas that same year, a judge lifted the outstanding CPLs, legally paving the way for the proposed sale to proceed. While the judgement definitively closed the door on Sun Wave reclaiming ownership of Watson Island, the judge went on to say that the decision "does not preclude financial damages being awarded to the company... damages are sought, however, and could be awarded in this action... I am satisfied here that damages will provide adequate compensation to Sun Wave."[43]

In August 2013, after years of court proceedings and over $400,000 in legal bills, Sun Wave and the City of Prince Rupert negotiated a settlement out of court.[44] While the city manager, Dr. Robert Long, described it as a "hard bargain," the agreement confirmed that the city had clear title on the lands from the tax sale process, which allowed decommissioning and the sale to Watco to proceed. As part of the settlement, the city and Sun Wave agreed that the municipality would manage the decommissioning process and that net profits from the sale of salvaged equipment and machinery would be divided.[45]

After the City of Prince Rupert and Watco signed an exclusivity agreement in 2012, Watco began paying for the city's monthly holding costs on Watson Island until the Sun Wave settlement was reached in 2013. The company also agreed to put $15 million towards site remediation, subject to approval of a remediation plan by the provincial government. After the city's settlement with Sun Wave, Watco and the city attempted to negotiate a definitive sales agreement before the exclusivity deadline of January 2014. During negotiations, Watco claimed that the updated estimate for remediation costs would exceed $50 to $60 million and proposed that Sun Wave or the province pay the difference.[46]

In February 2014, with no term sheet agreed to and the deadline passed, the Prince Rupert city council voted to terminate the exclusivity agreement with Watco and to no longer accept payment for maintenance costs. Watco claimed to have misunderstood the deadline and forwarded a new term sheet, but the council voted to reject the agreement. By that point, the company had paid the city approximately $2 million for the exclusive rights to purchase the island. After the city informed Watco that any further negotiations would be on a non-exclusive basis and that their term sheet was no longer acceptable, Watco responded by filing a request for an injunction to prevent the city from selling Watson Island to another party. A CPL was placed back on the property, meaning the city was once again legally barred from completing a sale.[47]

Seemingly undeterred by the setback, as local elections fast approached in the fall, the city announced in July 2014 that they had reached another exclusivity agreement, this time with the newly formed Watson Island LNG Corporation (WILNG). While mayor Jack Mussallem claimed that other offers were entertained over the course of multiple months,[48] less than two weeks later it was revealed that the company had only been incorporated in April 2014.[49] Furthermore, it was suggested that the deal required the city to obtain assistance from the provincial government to mitigate the environmental contamination. The WILNG exclusivity agreement with the city ran through to the end of 2014,[50] near the height of the province-wide LNG speculative boom. "Debt-Free BC" was promised by Premier Christy Clark in 2013, funded by any or all of more than a dozen projects proposed in the province. In the end, only one of those projects was built in Kitimat, while the rest, including WILNG, faded into oblivion.

By the end of 2014, Watson Island had completed its descent from the city's largest economic generator into its single biggest liability. The site was costing $90,000 per month and was wrapped up in multiple lawsuits with multiple companies. After years of supposed improvements from the container port opening, the City of Prince Rupert was again openly flirting with bankruptcy. Residential and business taxes were the highest rates in BC, more than 40 percent higher than the provincial average.[51] The roads budget had been cut in half. The parks budget and community groups had not received increases in years. And crucial infrastructure projects such as the RCMP station and water supply replacement were delayed indefinitely.

❧

In late 2014, Prince Rupert voted for a substantial change in leadership. Up against the incumbent mayor Jack Mussallem and two former city councillors, 28-year-old Lee Brain won a decisive victory, earning more votes than all 3 of his more experienced opponents combined. Furthermore, the polls were topped by four newcomers to the six-member city council.[52] Once the new mayor and majority new council were sworn into office, a dramatic change in strategy was soon apparent. Watson Island was still tied up in court from the botched attempted sale to Watco. The new civic administration launched an aggressive appeal to the courts to remove the CPL, whereby Watco would be required to post security of $3.24 million within three weeks in order to maintain the CPL. In their own words, "WatCo had insufficient available capital and also the Company considered it ill-advised to post security. Consequently, the [certificate of pending legislation] has now been removed from title."[53]

In 2015, the city proceeded with the demolition and salvage of the pulp mill infrastructure according to the terms of the settlement with Sun Wave. An arbitration provision proved to be incredibly important. Generally speaking, commercial arbitration is less time-consuming and costly than going to the Supreme Court. The arbitration clause was exercised in 2015 when the city hired NRI Global Inc. to dispose of tons of sulphur, hog fuel, asbestos, pulp, caustic soda, and other dangerous pulping chemicals left abandoned in the early 2000s. Sun Wave was ordered to pay the city $60,000 and to deposit $289,845 into a trust account. Despite this judgement, Sun Wave only provided $161,791. The arbitration clause was exercised again in 2017 by the city for approximately $2.3 million in reimbursement of costs associated with dismantling the pulp mill facilities. In both cases, the city's application was granted as the courts concluded that "it would be unfair and unjust for Sun Wave" to be allowed to withdraw from the 2013 agreement.[54]

During this time, Sun Wave had hired and fired at least five different legal firms, and the company's sole director, Ni Ritao, was in detention in China because of allegations of corruption.[55] As the city began finally moving forward on remediation, Sun Wave began claiming that the original settlement agreement was fraudulent because Ni's signature had been forged and his former legal counsel had acted without his authorization. The arbitrator dismissed this challenge and found Sun Wave in breach of the settlement agreement, at which point Sun Wave appealed to the Supreme Court.[56]

The ninety-five-page reasoning by the appeal judge categorically dismissed the claims, concluding that Sun Wave's actions "not only effectively constitutes an attack on the 2013 Settlement Agreement but also on three consent dismissal orders, [and] the 2015 Arbitration Award."[57] His definitive judgement addressed "the City's need for finality, to put this dispute behind them once and for all, and not to be dragged unduly back to square one."[58] For the first time in over a decade, Watson Island was free and clear of any legal issues and ready for its next lease on life.

In 2017, the city announced two milestones: 95 percent of the materials on the island had been recycled, including old pulping chemicals, which were re-utilized at other mills; and the city would lease Watson Island to Prince Rupert Legacy Inc., the municipality's wholly owned subsidiary, for a 30-year term for $100. In other words, the city was no longer entertaining offers to sell. Instead, the plan was to remediate and lease the property incrementally.

᯽

Watson Island "celebrated" its twenty-year anniversary of bankruptcy in 2017. It would seem a fitting gift that the city announced in April 2017 an agreement to lease part of the island to the Pembina Pipeline Corporation to construct a $275-million propane export facility. While the Rip Van Rupert curse had been broken by the container terminal a decade prior, the community's cautious optimism was still met with a healthy skepticism. For Pembina's proposed propane facility to be constructed, one final legal action had to be taken against Sun Wave. On the 93.1-hectare (230-acre) site on Watson Island, Sun Wave had continued to pay the taxes on a single lot of approximately 5.7 hectares (fourteen acres) since 2005. While equating to only 6 percent of the total land mass, the lot held by Sun Wave was strategically located adjacent to the CN Rail right-of-way. In July 2017, the city council unanimously approved the expropriation of the property. While Sun Wave again took the city to court, a judgement was awarded in the city's favour within a few months.[59] The City of Prince Rupert had officially re-gained complete and unequivocal legal ownership of Watson Island. While the City had initially been forced to become the unwilling owners through the 2009 tax sale, in 2017, it was by design.

Between 2017 and 2018, Pembina spent over $12 million demolishing and disposing of the former pulp mill's structures as well as removing over 77,000 cubic metres of contaminated soil.[60] In partnership with the city, over 5.7 million litres (1.5 million gallons) of black liquor, 500 tons of pulp, 23 tons of sulphur, and 30,000 barrels of bunker C fuel, among other things, were recycled. Over 95 percent of the waste, hazard, and surplus materials were recycled.[61] This was followed by a $250 million capital expenditure on the facility itself, which was designed to handle 20,000 barrels per day of propane.[62] The first shipment was handled in May 2021.

From a government buyout in the 1970s, a fire-sale privatization in the 1980s, bankruptcy and bailouts in the 1990s, a second bankruptcy, failed restart, tax sale, two failed sales, numerous court cases with multiple companies, hundreds of thousands of dollars in legal fees, plus millions spent on environmental remediation, the Watson Island saga was finally over. For its first fifty years, the Watson Island pulp mill had been Prince Rupert's single largest employer and tax contributor. In less than half that time, it had degenerated into the community's biggest liability. After nearly twenty years of holding the community hostage, Watson Island is now a national award-winner for brownfield revitalization. The remediation project was the first of its kind to be approved by the Province of BC as a proponent-driven process that is now being used as an example for other contaminated sites across the province.[63] With the commissioning of the propane export facility, the Watson Island saga has now become a textbook case study in economic and environmental innovation that other cities across BC and Canada are learning from. But closer to home, Watson Island is really an emotional touchstone for the city, an inter-dependent gauge of the whole community's health.

COLOURFUL CHARACTER: JACK MUSSALLEM

The man in charge during the late-1990 and mid-2000 to early 2010 periods of the Watson Island saga was former mayor Jack Mussallem. Descended from one of Prince Rupert's earliest immigrant families, Jack Mussallem is a third-generation Rupertite. His grandparents immigrated from Lebanon to Winnipeg before settling on Kaien Island in 1910. Hired as Prince Rupert's deputy city clerk, Mussallem worked in this capacity from 1981 to 1987 before being promoted to City Clerk in 1987.[64] In 1995, he was terminated as part of the city's cost cutting measures.[65]

The Mussallem name translates from Lebanese as "peaceful man."[66] Unfortunately for Jack, he chose an incredibly tumultuous time to sit in the mayor's chair. After winning a tight election in 1996 by only thirty-eight votes,[67] within his first few months in office, he received the call that the Watson Island pulp mill was shutting down. He described the news as "creating a lot of economic as well as emotional upheaval."[68] Just a few weeks later, when he voiced his stance against the Alaska Ferry blockade due to its negative impact on tourism, he was subsequently accused by local fishermen of "kissing Alaska's (expletive)."[69]

Mussallem lost his re-election bid in 1999. Perhaps in part for his controversial support for lifting the moratoriums on fish farming[70] or his opposition to the oil tanker moratorium,[71] Mussallem's stances and electoral misfortune were very likely caused in part by the des-peration and severity of the City's unfolding economic crisis. However, he was later re-elected as mayor in 2008 by less than two hundred votes before being handily re-elected in 2011. He served until 2014, when he was defeated by the young political newcomer Lee Brain.

As a former city clerk turned politician, Jack Mussallem's leader-ship approach is best described by one of his election campaign slo-gans, that it is "better to understand what is in the box rather than

Former Prince Rupert mayor Jack Mussallem.
PRINCE RUPERT CITY & REGIONAL ARCHIVES

to think outside of it."[72] Unfortunately for Mussallem, the box he found himself in was a city faced with unprecedented financial and legal troubles. To his supporters, Jack Mussallem was a calm leader who was dealt a bad hand in unprecedented times. His detractors judge the city's track record during his tenure against his word that "the mayor is basically the town's number one negotiator, spokesman and lobbyist."[73] Regardless of how much or how little stock one puts into the macroeconomic context in which he was operating, during Mussallem's time in the mayor's chair, Watson Island became, in his own words, "a hell hole… the thing never ends."[74] Therefore, perhaps his time in office is best summarized by the old adage that good timing is invisible, but bad timing sticks out a mile.

GLOBAL PANDEMIC

By the end of 2019, Prince Rupert was celebrating the launch of a new grand vision for the community. Finally with enough resources to plan for the future, the world-renowned planner Larry Beasley was hired to facilitate Vision 2030: an aggressive plan based on the community and the port complex growing in sync.[75] The vision was unveiled two weeks before Christmas 2019, adding to the growing momentum being generated by real, tangible progress. But the timing could not have been worse.

Just as Watson Island was poised to return to the municipal tax roll for the first time in more than two decades, in early 2020 the first cases of COVID-19 were detected in BC. After the provincial government called a state of emergency, schools were closed, many businesses were ordered to temporarily shutter their operations, and bans on in-person gatherings were enacted. Major events were forced to cancel. The federal government shut down all non-essential travel with the United States. Flights from many other countries were banned.

Before long, the Lower Mainland began reporting active outbreaks in multiple long-term care facilities and numerous deaths. A group of Prince Rupert physicians sounded the alarm, writing an appeal to the city hall for more action to be taken on top of the provincial guidelines. Prince Rupert was uniquely vulnerable to the virus. As a remote city, Prince Rupert had limited healthcare resources and only a handful of acute care beds, which were already at full capacity. The nearest hospital in Terrace was also operating overcapacity and transferring infected patients to Prince Rupert. Furthermore, early data had already shown a higher correlation of severe COVID-19 cases in the Indigenous population.

One of the local doctors explained at the time: "Ten people at the same time to ventilate, we can't. Ten people over three months, we can handle... this could be the most dramatic time any of us ever experience."[76] In response, the mayor and city council unanimously declared a local state of emergency on March 24, 2020. Unlike any other city in North America at the time, Rupertites were asked to self-isolate for fourteen days after any domestic travel.[77] The city activated an emergency operations centre and recommended that businesses limit entry, provide patrons with hand sanitizer, and encourage physical distancing.

Only three days after the declaration of a local state of emergency, the provincial government rescinded the local order.[78] The stated rationale was to offer a uniform provincial approach to fighting COVID-19. However, Prince Rupert had a fundamentally different experience with the pandemic than the rest of the BC. By the end of the 2020, BC tallied nearly 50,000 confirmed cases and more than eight hundred deaths while Prince Rupert was spared from virtually any community spread of COVID-19. With only a small handful of localized cases traced back to domestic travel, it is not a stretch to conclude that the early alarm bells raised by the local doctors, mayor, and council had a positive influence.

Unfortunately, Prince Rupert's reputation as a relative safe-haven from COVID-19 ended abruptly in early 2021, when the local long-term care facility declared an outbreak. Within just a few weeks, sixteen people lost their lives and two dozen front-line healthcare staff tested positive for the virus. Subsequent outbreaks were declared at the long-term care home and hospital, and multiple exposure advisories were announced at schools, workplaces, and the homeless shelter. By the middle of March 2021, after multiple weeks of escalating, triple-digit new case counts, Prince Rupert had the highest per-capita spread in the province.[79]

Luckily, Prince Rupert benefitted from an extraordinary piece of good timing. While local COVID-19 cases were accelerating, so too was the international vaccine supply. Provincial health authorities experimented with the first community-wide vaccination clinic in Prince Rupert, the largest for any city of its size in Canada at the time. With only one week's notice, the local civic centre auditorium was converted into a mass vaccination clinic thanks to four hundred volunteers. Within eight days, over 85 percent of eligible residents received their first dose of an mRNA vaccine, resulting in a quick drop to zero cases.[80] The results of the community-wide vaccination effort speak for themselves.

Unlike the divisive anti-mask, anti-vaccine, and anti-government protests experienced across Canada, the largest organized initiative in Prince Rupert during the pandemic was the more than five hundred homes who filled their front windows with rainbows and hearts as a tribute to healthcare workers.[81] Dubbed #RainbowResilience, the splash of colour and light displayed some much-needed solidarity during the dark days of the pandemic and demonstrated the uniquely colourful character of the community.

CHAPTER 16

WHERE ARE WE NOW?
WHERE ARE WE GOING?
2024 and Beyond

"A slogan is not, and never will be a means to an end in
the matter of Prince Rupert's destiny... it would be
a case of gilding the lily and painting the rainbow."
LETTER TO THE EDITOR, *PRINCE RUPERT*
DAILY NEWS, DECEMBER 12, 1927

ACTIONS SPEAK LOUDER THAN SLOGANS

Over the years, Prince Rupert has tried and failed to attach itself to
many slogans: the Golden City, the Dream City, the City of Certainties,
the Halibut Capital of the World, the Gloucester of the Pacific, the
Norway of North America, the Pulp City of Canada, the Gateway to
Alaska, the Prince of Ports, Trail Capital of BC,[1] and so many more.

Yet none of these nicknames are still used by local Rupertites.
So why does the moniker "City of Rainbows" seem to have staying
power that others have not?

None of the other slogans have stood the test of time because they
are either: too generic and could be applied to countless other places;
they aren't memorable or catchy; they are devoid of sentiment or
substance; they are too one-dimensional; or all of the above.

Most importantly, no other slogans have offered a meaningful and
timeless symbolism. The "City of Rainbows," on the other hand, is
a potent metaphor based on an enduring local reality. The rain and
clouds are not going anywhere anytime soon. The uplifting imag-
ery of the rainbow allows us to embrace the rain for what comes
after, knowing that "a fair share of rain makes the sunlight days the
sweeter."[2]

The City of Rainbows rebranding undertaken by the municipality
in 2022 resulted in a new logo designed by Ts'msyen artist Russell

Mather, new way finding signage, a new website, new advertising, and new apparel. None of these things will affect Prince Rupert's destiny, but they do help to tell the community's unique story. With the community in active recovery mode, the next chapter in the city's history depends on whether any lessons are learned from past mistakes—it will either be rejuvenation or regression.

The boom times in the 1960s and '70s were like a fever. Prince Rupert's overheated growth masked some underlying structural weaknesses with the local economy. And after the warnings signs in the 1980s of the economic bubble, the bust in the 1990s and 2000s was like the community experienced a triple-bypass level heart attack. The economic lifebloods of the city were disrupted, leading to a sudden and severe onset of consequences. The shocks to the system posed a risk of death and required significant intervention. And just like recovering from a heart-attack, time is needed for the city to fully rehabilitate itself, and significant lifestyle changes are required to prevent the bust from happening again in the future. The road to recovery is never painless or easy. There are setbacks and complications. Much in that same way, Prince Rupert's recovery has not been straightforward, and it is not yet complete.

Today, Prince Rupert is home to about 13,500 residents. Much like many other communities, persistent problems remain: housing shortage, poverty, food insecurity, substance abuse, healthcare service shortages, and crime. Substantially more resources and people are necessary for the city to move from recovery to remission. And yet, for the first time since the 1990s, there finally seem to be clear signs that the community is ready to turn the page on a new chapter of growth and prosperity. Not since the 1976 census has Prince Rupert's population stopped declining. Today, population numbers are growing slightly. More kids are being born. Immigration numbers and average household incomes are up. More housing is being built than at any time in the past twenty years. A rekindled sense of cautious optimism has emerged, tempered by the hard lessons of history, but buoyed by the unmistakable trademark Rupertite resilience.

Knowing where Prince Rupert and Kaien Island have come from gives some sense of where they might be headed. But as physicist Niels Bohr once allegedly said, "It's tough to make predictions, especially about the future." In that spirit, rather than attempting to prognosticate, the goal of this final chapter is to enliven the lessons learned from Prince Rupert's historical experience and offer some rainbow-related remedies to avoid repeating the mistakes of the past. What will become apparent is that Prince Rupert's story is really a story of the human condition.

DIVERSITY ENRICHES

From an economic standpoint, having all of Prince Rupert's metaphorical eggs in the same natural resource export basket was a recipe for the inevitable roller-coaster boom and bust. Fishermen have recognized that a single gear to harvest a single species leaves a vulnerability to seasonality, price fluctuations, and cyclical natural abundance. Many boats are now fitted with multiple gears for numerous fisheries, allowing them to earn a living year-round and mitigate risk. The built physical legacy of fishing is also diversified: the former Atlin Fish Plant is now the mixed-use anchor of Cow Bay. The Prince Rupert Fishermen's Cooperative lives on through Northern Savings Credit Union, and their 1940s supply store is now a waterfront pub. A former fishing net loft is home to a sushi restaurant. The largest salmon cannery warehouse plays host to local gymnastics. Prince Rupert will always be a fishing town thanks to its geography, infrastructure, culture, traditions, cuisine, and tourism.

The Port Authority continues to diversify cargoes and terminals with what they coin as an "intermodal ecosystem." With two logistics parks proposed for Ridley and Kaien Islands, the hope is to expand offerings to include transloading and warehousing for plastic pellets, cereal grains, speciality agricultural crops, lumber, and pulp.[3] And for the first time since 1982, a large-scale bulk liquid tank farm has received its environmental approvals.[4] Located on Ridley Island, the proposal is to ship liquified petroleum gas, diesel, and methanol.[5]

The former pulp mill site is now home to Pembina's propane export facility, an industrial testing laboratory, and a logistics transloading operation. Approximately twenty-eight hectares (seventy acres) of prime industrial land are ready for redevelopment on Watson Island. Options include converting the pulp mill's massive water clarifying tanks into on-land aquaculture, opening much-in-demand industrial lay-down areas, or even a hydrogen facility as proposed by a partnership of Pattern Energy, the City of Prince Rupert, Lax Kw'alaams, and Metlakatla in 2022.[6] The City of Prince Rupert has also opened submissions for biomass production, wind generation, and tidal energy projects around Watson Island.[7] Instead of one single, outsized "golden goose" industrial taxpayer, Prince Rupert now has a gander of major ratepayers to reduce over-reliance on any one industry.

Beyond the importance of economic diversity, a big part of Prince Rupert's growing strength is its multiculturalism. In a world experiencing a dramatic rise in anti-immigrant populist forces, Prince Rupert is a microcosm for the best results of the Canadian experiment. According to the 2021 federal census, 37 percent of residents identify as Indigenous and over 15 percent of the population identify as part of a visible minority. Sixteen percent of the city was not born in Canada, and another 16 percent are second-generation children of immigrants, predominantly from India, Vietnam, the Philippines, and China. This means that no one ethnic group makes up a majority of the community. And after years of expanding religious pluralism, the majority of residents now subscribe to "no religion/secular perspectives." For a remote city of 13,500 people, that is a profoundly different experience from the homogeneity found throughout most of the north.

Lastly, as the only municipality located within the Great Bear Rainforest, an area the size of Ireland that represents 25 percent of the world's remaining ancient coastal temperate rainforest, Prince Rupert is rich in biodiversity. Home to one of the largest concentrations of grizzly bears in North America and the world's only Spirit Bears,[8] to northern resident killer whales who like to rub their bellies on pebble beaches and migrating humpbacks that participate in bubble-net feeding, Kaien Island is an epicentre for some of the most spectacular species in the animal kingdom. The annual salmon runs support more than just humans, whales, and bears, but also otters, sea lions, seals, and countless species of birds such as eagles, herons, and kingfishers.[9] Furthermore, one hectare (2.5 acres) of the unique rainforest stores more than one thousand tons of carbon, making the protected region "a crucial shield against global climate instability."[10] Protecting this surrounding biodiversity is of paramount importance.

Economic diversification reduces the city's vulnerability to a downturn in any one industry. Embracing the complex cultural tapestry of Prince Rupert fosters a creative and dynamic social environment.

And the biodiversity of the Great Bear Rainforest contributes incalculable socio-economic, cultural, and environmental benefits. Ultimately, placing a high value on diversity will continue to enrich Prince Rupert's resilience, prosperity, and well-being.

CHASE RAINBOWS, BUT ONLY SOME

Depending on your perspective, someone who chases rainbows is engaged in either a futile pursuit or worthwhile wandering. In the case of Prince Rupert, the ever-elusive, unrealistic, and unattainable dream was Charles Hays's bombastic prediction that the city would one day become another Vancouver or San Francisco. Prince Rupert's struggle was never that the death of Charles Hays robbed the city of the pot of gold at the end of the rainbow. Rather, the struggle has been trying to live up to the impossible prophecy he left behind.

Chasing a rainbow in Prince Rupert means operating with the belief that something meaningful is worth the effort, even if a successful outcome is not guaranteed; to pursue something difficult or unconventional requires enthusiasm, hope, and optimism. Without such an attitude, Watson Island might still be tied up in never-ending court battles or would have been sold off for less than the taxes owed. The largest theatre in Northern BC may not have been built after the first referendum decisively failed. One of the tallest buildings in Northern BC would not remain a part of Prince Rupert's skyline without someone first proposing to build a skyscraper as tall as the Hotel Vancouver in a remote northern coastal rainforest. The cruise terminal was built on the sales pitch of attracting 250,000 cruise-ship tourists annually by 2014. While there were only 41,000 in 2022, the Port Authority has entered into a cruise terminal operations agreement with a global firm and has since doubled that number.[11]

Even the container terminal was at one point a rainbow to be chased, given how outlandish the idea was and the years of advocacy required. Before the first cranes had even arrived, Port Authority CEO Don Krusel was promising a third phase of expansion to 4 million TEUS within ten years. If true, that would have made Prince Rupert the fourth largest port in North America at the time.[12] The actual capacity at the tenth year was 1.35 million TEUS,[13] and by 2023 had increased to 1.6 million.[14] Despite the gap between prediction and reality, without that aggressive salesmanship and unyielding belief in the port's potential, the container terminal project plans would not have left paper.

However, there are certainly some rainbows not worth chasing. There are no offshore oil and gas rigs in Hecate Strait, despite years of lobbying to remove a moratorium.[15] Tens of billions of proposed investment in liquified natural gas (LNG) facilities have been announced since the 1980s to great fanfare before evaporating.[15] A ten-hectare (twenty-five-acre) mall development on the outskirts of town did not break ground despite years of promises.[16] But the bridge too far is a literal one. In politics, "a bridge to nowhere" implies that an expense is unnecessarily extravagant, or even useless. In Prince Rupert, "a bridge to Digby" suggests the same thing, but with the added twist of also being a champagne dream, an indulgence totally out of financial reach. As MLA, Dan Miller launched a campaign in 1994 for a fixed link between Digby and Kaien Islands. Amazingly, in 1996, the province pledged $27 million, or 25 percent towards what they estimated would be a total cost of $108 million.[18] Ignoring the huge road approaches and the more than sixty-metre (eighteen-storey) height clearance required, the shortest physical span across the Prince Rupert harbour is about seven hundred metres.[19] For comparison, that would mean building a suspension bridge 50 percent longer than the Lion's Gate Bridge in Vancouver.

There is a major difference between harbouring an unquenchable optimism versus entertaining widely unrealistic expectations. The sky may be the limit, but reaching for the clouds still needs solid ground. In the words of Nelson Mandela, "Vision without Action is merely a dream, Action without Vision is merely passing Time, but Action with vision can change the world."[20]

RAIN CHECK UNTIL THE RIGHT TIME

In 1800s baseball, when a game got postponed or cancelled due to rain, spectators received a check to attend a future game at no charge. In other words, timing is everything and patience is required. Similarly, there are projects in Prince Rupert's history that have been rain-checked over the decades due to a lack of funding or political will, poor planning, bad execution, or because the timing was just not right.

One example is the Ts'msyen Access Project. As an alternative route to a bridge to Digby, a road link to Lax Kw'alaams and Metlakatla has been studied since the 1960s.[21] By partnering the airport ferry with the Lax Kw'alaams and Metlakatla ferries, the cost savings would allow for a single dock across the harbour on the Ts'msyen Peninsula. Roads of approximately ten kilometres to each Indigenous community plus a bridge one-third the length to Digby Island across the Metlakatla Pass would complete connectivity between the communities.[22] The likelihood of this project coming to fruition is improving: the province funded a $20-million rebuild of the 17.5-kilometre access road into Lax Kw'alaams in 2016. The rapid expansion of the port complex opens opportunities for air cargoes, and the City of Prince Rupert is in the process of moving the Kaien Island airport ferry dock to a central location at Kwinitza/Rotary Waterfront Park.

Another project that is underway may have future implications for helping Prince Rupert become a technological hub on the North Coast. The municipality has owned its own telephone company since 1910, the CityWest Cable and Telephone Corporation, one of the last remaining publicly owned telecoms in the country. Rather than cave to the calls for privatization, the company is undertaking the Connected Coast Project, building out a 3,400-kilomtre subsea fibre-optic cable network around Vancouver Island, connecting 139 rural, remote, and Indigenous communities to high-speed internet.[23] For Prince Rupert, it means having the required redundancy of two fibre links to equip Kaien Island with speeds and reliability rivalling Vancouver. Furthermore, with world-class internet comes the potential to build data storage centres. Given the region's temperate climate, the fact that 40 percent of the average data centre's costs are for cooling systems,[24] and the emergence of subsea data centres,[25] Prince Rupert is uniquely positioned to leverage the tech wave by maximizing its cloud advantage.

Additionally, Prince Rupert is well placed to become a global clean energy contributor. Years before the city was connected to the provincial BC Hydro grid, the municipal water reservoir was once used to supply the city's power needs.[26] While the power generation equipment was removed decades ago, the dam was rebuilt in 2022 to an award-winning[27] standard that makes electricity generation possible again if and when the province grants permission for hydroelectricity within watershed conservancies.[28] As well, before any wind turbines were operating in BC, Mount Hays was slated to become the first wind farm in the province in 2006 after eighteen turbines were approved to power more than 10,000 homes.[29] The first iteration failed before another company acquired the investigative license in 2015. The proposal has since expanded to twenty-four turbines, but is more than six years behind the original schedule.[30] Kaien Island's unique geography has three sets of large tidal rapids that could be utilized for their energy potential. As early as 2006, the federal government highlighted Prince Rupert's massive tides as showing the most promise for tide-based power generation, behind only the famed Bay of Fundy.[31] A Vancouver-based start-up developed a 50-kilowatt generator for a pilot project in the Prince Rupert area in 2012,[32] and a Haida Gwaii company spent nearly $1 million piloting smaller prototypes for the area in 2017–18.[33] The potential is huge to provide clean energy for other nearby rural, remote, and Indigenous communities that are relying on increasingly expensive and dirty diesel or gasoline generators.

From its original boardwalks to the arrival of the Yellowhead Highway after the Second World War, the city has been in need of a safer and more accessible downtown area. With the city situated at the western terminus of Highway 16, the provincial department of highways has jurisdiction over the main thoroughfare that dissects Prince Rupert's downtown. Since the 1980s, a bypass road along Wantage Road has been proposed. In addition to allowing the highway to be relocated outside of the downtown core, a bypass road would open much-needed land for development, improve pedestrian and biker safety, and allow the municipality to finally take control of its downtown. While the current four-lane highway is the most dangerous stretch of road in the community, recent studies have shown that if it is reconfigured with angled parking, a bike path, and separated by medians, a people-oriented complete street is possible.[34]

Many of Prince Rupert's current problems have roots in the past. As more time passes, compelling opportunities are becoming more realistic thanks to the evolution of modern technologies, creative thinking, and patience.

PLAN FOR A RAINY DAY: RECESSION LESSON

In addition to taking advantage of the good times, we must also prepare for the bad times too. Setting aside resources when they are plentiful will save untold amounts of discomfort when the unexpected emergencies hit. Unfortunately, one of the greatest flaws in the human species is wishful thinking. There is an important lesson worth learning from Prince Rupert's case study. In the early 1980s, a single front page of the *Prince Rupert Daily News* had three major headlines: "Forest Industry in a State of Chaos"; "Salmon Stocks on Edge of a Disastrous Curve"; and "Mill Expansion at Risk."[35]

But instead of saving money to prepare for the inevitable storms, the city reacted with hubris. The Performing Arts Centre and Aquatic Centre were both built with millions in debt. Millions more were put up to build the Alaska Ferry Terminal. The city even offered to pay part of the salary of a speech pathologist and audiologist on behalf of the provincial health authority.[36] Fishing and forestry were considered "permanent and growing industries,"[37] and the only projected population trajectory was calling for the city to double in size.[38] Ironically, while councillors and residents thought the city was somehow fulfilling its long-awaited destiny, history repeated itself and Prince Rupert once again sank deep into the doldrums. Lesson learned: always look on the bright side, but not until you go blind.

There are plenty of storm clouds on Prince Rupert's horizon beyond 2024 that present risks that should not be overlooked.

Due to decades of infrastructure spending cuts, escalating debt, and deferred maintenance when times were good, followed by decades of having inadequate financial resources when times were bad, Prince Rupert's civic infrastructure as of the end of 2023 is in a semi-failure state. The estimated deficit to replace the dilapidated water pipes, sewer lines, roads, sidewalks, and turn-of-the-century wooden bridges exceeds $600 million. Even with record investments of $77 million from federal disaster mitigation fundng, $65 million from the Province, and $45 million borrowed by local taxpayers, only about one quarter of the city's most at-risk water system will be renewed.

Additionally, the local port complex in Prince Rupert faces several potential headwinds: geopolitical trade tensions with China, the threat of job losses from port automation, the phase out of thermal coal, and the impacts of climate change on wheat harvests or forestry health. In 2023, cargo volumes dropped for the second year in a row owing to supply chain challenges, shifting global energy needs, pandemic-related disruptions, and Asian economic growth slowing. The Port Authority has acknowledged that diversification will be their key to sustained success.

Being wedged between the North Pacific on one side and Mount Hays on the other, Prince Rupert has faced a housing crunch for most of its existence. In 2023, three out of every four houses in Prince Rupert were built before 1980. It is no surprise then that, compared to the provincial average, Prince Rupert has three times more houses in need of major repairs. There are more than one hundred people experiencing homelessness, and rental prices have increased substantially as the local economy has rebounded.[39] Thanks to provincial government investment, hundreds of new affordable and supportive housing units have been built over the past five years, and hundreds more are slated to begin construction in the coming one to two years. However, the waitlists on new affordable housing complexes still reaches the triple digits.

By saving for a rainy day while conditions are favourable, we can avoid reliving a boom-bust scenario where the cupboards are bare when we are most in need.

TAX PROBLEMS, RAIN OR SHINE

Right from the beginning, the city has had acrimonious relationships with its largest industrial taxpayers and has needed a strong determination to carry on when the going got tough. Charles Hays and the GTP fought to avoid contributing anything to the newly created municipality in the early 1900s. During the Great Depression, the city did not have enough tax revenue to afford its debt payments and was forced into bankruptcy in 1933. The pulp mill opposed joining the city's boundary in the 1960s and was bitterly against being treated as the big golden goose thereafter. Ridley Terminals Inc. sued the city and aggressively lobbied to lower their tax levy in the 1980s. The two recessions in the early 1980s and 1990s resulted in deep cuts to both infrastructure spending and taxes. Multiple failed restarts on Watson Island through the 2000s left local taxpayers holding the bag. And more recently, the city has been at odds with the Port Authority over their payment-in-lieu of taxes (PILT), settling a multi-year, multi-million dollar claim in 2016. But by 2023, another appeal was launched by the city due to the dramatic devaluation of Port Authority properties from $139 million to $26 million, resulting in double-digit tax increases on homeowners and small businesses.[40]

Provincial intervention through the years has always seemed to inflame tax tensions. When Watson Island was first included on the local tax roll in the 1960s, the provincial government exempted virtually all the mill's assets from taxation. When the Province of BC took control of the facility in the 1970s, their annual taxation appeals reduced the city's entire budget by 4 percent. In the 1980s, the provincial imposition of the Ridley Island Tax Sharing Agreement set off forty years of disputes between Prince Rupert and Port Edward. In 1995, new provincial tax regulations on railways saw CN's local property tax bill almost cut in half.[41] The 2005 tax sale of Watson Island saw the provincial government wash its hands of the facility after multiple failed bailouts and privatization, leaving Prince Rupert as the unwilling owners to inherit the liability and maintenance costs. Finally, the provincial government's imposed cap on municipal property taxes for port terminals has created an unsustainable decline of millions in annual revenues from what is now the city's primary industrial tax base.

Beware of fairweather friends, those industries and agencies who are supportive and friendly when things are going well but avoid taking on their fair share when the bill comes due.

NEVER JUDGE A DAY BY ITS WEATHER

The words of British author Alfred Wainwright are appropriate when applied to the story of Prince Rupert: "There's no such thing as bad weather, only unsuitable clothing."[42] In other words, do not allow less-than-ideal conditions to prevent or dictate decisions. Much like Prince Rupert weather can unpredictably change between all four seasons in a day, the circumstances of a situation can also shift over time.

The most pertinent local example is how Prince Rupert is confronting the irony of being a coastal city that has virtually no public beach access. As a city designed by industry, for industry, Prince Rupert's waterfront was purpose-built to serve the GTP, not the community. Over a century later, this unfavourable situation remains as the waterfront continues to be dominated by CN's rail yard and the Port Authority. As the port complex grew substantially since 2007,

CN shut down a one-kilometre stretch of waterfront pathway adjacent to their rail yard. The sand beaches on Ridley Island had public access cut off by the Port Authority in 2011.[43] Then in 2016, CN cut off access to the only accessible beach on Kaien Island after forty years of public use, citing illegal trespassing.[44] With projections for continued port development, the forecast for the possible opening of a new public waterfront in the seaside city looks grim.

Nonetheless, local tenacity has slowly but surely started to overcome this over-one-hundred-year-old problem. In 2016, thanks to a partnership between the municipality and Community Futures Pacific Northwest, the Port Authority donated a water lot after nearly $4 million in grant funds were secured to build a nearly 183-metre (six-hundred-foot) public wharf and breakwater and a fifty-one-slip marina.[45] The Cow Bay Marina is now home to a public kayak launch and is part of North America's Whale Trail. In 2018, after nearly fifteen years of work by the local Rotary Club, the 1.2-kilometre Rushbrook Trail was re-opened along the waterfront after being closed because safety issues from rockslides in 2003. In 2019, the City of Prince Rupert acquired 6.7 hectares (16.5 acres) of contaminated land in Cow Bay from CN to be remediated, stretching almost a full kilometre from the Cow Bay lagoon to the Hays Cove lagoon.[46] In 2020, Canfisco and the City of Prince Rupert reached an agreement for the municipality to lease the company's former warehouse space. Built right on the ocean, the site is strategic for recreation beside the Rushbrook Floats and public boat launch and is now sublet to the gymnastics club. In 2022, the Port Authority and the city celebrated the $4 million revitalization of the Seal Cove lagoon.[47] Then, in 2023, the heritage CN station was restored and converted into the local craft brewery as part of a $20 million waterfront redevelopment project that will later include a new dock for the airport ferry.[48]

Remaining motivated in the face of less-than-ideal conditions has revealed new paths that were not previously available for Prince Rupert.

EXPLORE EVERY GATEWAY

As the BC Ferries link to Haida Gwaii, Prince Rupert stands to gain immensely from the tens of thousands of tourists flocking to "Canada's Galapagos," with passenger numbers up almost 15 percent in 2023. The famed Inside Passage route from Vancouver Island brought approximately 37,000 visitors through Prince Rupert in 2022, a 62 percent jump after pandemic-related travel restrictions ended.[49] And after a five-month suspension of scheduled air services at the height of the pandemic, the Digby Island airport has returned to scheduling a daily flight to Vancouver.[50]

The future is a mixed bag when it comes to American visitors. Cruise tourism from Washington and California enroute to Alaska is increasing steadily, with more than 80,000 cruise passengers and more than fifty ships arriving in 2023, up from 41,000 in 2022 and the best result in over a decade.[51] The Cow Bay Marina is consistently filled with itinerant yachts destined for Alaska, creating millions in economic spin-off benefits. On the other hand, the storied Alaska Ferry link remains uncertain. After budget cuts, international disputes, and new regulations, the Ketchikan–Prince Rupert ferry service was stopped indefinitely in October 2019 after fifty-six years of service. A three-year hiatus over the pandemic saw the first Alaska ferry return in June 2022, but as a shell of its former self: only two trips per month in the summer of 2022, followed by no summer service at all in 2023 and 2024 due to a lack of vessels and crew.[52]

But the anchor for Prince Rupert is its status as the third-largest port in Canada, behind only Vancouver and Montreal. While cargo volumes dipped by 2 percent in 2022, this rural and remote city still processed over 25 million tons of cargo moving between the Asia-Pacific and American Midwest. A private road was opened in 2022 between the container terminal and Ridley Island, cutting emissions by 75 percent and dramatically reducing the amount of heavy truck traffic passing through the downtown core. The port complex has over $2 billion in potential new project investments under consideration, including a potential second container terminal.[53]

Without a doubt, Prince Rupert's strategic location will continue to play a vital role in shaping the community's future.

EVERY CLOUD HAS A SILVER LINING

How the city adapts to climate change will be a defining feature of this century. In BC, wildfires, droughts, and natural disasters are increasing in frequency and intensity. When flooding and landslides cut off all Vancouver rail services and vital road and port links for

weeks in 2021, the Prince Rupert port complex remained fully operational.[54] As wildfires sweep across British Columbia each summer,
burning communities and millions of acres of land to the ground,
Prince Rupert has not yet experienced an air quality advisory. With
other municipalities suffering from drought-like conditions and low
reservoirs, Prince Rupert has remained without water restrictions.
As heat waves cause hundreds of unnecessary deaths, Kaien Island
has never seen temperatures exceed 33 degrees Celsius, and has only
once gone three consecutive weeks without any precipitation.[55] The
potential for an earthquake-induced tsunami to cause significant
harm is considered to be "an event that probably won't happen,"
thanks to the protection of Digby Island, according to a detailed
2019 study.[56] And as the Northwest Passage increasingly becomes
available for shipping as the ice melts, Prince Rupert is positioned to
become a focal point of a new Arctic trade gateway. Climate change
adaptation presents a unique opportunity for Prince Rupert to offer
a place of refuge and play an outsized role in Canada's supply chain.

NO RAINDROPS, NO RAINBOWS

Ask any random person what they know about Prince Rupert and
the most typical answer will be that it rains a lot. And when it rains,
it really does pour, literally and figuratively. Murphy's Law is that
anything that can go wrong will go wrong. And in Prince Rupert's
case, when one bad thing happens, a whole series of additional difficulties tend to happen at the same time.

But Rupertites know that "our months of rain make some lives
dreary; but, our glorious rainbows rejoice the weary."[57] Through
some of the city's darkest days, the local "liquid sunshine state of
mind" confronted the tough times with positivity, joy, and humour.
The resilience of the people of Prince Rupert through challenging
times allowed the city to survive two world wars, the Great Depression, the Great Recession, the Watson Island saga, the millennium's
turmoil trifecta, the COVID-19 pandemic, and all the ups and downs
in between.

The residents of Prince Rupert today have retained a sometimes
ill-fated hopefulness that has endured through triumphs and trag-
edies. The relentless local spirit of optimism that has persisted for
over a century can best be described as cultivating an unshakeable

confidence in the city's potential through very difficult conditions. As an anonymous poet wrote in the *Prince Rupert Daily News* in 1943:

> Indeed with more sun we could do
> But has it ever occurred at least once to you
> How much we appreciate each little ray
> When the sun shines upon us some sunny day?[58]

❧

Rain has always shaped life on Kaien Island. The original Ts'msyen inhabitants, the first Europeans, and the most recent immigrants who have called this island home know the determination it takes to survive and thrive in the Great Bear Rainforest. From the Grease Trails to sea otter pelts, gold rushes, salmon canneries, the railway, two World Wars, the Halibut Capital of the World, the pulp mill, and now being home to the third biggest port in Canada, the history of Kaien Island is defined by trade. Much like the rain, trade has been crucial to a sustainable ecosystem, has fluctuated over time, knows no borders, and has contributed to growth.

Synonymous with that trade has been the exchange of cultures. From the Ts'msyen and their neighbours to the earliest European fur traders, the Chinese, Japanese, and Indigenous cannery workers, the multinational influx of immigrants for the pulp mill and commercial fishing, and now a community where no one ethnic group makes up a majority, Prince Rupert is a microcosm for British Columbia and Canada's diversity.

Cities, like people, have characters. And the unique character of the City of Rainbows is undoubtedly colourful. Prince Rupert is not a place for pessimists, the faint-hearted, or the close-minded. It takes imagination, hard work, and open-heartedness to remain an optimist on Kaien Island. For Rupertites, the rainbow stands as a symbol for an enduring hope through struggle, a spectrum of diversity, a gateway to other places, an enriching journey, and an unquenchable sense of optimism. As a crossroads for cultures and commerce, the forecast for the City of Rainbows may be shrouded in mist, but the future always looks bright.

ACKNOWLEDGEMENTS

To my wife, thank you for allowing me to spend countless evenings and weekends to complete this book the past three and a half years.

Newspapers are the first draft of history, so I am grateful to Black Press for preserving the archives of the *Prince Rupert Daily News*, to the *Northern View*, and to all the local reporters who did the legwork.

To the hundreds of authors whose works I have cited, I stand on your shoulders and owe a debt of gratitude.

To the staff at the Prince Rupert Library, thank you for showing me how to use a microfilm reader and always lending a helping hand.

To Marilyn Carr-Harris, your artistry in recolouring Prince Rupert archival photos provided much-needed inspiration.

To the Prince Rupert Regional Archives Society for maintaining such a phenomenal collection to choose from.

To Dr. Charles Menzies, Dr. Robert Long, and Dr. Michael Shoop for their time and insights when this book was just an idea in formation.

To Ceilidh Marlow for your edits and for suggesting I submit this idea to Heritage House in the first place.

To former mayor Lee Brain for the initial encouragement to expand this idea from a three-page pamphlet into a book.

And finally, thanks to my hometown and the countless friends, family, neighbours, and colleagues who call this special place home and have played a role in shaping its past, present, and future.

NOTES

Introduction
[1] Rowse, 2006.
[2] Bowman, 1982.
[3] CBC News, 2009.
[4] Kurjata, 2018.
[5] Statistics Canada, 2021.

Chapter 1: Trade: Since Time Immemorial
[1] Bowman, 1973.
[2] Hick, 2003.
[3] Menzies and Butler, 2008.
[4] Large, 1960.
[5] Bowman, 1989.
[6] Campbell, 2005.
[7] Turunan and Turunan, 2003; Meidinger and Pojard, 1991.
[8] Kitsumkalum Band, 2023.
[9] Marsden, 2002.
[10] Edinborough, Martindale, Cook, Supernant, and Ames, 2016.
[11] Ames and Martindale, 2014.
[12] Marshall, 2006.
[13] Ames and Martindale, 2014.
[14] Hebda and Matthews, 1985; Moss et al, 2007. The Holocene Period began around 9700 BCE.
[15] Banahan, 2005; Martindale et al 2009; McLaren 2008.
[16] Ames and Martindale, 2014.
[17] Martindale et al, 2009.
[18] Langdon, 2006.
[19] MacDonald and Cybulski, 2001.
[20] Langdon, 2006.
[21] Supernant and Cookson, 2014.
[22] MacDonald, 2006.
[23] Edinborough et al, 2016.
[24] Drucker, 1943.
[25] Ames, 1991, 1996, 2006; Marshall, 2006.
[26] Blanton, 1994; Coupland, 2006.
[27] Arnold 1996; Hayden 1990, 1996; Price and Brown, 1985.
[28] Deur and Turner, 2005.
[29] Campbell and Butler, 2010; Haggan et al, 2006.
[30] Coupland, Stewart, and Patton, 2010.
[31] Langdon, 2006.
[32] Coupland et al. 2010.
[33] Wissler, 1938.
[34] Anderson, 2006.
[35] Langdon, 2006.
[36] Garfield, 1932.
[37] Langdon, 2006.
[38] Patton, 2011.
[39] Cybulski, 1992.
[40] Cybulski, 2014ab; Martindale and Marsden, 2003.
[41] Ames, 2005.
[42] Marsden, 2000; Marsden, 2002; Martindale, Letham, Supernant, Brown, Edinborough, Duelks, and Ames, 2017; Archer 2001.
[43] Buddenhagen, 2017.
[44] Ames and Martindale, 2014.
[45] Buddenhagen, 2017.
[46] ibid.
[47] ibid.
[48] There are many discrepancies in the oral records of this event. There was a Hereditary Chief for each tribe within this alliance, each with their own unique responsibilities. Some were able to exert far more power and influence than others. Additionally, there were up to fourteen different tribes, not all of which remained a part of the alliance. Hence, some records mention more than nine Chiefs.
[49] Buddenhagen, 2017.
[50] ibid.
[51] Marsden, 2002.
[52] Buddenhagen, 2017.
[53] Supernant and Cookson, 2014.
[54] Martindale and Marsden, 2003.
[55] Marsden, 2000.
[56] Ames and Martindale, 2014.

57 MacDonald, 2006.
58 Langdon, 2006.
59 MacDonald, 2006; Anderson, 2006.
60 Campbell, 2005.
61 Barbeau and Benyon, **YEAR.
62 Millenia Research Limited, 2014.
63 Inglis, 1979.
64 Hutchison, 1995.
65 MacDonald, 1969.
66 Anderson, 2006.
67 Patton, 2011.
68 ibid.
69 Campbell, 2005.
70 Halpin and Seguin, 1990.
71 Carsten and Hugh-Jones, 1995.
72 Langdon, 2006.
73 Anderson, 2006.
74 Patton, 2011.
75 Murray, 1985.
76 Ames and Martindale, 2014.
77 Langdon, 2006.
78 Langdon, 2006.
79 MacDonald, 2006.

Chapter 2: International Exchange: 1770–1830

1 Nuffield, 1990.
2 Sanchez, 2004.
3 ibid.
4 Pethick, 1976; Fisher, 1992.
5 Pethick, 1976.
6 Hick, 2003.
7 Nuffield, 1990.
8 Allen, 2004; Menzies, 2016.
9 Allen, 2004.
10 1992. *Saaban: The Tsimshian and Europeans Meet.* Eds. Brown, Dorothy, Henry Reeves, Ken Campbell, et al. *Suwilaay'msga Na Ga'Niiyatgm (Teachings of Our Grandfathers)*, Vol. 3. Prince Rupert, BC: The Tsimshian Chief for Tsimshian Children Present and Future. 14–21.
11 Translation from *Saaban*, 14–21.
12 Marsden, 1992.
13 Menzies, 2016.
14 Allen, 2004.
15 Pethick, 1976.
16 Hayes, 1999.

17 Pethick, 1976; Nuffield, 1990.
18 Hayes, 1999.
19 Nuffield, 1990.
20 ibid.
21 Fisher, 1992.
22 Harris, 1990.
23 Hayes, 1999; Fisher, 1992.
24 Marsden and Galois, 1995.
25 Fisher, 1992.
26 Martindale, 1999.
27 Anderson, 2006.
28 Campbell, 2005.
29 Fisher, 1992.
30 Allen, 2004.
31 ibid.
32 Martindale, 2003; Martindale, 2006.
33 Hayes, 1999.
34 Brown, 2008.
35 Anderson, 1960.
36 Rowse, 2006.

Chapter 3: Fort Simpson: 1836–61

1 Martindale, 2009.
2 Rowse, 2006.
3 Meilleur, 1980.
4 Marsden and Galois, 1995.
5 Barr and Green, 2014.
6 Barr and Green, 2014.
7 Meilleur, 1980.
8 Marsden and Galois, 1995.
9 Province of BC, 2023.
10 Meilleur, 1980.
11 ibid.
12 Large, 1996.
13 Grumet, 1982.
14 Meilleur, 1980.
15 Campbell, 1992.
16 Anderson, 2006.
17 Pinkerton, 1987.
18 Carrothers, 1941.
19 Fisher, 1977.
20 Meilleurm 1980.
21 Davis, 1904.
22 Rowse, 2006.
23 Martindale, 1999.
24 Dean, 1994; Martindale, 2009; Dugg, 1969.
25 Boyd, 1999; Dean, 1994; Duff, 1969.
26 Martindale, 1999.

[27] Boyd, 1999.
[28] Duff, 1965; Garfield 1939; Murray, 1985.
[29] Fisher, 1977.
[30] MacDonald and Cove, 1987.
[31] Barman, 2014.
[32] Meilleur, 1980.
[33] Campbell, 1992.
[34] ibid.
[35] Atkinson, 2008.
[36] Meilleur, 1980.
[37] ibid.
[38] Peterson, 2012.
[39] Meilleur, 1980; Knight, 1996.
[40] Meilleur, 1980.
[41] Mackie, 1997.
[42] ibid.
[43] Meilleur, 1980.
[44] Sellers, 2005.
[45] Dean, 1994.
[46] Neylan, 2000.
[47] Siegel, 2023.
[48] Marsden and Galois, 1995.
[49] ibid.
[50] Martindale, 1999, 2000, 2003, 2006; Martindale and Jurakic, 2004, 2006.
[51] Martindale, 1999.
[52] Martindale, 2009.
[53] Neylan, 2000.
[54] Marsden, 1992. *Na Amwaaltga Ts'msiyeen: The Tsimshian, Trade, and the Northwest Coast Economy. Suwilaay'msga Na Ga'niiyatgm (Teachings of Our Grandfathers)*, Vol. 1. Prince Rupert, BC: The Tsimshian Chief for Tsimshian Children Present and Future. 61.
[55] Translation from Marsden, 1992.
[56] Atkinson, 2008.
[57] Campbell, 2005.
[58] Fisher, 1992.
[59] Meilleur, 1980.

Chapter 4: Metlakatla: 1862–70
[1] Hall, 2006.
[2] Tattrie, 2014.
[3] Murray, 1985.
[4] Murray, 1985.
[5] Davis, 1904.

[6] ibid.
[7] Atkinson, 2008.
[8] Davis, 1904.
[9] Menzies, 2016.
[10] Atkinson, 2008.
[11] Seguin, 1984.
[12] Drucker, 1965.
[13] Wentworth, 1968.
[14] ibid.
[15] Murray, 1985.
[16] Boyd, 1999.
[17] Murray, 1985.
[18] Campbell, 2005.
[19] Boyd, 1999.
[20] Murray, 1985.
[21] Atkinson, 2008.
[22] MacIvor, 1993.
[23] Wentworth, 1968.
[24] Retting, 1990.
[25] Neylan, 2000.
[26] ibid.
[27] Seguin, 1984.
[28] Campbell, 2005.
[29] Usher, 1964.
[30] Atkinson, 2011.
[31] Wentworth, 1968.
[32] Murray, 1985.
[33] ibid.
[34] ibid.
[35] Askren, 2006.
[36] Atkinson, 2008.
[37] Murray, 1985.
[38] ibid.
[39] ibid..
[40] ibid.
[41] Askren, 2006.
[42] Arctander, 1909.
[43] Murray, 1985.
[44] ibid.
[45] ibid.
[46] Arctander, 1909.
[47] Murray, 1985.
[48] Federal Indian Day School Class Action, 1997.
[49] Murray, 1985.
[50] Campbell, 2005.
[51] Dean, 1994; Fisher, 1977; Murray, 1985; Wolf, 1982.
[52] Duff, 1969.

53 Dunn, 1978.
54 Neylan, 1999.
55 Atkinson, 2008.
56 ibid.
57 ibid.
58 Barman, 2014.
59 Atkinson, 2008.
60 Atkinson, 2011.
61 Campbell, 2005.
62 Atkinson, 2008.
63 Fisher, 1992.

Chapter 5: Port Essington: 1871–1902
1 Lovisek, 2007.
2 Gough, 2016.
3 ibid.
4 Campbell, 2005.
5 Putnam, Taylor and Kettle, 2007.
6 Douglas, 1860.
7 Thomson, 2016.
8 BC Black History, 2023.
9 Ormsby, 2008.
10 ibid.
11 Ormsby, 1971.
12 Campbell, 2005.
13 Lovisek, 2007.
14 Boyd, 1999.
15 Barman, 2014.
16 Gough, 1971.
17 Bennett, 2000.
18 Chamberlin, 1888.
19 Large, 1958.
20 ibid.; Bowman, 1982.
21 Campbell, 2005.
22 Clayton, 1989.
23 Bowman, 1982.
24 Clayton, 1992; Appleyard, 1904.
25 Bowman, 1982; Large, 1958.
26 Harris, 1990.
27 Miller, 1998.
28 Rowse, 2006.
29 Seguin, 1984; Bennett, 2000.
30 Bowman, 1982.
31 Large, 1958.
32 *Prince Rupert Daily News*, 1961.
33 Bowman, 1982.
34 Campbell, 2005.
35 Anderson, 2006.
36 ibid.
37 Lovisek, 2007.
38 Menzies, 2016.
39 Anderson, 2006; Clayton, 1989.
40 Seguin, 1984.
41 Menzies, 2016.
42 Campbell, 2005.
43 Anderson, 2006.
44 Joint Indian Reserve Commission, 2023.
45 Harris, 2002.
46 ibid.
47 ibid.
48 ibid.
49 ibid.
50 Gadacz, 2006.
51 Menzies, 2016.
52 Cassidy, 1983.
53 ibid.
54 Harris, 2002.
55 Cassidy, 1983.
56 ibid.
57 Cassidy, 1983.
58 Clayton, 1992.
59 Harris, 2002.
60 Hayashi et al, 2016.
61 Chow, 2000.
62 Hayashi et al, 2016.
63 Discover Nikkei, n.d.
64 Hayashi et al, 2016.
65 ibid.
66 Chow, 2000.
67 Clayton, 1989.
68 Chow, 2000.
69 Greer, 1999.
70 Dorsey, 1897.
71 Appleyard, 1897.
72 Raptis, 2011.
73 Clayton, 1992.
74 Bowman, 1982.

Chapter 6: Full Steam Ahead: 1903–07
1 Dorsey, 1897.
2 Seguin, 1984.
3 Rowse, 2006.
4 Campbell, 1992.
5 Downs, 1971.
6 Bennett, 2006.
7 Downs, 1971.

[8] Large, 1996.
[9] ibid.
[10] ibid.
[11] Hick, 2003.
[12] Bowman, 1973.
[13] ibid.
[14] Rowse, 2006.
[15] Hick, 2003.
[16] Bowman, 1973.
[17] Butler, 2012.
[18] Grand Trunk Pacific Railway, 1912.
[19] Bowman, 1973.
[20] McDonald, 1990.
[21] Leonard, 1996.
[22] Roy, 1989.
[23] McDonald, 1990.
[24] Leonard, 1996.
[25] McDonald, 1990.
[26] Leonard, 1996.
[27] ibid.
[28] Report of Select Standing Committee, 1906.
[29] Leonard, 1996; McDonald, 1990.
[30] Spencer, 2007.
[31] ibid.
[32] Oxford Reference, 2023.
[33] Spencer, 2007.
[34] ibid.
[35] ibid.
[36] ibid.
[37] ibid.
[38] Pettigrew, 2013.
[39] Encyclopedia Britannica, 2023.
[40] Spencer, 2007.

Chapter 7: The Tip of the Rainbow: 1908–12

[1] Grand Trunk Pacific Railway, 1912.
[2] ibid.
[3] ibid.
[4] Greer, 1999.
[5] Hick, 2003.
[6] Canada Historic Places, 2008.
[7] Rowse, 2006.
[8] Leonard, 199.
[9] Bowman, 1973.
[10] Rowse, 2006.
[11] Kiffer, 2007.
[12] Leonard, 1996.

[13] *Prince Rupert Daily News*, 1927.
[14] Kiffer, 2010.
[15] Bowman, 1973.
[16] Bowman, 1989.
[17] Prince Rupert City and Regional Archives Society, 2010.
[18] Bowman, 1973.
[19] Large, 1960.
[20] *Prince Rupert Daily News*, 1911.
[21] Fisher, 1990.
[22] Leonard, 1996.
[23] Madsen, 2014.
[24] Leonard, 1996.
[25] Fisher, 1991.
[26] *Prince Rupert Daily News*, 1911.
[27] Fisher, 1991.
[28] ibid.
[29] Leonard, 1996.
[30] Siegel, 2023.
[31] Garden, 2021.
[32] Rowse, 2006.
[33] Leonard, 1996.
[34] Garden, 2021.
[35] Leonard, 1996.
[36] ibid.
[37] ibid.
[38] ibid.
[39] ibid.
[40] ibid.
[41] Greer, 1999.
[42] ibid.
[43] Prince Rupert, Daily News, 1911.
[44] The Empire, 1909.
[45] Hayashi et al, 2016.
[46] Roy, 1989.
[47] Leonard, 1996; Roy, 1989.
[48] Leonard, 1996.
[49] ibid.
[50] Roy, 1989.
[51] Greer, 1999; Roy, 1989.
[52] Greer, 1999.
[53] Prince Rupert City and Regional Archives Society, 2010.
[54] House of Commons, 1920.
[55] Davies, 1980.
[56] Prince Rupert City and Regional Archives Society, 2010.
[57] Large, 1960.

Chapter 8: A Titanic Loss: 1912–14

[1] Leonard, 1996.
[2] Murphy, 1992.
[3] Encyclopedia Titanica, 2023.
[4] Kiffer, 2012; Encyclopedia Titanica, 2023.
[5] Butler, 2012.
[6] Encyclopedia Titanic, 2023.
[7] Leonard, 1996.
[8] CN Rail, 1985.
[9] Large, 1960.
[10] Hacking, 1995.
[11] Campbell, 1981.
[12] Leonard, 1996.
[13] *Prince Rupert Daily News*, 1912.
[14] Bowman, 1982.
[15] McGovern, 1960.
[16] Marsh, 2006.
[17] Large, 1960.
[18] Bowman, 1973.
[19] Leonard, 1996.
[20] ibid.
[21] Davenport-Hines, 2012.
[22] Leonard, 1996.
[23] ibid.
[24] ibid.
[25] Warman, 1908.
[26] Leonard, 1996.
[27] Warman, 1908.
[28] Leonard, 1996.
[29] ibid.
[30] ibid.
[31] ibid.
[32] ibid.
[33] ibid.
[34] ibid.
[35] ibid.
[36] *Prince Rupert Daily News*, 1981.
[37] Murphy, 1992.
[38] ibid.
[39] Leonard, 1996.
[40] Murphy, 1992.
[41] ibid.
[42] ibid.
[43] ibid.
[44] Shannon, 2012.
[45] Regehr, 1920.
[46] Murphy, 1992.
[47] Peebles, 2021.
[48] Leonard, 1996.
[49] Prince Rupert Port Authority, 2021.
[50] Leonard, 1996.
[51] Murphy, 1992.
[52] Regehr, 1920.
[53] Hick, 2003.
[54] Bowman, 1982.
[55] *Prince Rupert Daily News*, 1956.
[56] Downs, 1971.

Chapter 9: Halibut Capital of the World: 1914–38

[1] *Prince Rupert Daily News*, 1917.
[2] *Prince Rupert Daily News*, 1916.
[3] ibid.
[4] Bowman, 1982.
[5] *Prince Rupert Daily News*, 1914.
[6] ibid.
[7] Greer, 1999.
[8] Scott, 1918.
[9] Winegard, 2012.
[10] Tattersfield, 2021.
[11] *Prince Rupert Daily News*, 1956.
[12] Zuehlke, 2017.
[13] ibid.
[14] Tattersfield, 2021.
[15] Zuehlke, 2017.
[16] *Prince Rupert Daily News*, 1920.
[17] House of Commons, 1920.
[18] ibid.
[19] BC Labour Heritage Centre, 2019.
[20] *Prince Rupert Daily News*, 1919.
[21] Madsen, 2014.
[22] *Prince Rupert Daily News*, 1922; *Prince Rupert Daily News*, 1923.
[23] Large, 1960.
[24] CN Rail, 1985.
[25] Large, 1996.
[26] *Prince Rupert Daily News*, 1942.
[27] Rowse, 2006.
[28] Butler and Campbell, 2003.
[29] *Prince Rupert Daily News*, 1922.
[30] Japanese Canadian History, 2023.
[31] *Prince Rupert Daily News* editorial, 1920.
[32] *Prince Rupert Daily News*, 1921.
[33] *Prince Rupert Daily News*, 1920–29.
[34] *Prince Rupert Daily News*, 1923.
[35] *Prince Rupert Daily News*, 1929.

36 ibid.
37 Large, 1960.
38 ibid.
39 Kiffer, 2007.
40 Bowman, 1982.
41 Fisher, 1991.
42 *Prince Rupert Daily News*, 1920.
43 Fisher, 1991.
44 ibid.
45 ibid.
46 Chow, 2000.
47 *Prince Rupert Daily News*, 1922.
48 Fisher, 1991.

Chapter 10: The Second World War: 1939–45

1 City of Prince Rupert, 2023.
2 Adams, 1938.
3 *Prince Rupert Daily News*, 1939.
4 Bowman, 1987.
5 *Prince Rupert Daily News*, 1939.
6 Abbott, 1994.
7 *Prince Rupert Daily News*, 1941.
8 Bowman, 1987.
9 *Prince Rupert Daily News*, 1941.
10 Bowman, 1987.
11 Kronbauer, 2021.
12 *Prince Rupert Daily News*, 1942.
13 Hayashi et al, 2016.
14 *Prince Rupert Daily News*, 1942.
15 ibid.
16 ibid.
17 Large, 1960.
18 Hayashi et al, 2016.
19 CBC Learning, 2001.
20 *Prince Rupert Daily News*, 1942.
21 *Prince Rupert Daily News*, 1944.
22 *Prince Rupert Daily News*, 1945.
23 *Prince Rupert Daily News*, 1942.
24 ibid.
25 Bowman, 1973; Bowman, 1987.
26 ibid.
27 *Prince Rupert Daily News*, 1942.
28 Cloe, 2017.
29 Bowman, 1987.
30 Savage, 2012.
31 Tucker, 1952.
32 Gedney, 1986.
33 Coyle, 2010.
34 Bowman, 1973.
35 Roy, 1976.
36 *Prince Rupert Daily News*, 1945.
37 Bowman, 1987.
38 ibid.
39 Bowman, 1989.
40 ibid.
41 Knight, 2005.
42 Canadian War Museum, 2023.
43 Adleman and Walton, 2004.
44 Roy, 1976.
45 history.com, 2009.
46 Stacey, 1948.
47 Bowman, 1987.
48 Grimshaw, 1992.
49 Kiffer, 2007.
50 Large, 1960.
51 *Prince Rupert Daily News*, 1944.
52 Province of BC, 1942.
53 Bowman, 1987.
54 *Prince Rupert Daily News*, 1944.
55 Bowman, 1973.
56 Edinburgh News, 2016.
57 Savage, 2012.
58 Bowman, 1982.
59 ibid.
60 *Prince Rupert Daily News*, 1945.
61 Bowman, 1982.
62 Savage, 2012.
63 Bowman, 1987.
64 Bowman, 1973.
65 *Prince Rupert Daily News*, 1945.
66 Bowman, 1975.
67 *Prince Rupert Northern View*, 2012.
68 Dalton, 2013.
69 Bowman, 1973.

Chapter 11: Here Comes the Boom: 1946–59

1 Bowman, 1987.
2 Bowman, 1973.
3 *Prince Rupert Daily News*, April 1947.
4 *Prince Rupert Daily News*, 1947.
5 Lax Kw'alaams, 2006.
6 Atkinson, 2017.
7 Harrington, 1949.
8 Bowman, 1996.
9 *Prince Rupert Daily News*, 1947.
10 Atkinson, 2017.

[11] Atkinson, 2017.
[12] Harrington, 1949.
[13] Bowman, 1982.
[14] *Prince Rupert Daily News*, 1947.
[15] *Prince Rupert Daily News*, 1948.
[16] *Prince Rupert Daily News*, 1949.
[17] *Prince Rupert Daily News*, 1949.
[18] *Prince Rupert Daily News*, 1953.
[19] Bowman, 1973.
[20] Prince Rupert City and Regional Archives, 2010.
[21] *Prince Rupert Daily News*, 1950.
[22] *Prince Rupert Daily News*, 1953.
[23] *Prince Rupert Daily News*, 1951.
[24] *Prince Rupert Daily News*, 1951.
[25] Brant, 2020.
[26] *Prince Rupert Daily News*, 1964.
[27] *Prince Rupert Daily News*, 1953.
[28] *Prince Rupert Daily News*, 1962; 1963.
[29] *Prince Rupert Daily News*, 1953.
[30] Barager, 2019.
[31] Lux, 2016.
[32] Barager, 2019.
[33] Wilt, 2020.
[34] Barager, 2019.
[35] Barager, 2019.
[36] Rudy Kelly, Episode 2, Apache Passing.
[37] Barager, 2019.
[38] Barager, 2019.
[39] Barager, 2019.
[40] Barager, 2019.
[41] *Prince Rupert Daily News*, 1957.
[42] *Prince Rupert Daily News*, 1957.
[43] Native Voice, 1958.
[44] *Prince Rupert Daily News*, 1958.
[45] Campbell, 2004.
[46] Barager, 2019.
[47] Campbell, 2004.
[48] *Prince Rupert Daily News*, 1958.
[49] *Prince Rupert Daily News*, 1958.
[50] *Prince Rupert Daily News*, 1958.
[51] Barager, 2019.
[52] Campbell, 2004.
[53] Barager, 2019.
[54] Barager, 2019.
[55] Barager, 2019.
[56] *Prince Rupert Daily News*, 1958.
[57] *Prince Rupert Daily News*, 1959.
[58] *Prince Rupert Daily News*, 1958.
[59] *Prince Rupert Daily News*, 1960.
[60] *Prince Rupert Daily News*, 1960.
[61] *Prince Rupert Daily News*, 1956.
[62] *Prince Rupert Daily News*, 1956-60.
[63] *Prince Rupert Daily News*, 1960.
[64] *Prince Rupert Daily News*, 1959; 1960.
[65] *Prince Rupert Daily News*, 1958.
[66] *Prince Rupert Daily News*, 1960.
[67] *Prince Rupert Daily News*, 1959-60.
[68] *Prince Rupert Daily News*, 1957.
[69] *Prince Rupert Daily News*, 1955-60.
[70] BC Labour Heritage Centre, 2019.
[71] *Prince Rupert Daily News*, 1960.
[72] *Prince Rupert Daily News*, 1960.
[73] *Prince Rupert Daily News*, 1957.
[74] *Prince Rupert Daily News*, 1953; 1957.
[75] *Prince Rupert Daily News*, 1957.
[76] Meissner, 2017.
[77] *Prince Rupert Daily News*, 1960.
[78] *Prince Rupert Daily News*, 1960.

Chapter 12: Boom: 1960–82

[1] *Prince Rupert Daily News*, 1961; 1963.
[2] *Prince Rupert Daily News*, 1962.
[3] *Prince Rupert Daily News*, 1961.
[4] *Prince Rupert Daily News*, 1968.
[5] *Prince Rupert Daily News*, 1966.
[6] *Prince Rupert Daily News*, 1961;62;63;64.
[7] *Prince Rupert Daily News*, 1965.
[8] *Prince Rupert Daily News*, 1964;67.
[9] *Prince Rupert Daily News*, 1971; 1972.
[10] Bowman, 1982.
[11] Alaska Marine Highway System, 2023; *Prince Rupert Daily News*, 1968.
[12] *Prince Rupert Daily News*, 1967; 1968.
[13] *Prince Rupert Daily News*, 1968.
[14] *Prince Rupert Daily News*, 1970.
[15] Bowman, 1982 + *Prince Rupert Daily News*, 1970; 1971.
[16] *Prince Rupert Daily News*, 1966; 1967.
[17] Bowman, 1982.
[18] *Prince Rupert Daily News*, 1971; Bowman, 1973.
[19] Hick, 2003.
[20] Byrne, 2015.
[21] *Prince Rupert Daily News*, 1973.
[22] *Prince Rupert Daily News*, 1971.

23 Menzies, 2008.
24 Millenia Research Limited, 2014.
25 Millenia Research Limited, 2014.
26 *Prince Rupert Daily News*, 1975.
27 Prince Rupert Port Authority, 2023.
28 *Prince Rupert Daily News*, 1981.
29 *Prince Rupert Daily News*, 1982.
30 *Prince Rupert Daily News*, 1963; Macrotrends, 2023.
31 *Prince Rupert Daily News*, 1969.
32 *Prince Rupert Daily News*, 1968.
33 *Prince Rupert Daily News*, 1983; 1980.
34 *Prince Rupert Daily News*, 1981.
35 Stanger, 2013.
36 *Prince Rupert Daily News*, 1972.
37 Governor General of Canada, 2022.
38 Northern British Columbia Archives and Special Collections, 2009.
39 *Prince Rupert Daily News*, 1972.
40 *Prince Rupert Daily News*, 1977; Northern British Columbia Archives and Special Collections, 2009.
41 *Prince Rupert Daily News*, 1975.
42 Taylor, 2022.
43 *Prince Rupert Daily News*, 1975.
44 *Prince Rupert Daily News*, 1974.
45 *Prince Rupert Daily News*, 1975.
46 Hume, 2017.
47 Northern British Columbia Archives and Special Collections, 2009.
48 Comox Valley Walk of Achievement, 2012.
49 Hume, 2017.
50 Roy, 2008.
51 Stanger, 2013.
52 Powell and Sullivan, 2006.
53 Mussett, 2021.
54 Chow, 2000.
55 *Prince Rupert Daily News*, 1961.
56 Memory BC, 2023.
57 Wahl, 2008.
58 Huculak, 1984.
59 Nayar, 2012.
60 Melegrito, 2015.
61 Mussett, 2021.
62 Norris and Clatworthy, 2010.
63 Friendship House, 2023.
64 Mulder, 1994.
65 CPTDB Wiki, 2023.
66 Gitmaxmak'ay Nisga'a Society, 2023.
67 Haida Nation, 2023; Statistics Canada, 2016.
68 Nayar, 2012.
69 *Prince Rupert Daily News*, 1976.

Chapter 13: Bubble: 1982–93
1 *Prince Rupert Daily News*, 1982.
2 *Prince Rupert Daily News*, 1977.
3 *Prince Rupert Daily News*, 1975; 1979.
4 *Prince Rupert Daily News*, 1974.
5 *Prince Rupert Daily News*, 1976; 1977.
6 *Prince Rupert Daily News*, 1980.
7 *Prince Rupert Daily News*, 1982; 1983; 1984; 1985; 1986.
8 *Prince Rupert Daily News*, 1992; 1995.
9 *Prince Rupert Daily News*, 1994.
10 *Prince Rupert Daily News*, 1981.
11 *Prince Rupert Daily News*, 1982.
12 *Prince Rupert Daily News*, 1979.
13 *Prince Rupert Daily News*, 1981.
14 Al-Kodmary, Kheir, Mir, Ali, 2013.
15 *Prince Rupert Daily News*, 1981.
16 *Prince Rupert Daily News*, 1982.
17 *Prince Rupert Daily News*, 1976.
18 *Prince Rupert Daily News*, 1983.
19 *Prince Rupert Daily News*, 1982.
20 *Prince Rupert Daily News*, 1982.
21 *Prince Rupert Daily News*, 1986.
22 *Prince Rupert Daily News*, 1982.
23 *Prince Rupert Daily News*, 1974; 1975; 1981; 1983.
24 *Prince Rupert Daily News*, 1982; 1983.
25 *Prince Rupert Daily News*, 1982.
26 *Prince Rupert Daily News*, 1982.
27 *Prince Rupert Daily News*, 1978.
28 *Prince Rupert Daily News*, 1982.
29 Prince Rupert City and Regional Archives, 2023.
30 *Prince Rupert Daily News*, 1981.
31 Bowman, 1982.
32 *Prince Rupert Daily News*, 1983.
33 *Prince Rupert Daily News*, 1981.
34 *Prince Rupert Daily News*, 1982.
35 *Prince Rupert Daily News*, 1972; 1974; 1979.
36 *Prince Rupert Daily News*, 1980.

[37] *Prince Rupert Daily News*, 1978.

[38] *Prince Rupert Daily News*, 1982.

[39] *Prince Rupert Daily News*, 1984.

[40] *Prince Rupert Daily News*, 1984.

[41] *Prince Rupert Daily News*, 1984.

[42] CN Rail, 1985.

[43] *Prince Rupert Daily News*, 1985.

[44] McIver, 1985.

[45] *Prince Rupert Daily News*, 1984.

[46] *Prince Rupert Daily News*, 1984.

[47] *Prince Rupert Daily News*, 1985.

[48] *Prince Rupert Daily News*, 1984;1985.

[49] *Prince Rupert Daily News*, 1981.

[50] *Prince Rupert Daily News*, 1985.

[51] *Prince Rupert Daily News*, 1985; 1986.

[52] *Prince Rupert Daily News*, 1987.

[53] *Prince Rupert Daily News*, 1990.

[54] *Prince Rupert Daily News*, 1990.

[55] *Prince Rupert Daily News*, 1958; 1979.

[56] *Prince Rupert Daily News*, 1957.

[57] *Prince Rupert Daily News*, 1993.

[58] *Prince Rupert Daily News*, 1975.

[59] *Prince Rupert Daily News*, 1983.

[60] *Prince Rupert Daily News*, 1981.

[61] *Prince Rupert Daily News*, 1982.

[62] *Prince Rupert Daily News*, 1969.

[63] *Prince Rupert Daily News*, 1969.

[64] *Prince Rupert Daily News*, 1969.

[65] *Prince Rupert Daily News*, 1972.

[66] *Prince Rupert Daily News*, 1973.

[67] https://www.thefreelibrary.com/
Lester+was+B.C.%27s+longest-
serving+mayor.-a0153191202.

[68] *Prince Rupert Daily News*, 1990.

[69] *Prince Rupert Daily News*, 1964.

[70] *Prince Rupert Daily News*, 1981.

[71] *Prince Rupert Daily News*, 1975; 1979.

[72] *Prince Rupert Daily News*, 1965.

[73] *Prince Rupert Daily News*, 1982.

[74] *Prince Rupert Daily News*, 1977; 1983.

[75] *Prince Rupert Daily News*, 1983.

[76] *Prince Rupert Daily News*, 1987.

[77] *Prince Rupert Daily News*, 1982.

[78] *Prince Rupert Daily News*, 1983.

[79] *Prince Rupert Daily News*, 1984.

[80] *Prince Rupert Daily News*, 1990.

[81] *Prince Rupert Daily News*, 1985.

[82] Memory BC, 2023.

Chapter 14: Bust: 1993–2006

[1] https://anglicanjournal.com/
caledonia-faces-challenge-with-
hope-424/

[2] https://www.ctvnews.ca/b-c-towns-
suffer-as-major-paper-companies-
refuse-to-pay-tax-1.461569?cache=yes
%3FclipId%3D375756.

[3] *Prince Rupert Daily News*, 1990; 1991.

[4] *Prince Rupert Daily News*, 1992.

[5] Gordon and McCormack, 2020.

[6] *Prince Rupert Daily News*, 1993.

[7] *Prince Rupert Daily News*, 1964.

[8] Prince Rupert Daily New, 1965.

[9] *Prince Rupert Daily News*, 1966.

[10] *Prince Rupert Daily News*, 1966.

[11] *Prince Rupert Daily News*, 1970.

[12] *Prince Rupert Daily News*, 1970.

[13] *Prince Rupert Daily News*, 1970; 1971.

[14] Sexty, 1981.

[15] *Prince Rupert Daily News*, 1973.

[16] Sexty, 1981.

[17] *Prince Rupert Daily News*, 1973.

[18] Sexty, 1981.

[19] *Prince Rupert Daily News*, 1975.

[20] *Prince Rupert Daily News*, 1974, 1975.

[21] *Prince Rupert Daily News*, 1976.

[22] Sexty, 1981.

[23] *Prince Rupert Daily News*, 1979.

[24] *Prince Rupert Daily News*, 1978.

[25] Packman, 1977.

[26] Waldichuk, 1962.

[27] Raedemaecker, 2003.

[28] Raedemaecker, 2003.

[29] *Prince Rupert Daily News*, 1970;1973;
1977; Packman, 1977.

[30] *Prince Rupert Daily News*, 1974.

[31] *Prince Rupert Daily News*, 1973.

[32] *Prince Rupert Daily News*, 1979.

[33] *Prince Rupert Daily News*, 1979.

[34] Ombudsman of British Columbia,
1985.

[35] *Prince Rupert Daily News*, 1981; 1985.

[36] *Prince Rupert Daily News*, 1982.

[37] *Prince Rupert Daily News*, 1983.

[38] *Prince Rupert Daily News*, 1984.

[39] *Prince Rupert Daily News*, 1983.

[40] *Prince Rupert Daily News*, 1983.

41 *Prince Rupert Daily News*, 1982.

42 *Prince Rupert Daily News*, 1984.

43 Ombudsman of British Columbia, 1985.

44 Ombudsman of British Columbia, 1985.

45 Province of BC, 1999; Hunter, 1998.

46 *Prince Rupert Daily News*, 1986.

47 *Prince Rupert Daily News*, 1991; 1992; 1993.

48 *Prince Rupert Daily News*, 1993.

49 *Prince Rupert Daily News*, 1994.

50 *Prince Rupert Daily News*, 1997.

51 *Prince Rupert Daily News*, 1994.

52 *Prince Rupert Daily News*, 1997.

53 Hunter, 1998.

54 *Prince Rupert Daily News*, 1997.

55 Province of BC, 2002.

56 *Prince Rupert Daily News*, 1997.

57 Province of BC, 2002.

58 Schneider, 1997.

59 Hunter, 1998.

60 Province of BC, 2002.

61 Hunter, 1998.

62 Stirling, 2005.

63 Prince Rupert Economic Development Commission, 2002.

64 Province of BC, 1999.

65 Province of BC, 2002.

66 Stirling, 2005.

67 *Prince Rupert Daily News*, 2005.

68 Brown, 2019.

69 Thomas, 2015.

70 *Prince Rupert Daily News*, 2005.

71 Stirling, 2005; *Prince Rupert Daily News*, 2005.

72 Stirling, 2005.

73 *Prince Rupert Daily News*, 2005.

74 *Prince Rupert Daily News*, 2005.

75 Supreme Court of British Columbia, 2013; *Prince Rupert Daily News*, 2005.

76 Urbas, 2022.

77 Supreme Court of British Columbia, 2013.

78 *Prince Rupert Daily News*, 2008.

79 Thomas, 2012.

80 *Prince Rupert Daily News*, 2009.

81 Urbas, 2022.

82 *Prince Rupert Daily News*, 1977.

83 *Prince Rupert Daily News*, 1977 – 1983.

84 *Prince Rupert Daily News*, 1996, 1997; Powroznik and Sandy, 1993.

85 Dal Monte, 2021.

86 Mickleburgh, 2000.

87 Braid, 2016.

88 Province of BC, 2018.

89 Mickleburgh, 2000. https://www.theglobeandmail.com/news/national/miller-provides-oasis-of-calm-in-stormy-bc/article1036852/.

90 BC Stats, 2001.

91 *Prince Rupert Daily News*, 1996.

92 Nelson and Turris, 2004.

93 Gislason, 2006.

94 BC Conservation Data Centre, 2022.

95 Olesiuk, Ellis and Ford, 2005.

96 *Prince Rupert Daily News*, 1981.

97 *Prince Rupert Daily News*, 1994.

98 *Prince Rupert Daily News*, 1994.

99 Depalma, 1998.

100 Brown, 2005.

101 Kiffer, 2007.

102 Kiffer, 2007.

103 Brown, 2005.

104 Brown, 2005.

105 Wood, 1997.

106 *Prince Rupert Daily News*, 1997.

107 Germina, 1997.

108 Brown, 2005.

109 Brown, 2005.

110 Brown, 2005.

111 Anderson and Keene, 1997; Wood, 1997.

112 Wood, 1997.

113 ABC News, 2001.

114 Butler, 2005; Gislason, 2006; Pinkerton et al., 2014.

115 Byrne, 2015.

116 Ewins, 1999.

117 Byrne, 2015.

118 Whiteley, 2007.

119 *Prince Rupert Daily News*, 1997; 1999; Halseth, Ryser and Durken, 2005.

120 Spelter and Alderman, 2005.

121 Kolenko, 2013.

122 Kolenko, 2013.

123 Ecotrust Canada, 2004.

124 *Prince Rupert Daily News*, 1993.

125 *Prince Rupert Daily News*, 2005; 2008.

126 Canadian Press, 2007.

127 Statistics Canada, 2010.

128 Ryser et al, 2008.

129 Statistics Canada, 2006.

130 *Prince Rupert Daily News*, 2008; 2010.

131 *Prince Rupert Daily News*, 1995.

132 *Prince Rupert Daily News*, 1995; 1996.

133 *Prince Rupert Daily News*, 2006.

134 *Prince Rupert Daily News*, 1995.

135 Vassallo, 2004.

136 Statistics Canada, 2006a.

137 Statistics Canada, 2006b.

138 prspecialevents.com/seafest-2023.html.

Chapter 15: Recovery: 2007–23

1 *Prince Rupert Daily News*, 1990.

2 *Prince Rupert Daily News*, 1969.

3 Lough, 2017a.

4 Whiteley, 2007.

5 Lough, 2017a.

6 Lough, 2017b.

7 Whiteley, 2007.

8 California Apparel News, 2007.

9 *Prince Rupert Daily News*, 2010.

10 Wilson and Summerville, 2008.

11 *Prince George Citizen*, April 15, 2006.

12 *Prince Rupert Daily News*, 2006.

13 Byrne, 2015.

14 Government of Canada (2008).

15 Menzies, 2008.

16 *Prince Rupert Daily News*, 2008.

17 *Prince Rupert Daily News*, 2008 [Ritchie, L. Coast Ts'msyen hopeful port talks moving ahead] July 03.

18 Baker, T. (2008). RTI and Coast Ts'msyen make history on the dotted line. June 26th.

19 Hoekstra, 2011.

20 *Prince Rupert Daily News*, 2006.

21 *Prince Rupert Daily News*, 2013.

22 Statistics Canada, 2015.

23 BC Ministry of Agriculture and Food, 2020.

24 Thomas, 2011.

25 Thomas, 2012.

26 Campbell, 2015.

27 Butler, C.

28 Campbell, 2016.

29 *Prince Rupert Northern View*, 2013.

30 Statistics Canada 2013, 2013.

31 Union of BC Municipalities, 2014.

32 *Prince Rupert Daily News*, 2010.

33 Altagas, 2017.

34 Crawford, 2017.

35 *Prince Rupert Northern View*, 2018.

36 Grant Thornton, 2017.

37 BC Ministry of Agriculture and Food, 2020.

38 Kelly, 2017; Gareau, 2017.

39 Lough, 2018.

40 Province of BC, 2019.

41 Supreme Court of British Columbia, 2012.

42 Canadian Press, 2013.

43 Thomas, 2012.

44 City of Prince Rupert, 2013.

45 Supreme Court of British Columbia, 2019.

46 Thomas, 2014.

47 Supreme Court of British Columbia, 2015.

48 Thomas, July 16, 2014.

49 Perry, 2014.

50 Thomas, July 16, 2014.

51 Civicinfo, 2014.

52 Global News, 2014.

53 Colonial Coal, 2018.

54 Supreme Court of British Columbia, 2019.

55 Supreme Court of British Columbia, 2019.

56 Urbas, 2019.

57 Supreme Court of British Columbia, 2019.

58 Brown, 2019.

59 Bartlett, 2018.

60 Pembina, 2021.

61 Millar, 2022.

62 Richesson, 2021.

63 McElhanney, 2022.

64 Prince Rupert City and Regional Archives, 2013.

[65] *Prince Rupert Daily News*, 1995.
[66] Moyer, 1954.
[67] Prince Rupert Archives, 2013.
[68] Orton, 2014.
[69] Kiffer, 2007.
[70] Lornie et al, 1999.
[71] House of Commons, 1999.
[72] Hale, November 19, 2011.
[73] Hale, November 16, 2011.
[74] City of Prince Rupert, 2014.
[75] ReDesign Rupert, 2019.
[76] Kurjata, 2020.
[77] ibid.
[78] Millar, March 26, 2020.
[79] CBC News, 2021.
[80] Holliday, 2021.
[81] Millar, April 20, 2020.

Chapter 16: Where Are We Now? Where Are We Going?: 2024 and Beyond

[1] *Prince Rupert Daily News*, 1991.
[2] *Prince Rupert Daily News*, 1943.
[3] Prince Rupert Port Authority, 2023.
[4] *Prince Rupert Daily News*, 1981; 1982; 1984.
[5] Vopak, 2023.
[6] Statistics Canada, 2021.
[7] City of Prince Rupert, 2024.
[8] Canopy Planet, 2023.
[9] Great Bear Rainforest Education and Awareness Trust, 2020.
[10] Canopy Planet, 2023.
[11] Cruise Industry News, 2022.
[12] *Prince Rupert Daily News*, 2006.
[13] Cocullo, 2019.
[14] Prince Rupert Port Authority, 2023.
[15] *Prince Rupert Daily News*, 2003; 2004; 2005.
[16] *Prince Rupert Daily News*, 2006.
[17] ibid.
[18] *Prince Rupert Daily News*, 1996.
[19] Trillium Business Strategies Inc., 2003.
[20] UNESCO, 2023.
[21] *Prince Rupert Daily News*, 1965.
[22] Thomas, 2011.
[23] Connected Coast, 2023.
[24] Dataspan, 2023.
[25] Roach, 2020.

[26] *Prince Rupert Daily News*, 1983.
[27] ACEC-BC Awards, 2023.
[28] Millar, 2023b.
[29] Thomas, 2006; Canadian Environmental Assessment Agency, 2012.
[30] Sea Breeze Power Corp, 2023.
[31] Cornett, 2006.
[32] Bennett, 2012.
[33] Callaghan, 2017; Wouters, 2018.
[34] City of Prince Rupert, 2023; Lough, 2018.
[35] *Prince Rupert Daily News*, 1981.
[36] *Prince Rupert Daily News*, 1987.
[37] *Prince Rupert Daily News*, 1963.
[38] *Prince Rupert Daily News*, 1984.
[39] City Spaces, 2022.
[40] Millar, January 11, 2023.
[41] *Prince Rupert Daily News*, 1995.
[42] Wainwright, 2003.
[43] *Prince Rupert Northern View*, 2011.
[44] Lough, 2017.
[45] Cow Bay Marina, 2023.
[46] Cocullo, July 24, 2019.
[47] Millar, 2022.
[48] Millar, 2021.
[49] BC Ferries, 2022.
[50] Prince Rupert Airport, 2021.
[51] Prince Rupert Port Authority, 2022.
[52] CBC Daybreak North, 2023.
[53] Bailey, 2023.
[54] Azizi, 2021.
[55] Extreme Weather Watch, 2023.
[56] Cocullo, 2019b.
[57] Silverthorn, G. (1944). June 09. *Prince Rupert Daily News*.
[58] Anonymous poet, *Prince Rupert Daily News* March 13th, 1943.

BIBLIOGRAPHY

[Unknown]. 1910. "Prince Rupert Journal." N. Newspapers - Prince Rupert Journal.
Prince Rupert, B.C. : O. H. Nelson. August 22. doi:http://dx.doi.org/10.14288/
1.0311863.

Abbott, George M. 1994. "Duff Pattullo and the Coalition Controversy of 1941." *BC
Studies* 102 (Summer 1994).

ABC News. 2001. "Canada, U.S. Declare End to Salmon War." Last modified January 3,
2001. https://abcnews.go.com/Technology/story?id=99350&page=1.

ACEC-BC Awards. 2023. "Woodworth Dam Optimization." https://acecbcawards.com/
2023-awards/2023-municipal-civil-infrastructure/woodworth-dam-optimization/.

Adams, John Q. 1938. "Prince Rupert, British Columbia." *Economic Geography* 14:2.
167–83.

Akrigg, G.P.V, and Helen Akrigg. 1975. *British Columbia Chronicle, 1778–1846:
Adventures by Sea and Land.* Vancouver: Discovery Press.

Al-Kodmany, Kheir, and Mir M. Ali. 2013. *The Future of the City: Tall Buildings and
Urban Design.* Ashurst, UK: WIT Press. 369.

Altagas. 2017. "Altagas Announces Positive FID on Canada's First West Coast Propane
Export Terminal." Press release, January 3, 2017. https://www.altagas.ca/
newsroom/news-releases/altagas-announces-positive-fid-canadas-first-west-
coast-propane-export.

Ames, Kenneth A. 1991. "The Archaeology of the Longue Durée: Temporal and
Spatial Scale in the Evolution of Social Complexity on the Southern Northwest
Coast." *Antiquity* 65:935–45.

———. 1996. "Life in the Big House: Household Labour and Dwelling Size on the
Northwest Coast." *People who Lived in Big Houses: Archaeological Perspectives on
Large Domestic Structures.* Gary G. Coupland and E.B. Banning, eds. Madison,
WI: Prehistory Press. 131–50.

———. 2005. *The North Coast Prehistory Project Excavations in Prince Rupert Harbour,
British Columbia: The Artifacts.* Oxford: BAR Publishing.

———. 2006. "Thinking about Household Archaeology on the Northwest Coast."
Household Archaeology on the Northwest Coast. 1st ed. Sobel, Elizabeth A., D. Ann
Trieu Gahr, and Kenneth M. Ames, eds. Ann Arbor, MI: Berghahn Books. 16–36.
https://doi.org/10.2307/j.ctv8bt3gt.

Ames, Kenneth M., and Andrew Martindale. 2014. "Rope Bridges and Cables:
A Synthesis of Prince Rupert Harbour Archaeology. *Canadian Journal of
Archaeology* 38(1). 140–78.

Ames, Kenneth M., and Herbert D.G. Maschner. 1999. *Peoples of the Northwest
Coast: Their Archeology and Prehistory.* London: Thames & Hudson.

Anderson, Bern. 1960. *The Life and Voyages of Captain George Vancouver: Surveyor
of the Sea.* Toronto: University of Toronto Press

Anderson, Margaret. 1984. "The Tsimshian: Images of the Past, Views for the
Present." Vancouver, BC: UBC Press

———. 2006. "The Allied Tribes Tsimshian of North Coastal British Columbia: Social Organization, Economy and Trade." Vancouver, BC. https://faculty.arts.ubc.ca/menzies/documents/anderson.pdf.

Anderson, Ross and Linda Keene. 1997. "Alaska Drops BC Ferry—Retaliation for Prince Rupert Fish-War Blockade." *The Seattle Times*, July 23, 1997. https://archive.seattletimes.com/archive/?date=19970723&slug=2550958.

Appleyard, B. 1897. "Port Essington, British Columbia: Whites and Indians." *Mission Field*, October 1, 1897. 361–71.

Archer, David. 2001. "Village Patterns and the Emergence of Ranked Society in the Prince Rupert Area." *Perspectives on Northern Northwest Coast Prehistory.* Jerome S. Cybulski, ed. 203–22. Ottawa: University of Ottawa Press. https://doi.org/10.2307/j.ctt22zmcv8.12

Arnold, Jeanne E. 1996. "The Archaeology of Complex Hunter-Gatherers." *Journal of Archaeological Method and Theory* 3(1):77–125.

Atkinson, Maureen L. (2008). "One Sided Conversations: Chapters in the Life of Odille Morison." Athabasca University Master of Arts Integrated Studies Project. http://dtpr.lib.athabascau.ca/action/download.php?filename=mais/atkinsononesidedconversations0508.pdf

———. 2011. "The 'Accomplished' Odille Quintal Morison: Tsimshian Cultural Intermediary of Metlakatla, British Columbia." *Recollecting: Lives of Aboriginal Women of the Canadian Northwest and Borderlands.* Eds. Sarah Carter and Patricia McCormack. Edmonton: AU Press. 135–56.

———. 2017. "Replacing Sound Assumptions: Rediscovered Narratives of Post War Northern British Columbia." Thesis, University of Waterloo. http://hdl.handle.net/10012/12571.

Azizi, Joshua. 2021. "Prince Rupert Port Authority says it's ready to support disrupted supply chains in southern B.C." *CFTK-TV News.* https://www.cftktv.com/prince-rupert-port-authority-says-it-s-ready-to-support-disrupted-supply-chains-in-southern-b-c-1.5671838

Bailey, K. 2023. "Port of Prince Rupert sees drop in cargo volume in 2022." *Prince Rupert Northern View.* https://www.thenorthernview.com/news/port-of-prince-rupert-sees-drop-in-cargo-volume-in-2022/

Banahan, Joan. 2005. "Small Site Archaeology on the Northern Northwest Coast." Conference paper. *Canadian Journal of Archaeology.*

Banner, Allen, J. Pojar, and G.E. Rouse. 1983. "Postglacial paleoecology and successional relationships of a bog woodland near Prince Rupert, British Columbia." *Canadian Journal of Forest Research* 13(5):938–47.

Barager, Matthew. 2019. "'No Indians Allowed': Challenging Aboriginal Segregation in Northern British Columbia, 1945–1965." MA thesis, University of Northern British Columbia. https://core.ac.uk/download/236983858.pdf

Barman, Jean. 2015. *French Canadians, Furs, and Indigenous Women in the Making of the Pacific Northwest.* Vancouver: UBC Press.

———. 2020. *On the Cusp of Contact: Gender, Space and Race in the Colonization of British Columbia.* Madeira Park, BC: Harbour Publishing.

Barman, Jean and Mike Evans. 2009. "Reflections on Being, and Becoming, Métis in British Columbia." BC Studies 161. 59–91.

Bartlett, Keili. 2018. "City of Prince Rupert gains complete ownership of Watson Island." *Prince Rupert Northern View.* https://www.thenorthernview.com/news/city-of-prince-rupert-gains-complete-ownership-of-watson-island/.

BC Black History Awareness Society. 2023. "Earliest Pioneers (1858–1899): Stories— Sir James Douglas." https://bcblackhistory.ca/sir-james-douglas/.

BC Conservation Data Centre. 2013. "Conservation Status Report: *Eumetopias jubatus*." BC Ministry of Environment. Available: https://a100.gov.bc.ca/pub/eswp/.

BC Ferries. 2022. "Traffic Statistics System Total Vehicle and Passenger Counts by Route for December 2022." https://www.bcferries.com/web_image/hb3/h56/8920295079966.pdf

Beasley & Associates, Planning Inc. and CIVITAS Studio - Urban Design and Planning & Architecture. 2019. "Prince Rupert 2030 Vision: A Vibrant City Hosting a Vibrant Port." *redesign rupert*. December 2019. https://www.redesignrupert.ca/prince-rupert-2030.

Bennett, Nelson. 2012. "BC tidal power plays scoring in east. Business in Vancouver." *Business Intelligence for BC*. https://biv.com/article/2012/01/bc-tidal-power-plays-scoring-in-east

Bennett, Norma V. 2000. *Pioneer Legacy: Chronicles of the Lower Skeena River*. Terrace, BC: Dr. R.E.M. Lee Hospital Foundation.

Black Press Media. 2021. Turning the Pages: the Prince Rupert Newspaper Archives. https://prnewspaperarchives.ca/islandora/object/islandora%3A1

Blanton, Richard. 1994. *Houses and Households: A Comparative Study*. New York: Plenum Press.

Black Press Media. 2013. "Prince Rupert's Year in Review: July to September." *The Norther View*. January 3, 2013. https://www.thenorthernview.com/news/prince-ruperts-year-in-review-july-to-september/.

Bolt, Clarence R. 1992. *Thomas Crosby and the Tsimshian: Small Shoes for Feet Too Large*. Vancouver: UBC Press.

Bowman, Phylis. 1973. *Muskeg, Rocks and Rain!*. Sunrise Printing: Chilliwack, BC

———. 1982. *The City of Rainbows!*. Sunrise Printing: Chilliwack, BC

———. 1982. *Klondike of the Skeena!*. Sunrise Printing: Chilliwack, BC

———. 1982. *Land of Liquid Sunshine!*. Sunrise Printing: Chilliwack, BC

———. 1981. *Road, Rail and River!*. Sunrise Printing: Chilliwack, BC

———. 1989. *Trace Trails of History!*. Sunrise Printing: Chilliwack, BC

———. 1996. "The Mayors of Prince Rupert." BC Historical News: *Journal of the BC Historical Federation* 30(1):27–29. https://open.library.ubc.ca/viewer/bch/1.0190635#p28z-3rof:Phylis%20bowman.

Bown, Steven R. 2012. *Madness, Betrayal and the Lash: The Epic Voyage of Captain George Vancouver*. Madeira Park, BC: Douglas & McIntyre.

Boyd, Robert T. 1999. *The Coming of the Spirit of Pestilence: Introduced Infectious Diseases and Population Decline among Northwest Indians, 1774–1874*. Vancouver: UBC Press

Braham, Michael. 1965. "Fact Sheet #67: Lieutenant-Colonel Cyrus Wesley Peck, VC, DSO*." The Friends of the Canadian War Museum. https://friends-amis.org/wp-content/uploads/2020/10/FS67_LcolCyrusPeckvc.pdf.

Braid, Don. 2016. "Ex-B.C. Premier backs pipeline—and he's a New Democrat." *Calgary Herald*, December 12, 2016. https://calgaryherald.com/news/politics/braid-ex-b-c-premier-backs-pipeline-and-hes-a-new-democrat.

Brant, Jennifer. 2020. "Racial Segregation of Indigenous Peoples in Canada." *The Canadian Encyclopedia*. https://www.thecanadianencyclopedia.ca/en/article/racial-segregation-of-indigenous-peoples-in-canada.

Brown, Dennis. 2005. *Salmon Wars: The Battle for the West Coast Salmon Fishery.* Madeira Park, BC: Harbour Publishing.

Brown, Dorothy, Henry Reeves, Ken Campbell, et al, eds. 1992. *Saaban: The Tsimshian and Europeans Meet. Suwilaay'msga Na Ga'Niiyatgm (Teachings of Our Grandfathers),* Vol. 3. Prince Rupert, BC: The Tsimshian Chief for Tsimshian Children Present and Future.

Buddenhagen, Jeremy. 2017. Tsemsyaenhl-get: Sixteen battles in the military history of the Nine Allied Tsimshian Tribes. MA thesis, University of Victoria. http://hdl. handle.net/1828/9043.

Butler, Caroline F. 2005. "More Than Fish: Political Knowledge in the Commercial Fisheries of British Columbia." PhD dissertation, University of British Columbia. https://dx.doi.org/10.14288/1.0092323.

Butler, Caroline F. and Kenneth Campbell. 2003. "The River People: Living and Working in Oona River." Forests for the Future, Unit 6. University of British Columbia. https://ecoknow.ca/documents/OonaBook.pdf.

Butler, Don. 2012. "In Charles Melville Hays' Tracks." *The Ottawa Citizen,* April 7, 2012. https://web.archive.org/web/20150915031334/http://www.railfame.ca/documents/news/20/2012_04_07_Hays1.pdf.

Byrne, Nicholas. 2015. "The Little Port that Could: Changing Port Governance in Prince Rupert, British Columbia, 1945–2014." MA thesis, University of British Columbia. https://dx.doi.org/10.14288/1.0166345.

California Apparel News. 2007. "Prince Rupert Port Prepares for Container Ships to Call Soon." https://www.apparelnews.net/news/2007/sep/21/prince-rupert-port-prepares-for-container-ships/.

Callaghan, Corey. 2017. "Company Testing Tidal Energy Prototype on Haida Gwaii." Marine Renewables Canada. https://supplychain.marinerenewables.ca/updates/2017-07-11/company-testing-tidal-energy-prototype-on-haida-gwaii

Campbell, Kenneth. 1981. *Charles M. Hays: Death of a Dream.* North Coast Memories.

———. 1992. *Fort Simpson, Fur Fort at Laxlgu'alaams.* Canada: The Tsimshian Chiefs.

———. 2005. *Persistence and Change: A History of the Ts'msyen Nation.* First Nations Education Council.

Campbell, Kevin. 2016. 2015. "Sad day for Rupert as cannery closes." *Prince Rupert Northern View.* : https://www.thenorthernview.com/news/sad-day-for-rupert-as-cannery-closes/.

———. "Prince Rupert second-worst in B.C. for child poverty." *Prince Rupert Northern View.* https://www.thenorthernview.com/news/prince-rupert-second-worst-in-b-c-for-child-poverty/.

Campbell, Robert A. 2004. "A 'Fantastic Rigmarole': Deregulating Aboriginal Drinking in British Columbia, 1945–62." BC Studies 141 (Spring 2004). 81–104.

Campbell, Sarah K. and Virginia Butler. 2010. "Archaeological Evidence for Resilience of Pacific Northwest Salmon Populations and the Socioecological System over the last ~7,500 years." *Ecology and Society* 15(1): 17. https://www.jstor.org/stable/26268107.

Canada's Historic Places. 2008. "MacDonald Hotel." https://www.historicplaces.ca/en/rep-reg/place-lieu.aspx?id=8791&pid=0.

Canadian Environmental Assessment Agency. 2012. Archived: Mount Hays Wind Farm Project. Canadian Environmental Assessment Registry: 07-01-36046. https://ceaa-acee.gc.ca/052/details-eng.cfm?pid=36046.

Canadian Press. 2007. Northern B.C. towns lead in population declines. *CTV News.* https://www.ctvnews.ca/northern-b-c-towns-lead-in-population-declines-1.233021

———. 2009. "B.C. towns suffer as major paper companies refuse to pay tax." *CTV News.* https://www.ctvnews.ca/b-c-towns-suffer-as-major-paper-companies-refuse-to-pay-tax-1.461569?cache=yes%3FclipId%3D375756.

Canadian War Museum. 2023. "The Aleutians Campaign, 1942–43." *Democracy at War: Canadian Newspapers and the Second World War.* https://www.warmuseum.ca/cwm/exhibitions/newspapers/operations/aleutian_e.html

Canopy Planet. 2023. "The Great Bear Rainforest." https://canopyplanet.org/campaigns/protecting-forests/the-coastal-temperate-rainforest/protecting-the-great-bear-rainforest/.

Carsten, Janet and Stephen Hugh-Jones. 1995. *About the House: Lévi-Strauss and Beyond.* New York: Cambridge University Press.

Cassidy, Maureen. 1983. "The Skeena River Uprising of 1888." *British Columbia Historical News* 16:3 (Winter 1983). https://www.library.ubc.ca/archives/pdfs/bchf/bchn_1983_spring.pdf.

CBC Daybreak North (2023). No Alaska Ferry Service to Prince Rupert this Summer. : https://www.cbc.ca/player/play/2182374979741

CBC Learning. 2001. "Japanese Internment: British Columbia wages war against Japanese Canadians." https://www.cbc.ca/history/EPISCONTENTSE1EP14CH3PA3LE.html.

CBC News. 2009. "Allergic to sun, family wins B.C. residency." https://www.cbc.ca/news/canada/british-columbia/allergic-to-sun-family-wins-b-c-residency-1.862690

———. 2021. "COVID-19 patients in B.C.'s north being flown elsewhere for care as local hospitals hit limits." https://www.cbc.ca/news/canada/british-columbia/covid-19-update-sept-21-1.6184078.

Chow, Lily. 2001. *Chasing Their Dreams: Chinese Settlement in the Northwest Region of British Columbia.* Qualicum Beach, BC: Caitlin Press.

City of Prince Rupert. 2013. News Release: GlobeNewswire. https://www.globenewswire.com/en/news-release/2013/08/30/1344267/0/en/News-Release.html.

———. 2014. Council meeting, November 24, 2014. https://www.youtube.com/watch?v=pnfIPoeUbcM&t=8015s.

———. 2023. "Council History." https://www.princerupert.ca/city-hall/mayor-and-council/council-history?bcgovtm=buffer.

———. 2024. "Prince Rupert Seeking Partners for Innovative Energy Projects." https://www.princerupert.ca/index-pages/news/prince-rupert-seeking-partners-innovative-energy-projects

———. 2023. "Transportation Plan." https://www.princerupert.ca/building-development/community-planning/transportation-plan#:~:text=In%20July%20of%202023%2C%20Prince,the%20airport%20ferry%20and%20beyond.

City Spaces. 2022. "Housing Needs Report: City of Prince Rupert, December 2022." https://www.princerupert.ca/media/19.

CivicInfo BC. 2024. https://www.civicinfo.bc.ca/.

Clayton, Daniel Wright. 1989. "Geographies of the Lower Skeena 1830-1920." MA thesis, University of British Columbia. https://dx.doi.org/10.14288/1.0097752.

CN Rail. 1985. *Growing with Prince Rupert.* Montreal: Canadian National Railway.

Cocullo, Jenna. 2019. "A new vision unveiled for Prince Rupert." *Prince Rupert Northern View*, December 13, 2019. https://www.thenorthernview.com/news/a-new-vision-unveiled-for-prince-rupert/.

———. 2019. "Prince Rupert Port Authority hits record cargo volume but a decline in revenues for 2018." *Prince Rupert Northern View*. https://www.thenorthernview. com/business/prince-rupert-port-authority-hits-record-cargo-volume-but-a-decline-in-revenues-for-2018/.

———. 2019. "City releases the Prince Rupert Tsunami Study results." *Prince Rupert Northern View*, May 28, 2019. https://www.thenorthernview.com/news/city-releases-the-prince-rupert-tsunami-study-results/.

Colonial Coal. 2018. "Management's Discussion and Analysis of Financial Position and Results of Operations." https://www.ccoal.ca/wp-content/uploads/2018/11/ccic-mda-q4-nov-8-18-final-to-file.pdf.

Comox Valley Walk of Achievement. 2012. "The Honourable Iona Campagnolo." https://www.walkofachievement.com/honourees/iona-campagnolo/.

Connected Coast. 2023. "About." https://connectedcoast.ca/about/.

Cornett, Andrew and Michael Tarbotton. 2006. "Inventory of Canada's Marine Renewable Energy Resources." National Research Council Canada. https://ressources-naturelles.canada.ca/sites/www.nrcan.gc.ca/files/canmetenergy/files/pubs/CHC-TR-041.pdf.

Coupland, Gary. 2006. "A Chief's House Speaks: Communicating Power on the Northern Northwest Coast." *Household Archaeology on the Northwest Coast*. 1st ed. Sobel, Elizabeth A., D. Ann Trieu Gahr, and Kenneth M. Ames, eds. Ann Arbor, MI: Berghahn Books. 80–96. https://doi.org/10.2307/j.ctv8bt3gt.

Coupland, Gary, Kathlyn Stewart, and Katherine Patton. 2010. "Do You Never Get Tired of Salmon?: Evidence for Extreme Salmon Specialization at Prince Rupert Harbour, British Columbia." *Journal of Anthropological Archaeology* 29(2):189–207.

Cow Bay Marina. 2023. "Welcome to Our Marina." https://cowbaymarina.ca/.

Canadian Public Transit Discussion Board. 2023. "Independently operated but owned by BC Ferries." https://cptdb.ca/wiki/index.php?title=BC_Ferries&mobileaction=toggle_view_desktop#Current.

Crawford, John. 2017. "Wolverine hosts open houses on Prince Rupert terminal proposal." iHeart Radio News. https://www.iheartradio.ca/wolverine-hosts-open-houses-on-prince-rupert-terminal-proposal-1.3366157.

Cruise Industry News. 2022. "Global Ports Holding Enters North American Market with Prince Rupert Deal." November 14, 2022. https://cruiseindustrynews.com/cruise-news/2022/11/global-ports-holding-enters-north-american-market-with-prince-rupert-deal/

Cybulski, Jerome S. 1992. *A Greenville Burial Ground: Human Remains and Mortuary Elements in British Columbia Coast Prehistory*. Ottawa: University of Ottawa Press.

Dal Monte, Richard. 2021. "Dan Miller helped create Royal Roads." Royal Roads University. https://www.royalroads.ca/news/dan-miller-helped-create-royal-roads.

Dalton, Danielle. 2013. *Book of Rainbows: Stories of Cultural Diversity Making a Difference*. Prince Rupert, BC: Hecate Strait Employment Development Society.

DataSpan. 2023. "Data Centre Cooling Costs." https://dataspan.com/blog/data-center-cooling-costs/

Davenport-Hines, Richard. 2012. *Voyagers of the Titanic: Passengers, Sailors, Shipbuilders, Aristocrats, and the Worlds They Came From*. New York: William Morrow.

Davies, Megan J. 2005. "Night Soil, Cesspools, and Smelly Hogs on the Streets: Sanitation, Race, and Governance in Early British Columbia." *Histoire sociale/ Social History*, 38:75 (2005). https://hssh.journals.yorku.ca/index.php/hssh/article/view/4290.

Davis, George T.B. 1904. *Metlakahtla: a true narrative of the red man*. Chicago: Ram's Horn Company.

Dean, Jonathan R. 1994. "'These Rascally Spackaloids': The Rise of Gispaxlots Hegemony at Fort Simpson, 1832–40." *BC Studies* 101 (Spring 1994). 41–78.

Depalma, Anthony. 1997. "Canadians End Blockade In Salmon-Fishing Dispute." *New York Times*, July 22, 1997. https://www.nytimes.com/1997/07/22/world/canadians-end-blockade-in-salmon-fishing-dispute.html.

Deur, Douglas and Turner, Nancy J. eds. 2005. *Keeping It Living: Traditions of Plant Use and Cultivation on the Northwest Coast of North America*. Vancouver: UBC Press.

Discover Nikkei. n.d. "Nisei immigration to Canada." https://discovernikkei.org/en/journal/2017/3/24/nisei-immigration-to-canada/.

Dorsey, George A. (1897). "Up the Skeena River to the Home of Tsimshians." *Popular Science Monthly* 54. 181–93.

Douglas, James. 1860. James Douglas to Pelham-Clinton, Henry Pelham Fiennes, January 27, 1860, CO 60:5, 243.*The Colonial Despatches of Vancouver Island and British Columbia 1846–1871*, Edition 2.4. Colonial Despatches project. James Hendrickson ed. Victoria, B.C.: University of Victoria.

Downie, William. 1893. *Hunting for Gold: Reminiscences of Personal Experience and Research in the Early Days of the Pacific Coast from Alaska to Panama*. San Fransisco: California Pub. Co.

Downs, Art. 1971. *Paddlewheels on the Frontier: The Story of BC Sternwheelers and Steamers*. Vols. 1 and 2. Cloverdale, BC: BC Outdoors Magazine.

Drucker, Philip. 1944. "Archaeological Survey on the Northern Northwest Coast." *Bureau of American Ethnology Bulletin* 133 (20): 17–142.

Dunn, John Asher. 1978. A *Practical Dictionary of the Coast Tsimshian Language*. Ottawa: University of Ottawa Press.

Ecotrust Canada. 2004. "Catch-22: Conservation, Communities and the Privatization of BC Fisheries—An Economic, Social and Ecological Impact Study." /hdl.handle.net/1834/19548.

Edinborough, Kevan, A. Martindale, G.T. Cook, K. Supernant, and K.M. Ames. 2016. "A Marine Reservoir Effect ΔR Value for Kitandach, in Prince Rupert Harbour, British Columbia, Canada." *Radiocarbon* 58:4: 885–91. https://doi.org/10.1017/RDC.2016.46.

Encyclopedia Britannica. 2023. "Rupert River." https://www.britannica.com/place/Rupert-River.

Encyclopedia Titanica. 2021. "Charles Melville Hays." https://www.encyclopedia-titanica.org/titanic-victim/charles-melville-hays.html.

Ewins, Adrian. 1999. "Prince Rupert terminal closes for unknown period." *The Western Producer*, March 4, 1999. https://www.producer.com/news/prince-rupert-terminal-closes-for-unknown-period/.

Extreme Weather Watch. 2023. "Prince Rupert Weather Records." https://www.extremeweatherwatch.com/cities/prince-rupert.

Federal Indian Day School Class Action. 1997. "Appendix K: List of Federal Indian Day Schools." https://indiandayschools.com/en/wp-content/uploads/schedule-k.pdf.

Fisher, Robin. 1990. "T.D. Pattullo and the North: The Significance of the Periphery in British Columbia Politics." *The Pacific Northwest Quarterly* 81(3), 101–11.

———. 1991. *Duff Pattullo of British Columbia*. University of Toronto Press.

———. 1992. *Contact and Conflict: Indian-European Relations in British Columbia, 1774–1890*, 2nd ed. Vancouver: UBC Press.

———. 1992. *Vancouver's Voyage: Charting the Northwest Coast, 1791–1795*. Maderia Park: Douglas and McIntyre.

Friendship House. 2023. "Friendship House (1958–present)." https://friendshiphouse. ca/history/

Gadacz, René R. 2006. "Potlatch." *The Canadian Encyclopedia*. https://www. thecanadianencyclopedia.ca/en/article/potlatch.

Galois, Robert. 2003. *A Voyage to the North West Side of America: The Journals of James Colnett, 1786–89*. Vancouver: UBC Press.

Garden, Bailey. 2021. "The Battle of Kelly's Cut." BC Labour Heritage Centre. https:// www.labourheritagecentre.ca/the-battle-of-kellys-cut/.

Gareau, Chris. 2017. "Recreational salmon fishing shut down." *Prince Rupert Northern View*, June 20, 2017. https://www.thenorthernview.com/news/recreational-salmon-fishing-shut-down/.

Garfield, Viola. 1932. Field notebooks from Coast Tsimshian interviews in Port Simpson. 9 vols. Seattle: University of Washington, Special Collections.

Garland, Hamlin. 1800. *Ho, for the Klondike!* https://www.canadiana.ca/view/oocihm. 16250.

Germain, David. 1997. "Alaska ferry leaves Canadian port after three-day blockade." *Kitsap Sun*, July 22, 1997. https://products.kitsapsun.com/archive/1997/07-22/ 0031_alaska_ferry_leaves_canadian_port.html.

Gislason, Gordon. 2006. "Commercial vs. Recreational Fisheries Allocation in Canada: Pacific Herring, Salmon and Halibut." Conference paper. https://www.npfmc.org/ wp-content/PDFdocuments/halibut/CommercialRecreationalCanada.pdf.

Gitmaxmak'ay Nisga'a Society. 2023. "About Us." https://gitmaxmakay.ca/about-us.

Global News (2014). "Prince Rupert election results 2014: Full results." November 15, 2014. https://globalnews.ca/news/1669607/prince-rupert-election-results-2014-full-results-in-the-mayoral-race/.

Gordon, Todd and Geoffrey McCormack. 2020. "Canada and the crisis of capitalism." *Briarpatch*, February 25, 2020. https://briarpatchmagazine.com/articles/view/ canada-and-the-crisis-of-capitalism.

Gough, Barry. 1971. *The Royal Navy and the Northwest Coast of North America, 1810–1914: A Study of British Maritime Ascendancy*. Vancouver: UBC Press.

Government of BC. 2001. "BC Stats: British Columbia's Fish Product and Seafood Industry in the 1990s." Ministry of Finance and Corporate Relations. https://www. for.gov.bc.ca/hfd/library/documents/bib107055.pdf.

———. 2020. "British Columbia Seafood Processing Employment Survey Results 2019 and 2020." BC Ministry of Agriculture and Food. https://www2.gov.bc.ca/assets/ gov/farming-natural-resources-and-industry/agriculture-and-seafood/statistics/ industry-and-sector-profiles/employment/bc_seafood_processing_employment_ survey_report_2019_2020.pdf

Government of Canada. 2008. "Douglas Eyford Appointed to Negotiate with First Nations on Prince Rupert Fairview Container Terminal Issues." Press Release No. H 005/08. https://www.canada.ca/en/news/archive/2008/01/douglas-eyford-appointed-negotiate-first-nations-prince-rupert-container-terminal-issues.html.

———. 2021. "Cyrus Wesley Peck." https://www.canada.ca/en/department-national-defence/services/medals/victoria-cross-recipients/cyrus-wesley-peck.html.

Grand Trunk Pacific Railway. 1912. *Prince Rupert, British Columbia: The Pacific Coast terminus of the Grand Trunk Railway.* Montreal: The Railway.

Grant, D. (1979). T.D. Pattullo's Early Career. British Columbia Historical News. Volume 13(1). : https://www.library.ubc.ca/archives/pdfs/bchf/bchn_1979_fall.pdf

Grant Thornton. 2017. "Consolidated financial statements, Prince Rupert Port Authority, December 31, 2017." https://www.rupertport.com/wp-content/uploads/2019/12/port-of-prince-rupert-2017-financial-statements.pdf.

Great Bear Rainforest Education and Awareness Trust (2020). Biodiversity. : https://greatbearrainforesttrust.org/biodiversity/

Greer, Karla. 1999. *Race, Riot, and Rail: The Process of Racialisation in Prince Rupert, BC, 1906–1919.* MA thesis, University of Victoria.

Grimshaw, L. (1992). "No. 1 Armoured Train." *Branchline* 31(8). 8–12. https://bytownrailwaysociety.ca/phocadownload/branchline/1992/1992-09.pdf.

Hacking, Norman. 1995. *Prince Ships of Northern BC: Ships of the Grand Trunk Pacific and Canadian National Railways.* Victoria: Heritage House Publishing.

Haggan, Nigel, N. Turner, J. Carpenter, J. Jones, Q. Mackie, and C. Menzies. 2006. "12,000+ Years of Change: Linking Traditional and Modern Ecosystem Science in the Pacific Northwest." UBC Fisheries Centre Working Paper #2006-02.

Haida Nation. 2023. "Council of the Haida Nation/Secretariat of the Haida Nation." https://www.haidanation.ca/secretariat-of-the-haida-nation/.

Hale, Alan S. 2011. (2011). Sparks fly as Prince Rupert mayoral candidates participate in forum. The *Prince Rupert Northern View*, November 16, 2011. https://www.thenorthernview.com/news/sparks-fly-as-prince-rupert-mayoral-candidates-participate-in-forum/

———. "Election Results: Jack Mussallem Re-elected." *The Prince Rupert Northern View*, November 19, 2011. https://www.thenorthernview.com/news/election-results-jack-mussallem-re-elected/.

Hall, Roger. 2006. "Upper Canada." *The Canadian Encyclopedia.* https://www.thecanadianencyclopedia.ca/en/article/upper-canada.

Halpin, Marjorie and Seguin. 1990. "Tsimshian Peoples: Southern Tsimshian, Coast Tsimshian, Nishga, and Gitksan." *Handbook of North American Indians: Northwest Coast* (Vol. 7). Wayne Suttles, ed. Washington: Smithsonian Institution, Washington. 267–84.

Halseth, Greg, Laura, Ryser, and Shiloh Durkee. 2005. "Shopping and Commuting Patterns in Prince Rupert, B.C." https://www2.unbc.ca/sites/default/files/sections/greg-halseth/finalshoppingreportprincerupert.pdf.

Harrington, L. 1949. "Prince Rupert's Leading Lady." *Saturday Night.*

Harris, E.A. 1990. *Spokeshute: Skeena River memory.* Victoria: Orca Book Publishers.

Harris, Cole. 2003. *Making Native Space: Colonialism, Resistance, and Reserves in British Columbia.* Vancouver: UBC Press.

Hayashi, Jim Kotaro, Fumio Kanno, and Henry Tanaka. 2017. *Changing Tides: Vanishing Voices of Nikkei Fishermen and Their Families.* Burnaby, BC: Nikkei National Museum & Cultural Centre.

Hayden, Brian. 1990. "Nimrods, Piscators, Pluckers and Planters: The Emergence of Food Production." *Journal of Anthropological Archaeology* 9(1):31–69.

Hayes, Derek. 2001. *Historical Atlas of British Columbia and the Pacific Northwest.* Madeira Park, BC: Douglas and McIntyre.

Hebda, Richard and Rolf Matthews. 1984. "Holocene History of Cedar and Native Indian Cultures of the North American Pacific Coast." *Science* 225:711–13.

Hick, W.B.M. 2003. *Hays' Orphan: The Story of the Port of Prince Rupert.* Prince Rupert, BC: Prince Rupert Port Authority.

History Channel. 2009. https://www.history.com.

Hoekstra, Gordon. 2011. "Prince Rupert port reaches key deal with First Nations. Prince George Citizen." https://www.princegeorgecitizen.com/local-news/prince-rupert-port-reaches-key-deal-with-first-nations-3710976.

Holiday, Ian. 2021. "85% of Prince Rupert residents vaccinated as B.C. adds tourism workers to clinic staff." CTV News. https://bc.ctvnews.ca/85-of-prince-rupert-residents-vaccinated-as-b-c-adds-tourism-workers-to-clinic-staff-1.5360799.

Horetzky, Charles. 1874. *Canada on the Pacific: Being an Account of the Journey from Edmonton to the Pacific.* Montreal: Dawson Brothers.

House of Commons. 1999. "Standing Committee on Canadian Heritage." Audio recording. https://www.ourcommons.ca/DocumentViewer/en/36-1/CHER/meeting-67/evidence.

Houston, John, ed. *The Empire.* 1909. Prince Rupert, BC Police Day Book, Port Essington, Year 1909. Prince Rupert, BC: Prince Rupert City & Regional Archives.

Huculak, Michael. 1984. *Ukrainians in British Columbia and Their Contribution to the Cultural Life of the Province.* Marta D. Olynyk, trans. Richmond, BC: Ivan Franko Cultural Society.

Hume, Stephen. 2017. "Campagnolo served BC in many capacities." *The Province,* February 17, 2017. https://www.pressreader.com/canada/the-province/20170217/281556585585889.

Hunter, Jennifer. 1998. "Pulp and politics: the B.C. government keeps on bailing at Skeena." *Maclean's.* https://archive.macleans.ca/article/1998/3/2/pulp-and-politics.

Hutchinson, I., and A.D. McMillan. 1997. "Archaeological Evidence for Village Abandonment Associated with Late Holocene Earthquakes at the Northern Cascadia Subduction Zone." Quaternary Research 48 (1): 79-87. Meidinger, D. & Pojar, J. (1991). Ecosystems of British Columbia. Special Report Series 6, Province of British Columbia, Victoria.

Inglis, Richard. 1972. "Archaeological Project in the Prince Rupert Harbour, 1972." *Bulletin (Canadian Archaeological Association)* 4 (1972): 101–105.

Inglis, Richard and George F. MacDonald. 1979. *Skeena River Prehistory.* Ottawa: University of Ottawa Press.

Jack Mussallem Collection. Prince Rupert City and Regional Archives. https://princerupertarchives.ca/search/detail-bare.php?ID=8825.

Jack Mussallem collection 1977-1986 Fonds. 2013. Prince Rupert Archives

Japanese Canadian History. 2023. "Reference Timeline." https://japanesecanadianhistory.net/historical-overview/reference-timeline/.

Joint Indian Reserve Commission. 2023. "Peter O'Reilly." *Federal and Provincial Collections of Minutes and Decision, Correspondence and Sketches.* https://jirc.ubcic.bc.ca/node/49.

Kelly, Ash. 2017. "Skeena River sockeye returns at historic lows." CBC News, June 28, 2017. https://www.cbc.ca/news/canada/british-columbia/skeena-river-sockeye-returns-at-historic-lows-1.4176967.

Kiffer, Dave. 2007. "Prince Rupert: Hays' 'Orphan' Looks to the Future." *SitNews*, February 28, 2007. http://www.sitnews.us/Kiffer/PrinceRupert/022807_prince_rupert.html.

———. 2007. "Alaska/Canada Salmon 'war' 10 years ago." *SitNews*, July 19, 2007. http://www.sitnews.us/Kiffer/SalmonWars/071907_salmonwars.html.

———. 2010. "Prince Rupert Turns 100." SitNews, March 08, 2010. http://www.sitnews.us/Kiffer/PrinceRupert100/030810_prince_rupert.html.

———. 2012. "Founder of Prince Rupert died on Titanic 100 years ago." *SitNews*, April 09, 2012. http://www.sitnews.us/Kiffer/Titanic/040912_titanic.html.

Kitsumkalum Band. 2023. "Our Culture." https://kitsumkalum.com/about/our-culture/#:~:text=These%20are%20oral%20laws%2C%20passed,of%20the%20law%20are%20illustrated.

Knight, Rolf. 1996. *Indians at Work: An Informal History of Native Labour in British Columbia 1858–1930*. Vancouver: New Star Books.

Kolenko, Sean. 2013. "Northern Exposure, part 2: Prince Rupert in the eye of the energy storm. Business in Vancouver." *Business in Vancouver*, October 14, 2013. https://www.biv.com/news/economy-law-politics/northern-exposure-part-2-prince-rupert-in-the-eye-8237803.

Kronbauer, Bob. 2021. "This secret armoured train patrolled a B.C. river during WWII." *Prince George Citizen*, January 12, 2021. https://www.princegeorgecitizen.com/highlights/skeena-armoured-train-wwii-3253341.

Kurjata, Andrew. 2018. "Safe Place program for LGBTQ community launches in Prince Rupert, B.C. CBC News British Columbia." CBC News, January 1, 2018. https://www.cbc.ca/news/canada/british-columbia/rcmp-safe-place-prince-rupert-1.4491660.

———. 2020. "Prince Rupert orders anyone entering city to self-isolate for 14 days." CBC News, March 24, 2020. https://www.cbc.ca/news/canada/british-columbia/covid-19-prince-rupert-north-coast-1.5508495.

Langdon, Steve J. 2006. "Trade in Precontact Coast Tsimshian Society: Expert Witness Report prepared for plaintiffs in Lax Kw'alaams Indian Band v Canada (Attorney General)." University of Alaska Anchorage.

Large, Richard Geddes. 1960. *Prince Rupert: a gateway to Alaska and the Pacific*. Vancouver: Mitchell Press Ltd.

———. 1996. *The Skeena: River of Destiny*. Victoria: Heritage House Publishing.

Lax Kw'alaams. 2006. "The History of Tree Farm License 1." https://www2.gov.bc.ca/assets/gov/farming-natural-resources-and-industry/forestry/timber-tenures/tree-farm-licence/management-plans/appendix__1__mp_10__history_tfl_1_july_15.pdf.

Leonard, F. 1996. *A Thousand Blunders: The Grand Trunk Pacific Railway and Northern British Columbia*. Vancouver: UBC Press.

Lewis, Suzzane. 2023. "Vision Action Can Change the World." UNESCO. https://www.iiep.unesco.org/en/vision-action-can-change-world.

Lornie, Jim, et al. 1999. "An open letter to the Premier from B.C.'s Coastal Mayors on the future of salmon aquaculture in British Columbia." October 15, 1999. http://www.nanfa.org/archive/nanfa/nanfaoct99/0046.html.

Lough, Shannon. 2017. "No beach access for Seafest activities, CN refuses to negotiate with city." *Prince Rupert Northern View*, May 21, 2017. https://www.thenorthernview.com/news/no-beach-access-for-seafest-activities-cn-refuses-to-negotiate-with-city/.

———. 2017. "Victoria Cross recipient remembered with stone memorial." *Prince Rupert Northern View*, September 5, 2017. https://www.thenorthernview.com/community/victoria-cross-recipient-remembered-with-stone-memorial/.

———. 2018. "Thirteen pedestrians hit in 14 months in Prince Rupert." *Prince Rupert Northern View*, February 15, 2018. https://www.trailtimes.ca/news/thirteen-pedestrians-hit-in-14-months-in-prince-rupert/.

———. 2018. "Commercial fishing is Canada's most dangerous job, report states." *Prince Rupert Northern View*, November 29, 2018. https://www.thenorthernview.com/news/commercial-fishing-is-canadas-most-dangerous-job-report-states/.

Lower, Joseph Arthur. 1939. "The Grand Trunk Pacific Railway and British Columbia." MA thesis, University of British Columbia. https://dx.doi.org/10.14288/1.0098676

MacDonald, George F. 1969. "Preliminary culture sequence from the Coast Tsimshian area, British Columbia." *Northwest Anthropol. Res. Notes* 3:240–54.

———. 2006. "Coast Tsimshian Pre-Contact Economics and Trade: An Archeological and Ethno-Historic Reconstruction." Submission to Ratliff & Co. Metlakatla/Lax Kw'alaams Land Claim File.

Macdonald, George F. and David Archer. n.d. *Violence vs. Trade.*

MacDonald, George F. and John J. Cove (1987) *Tsimshian Narratives, vol. 2: Trade and Warfare*. Barbeau, Marius and William Benyon, eds. Ottawa: Canadian Museum of Civilization.

MacDonald, G. and Jerome Cybulski. 2001. "Introduction: The Prince Rupert Harbour Project." *Perspectives on Northern Northwest Coast Prehistory*. Jerome S. Cybulski, ed. Ottawa: University of Ottawa Press. 1–24.

MacIvor, Madeline. 1993. "Science and Technology Education in a Civilizing Mission." MA thesis, University of British Columbia. https://dx.doi.org/10.14288/1.0086448.

Mackie, Richard. 1997. *Trading Beyond the Mountains: the British fur trade on the Pacific 1793–1843*. Vancouver: UBC Press.

Macrotrends. 2023. "Canada Infant Mortality Rate 1950-2023." https://www.macrotrends.net/countries/CAN/canada/infant-mortality-rate.

Madsen, Chris M.V. 2014. "Wages, Work and Wartime Demands in British Columbia Shipbuilding, 1916–19." *BC Studies* 182 (Summer 2014). 73–111.

Marsden, Susan. 1992. *Na Amwaaltga Ts'msiyeen: The Tsimshian, Trade, and the Northwest Coast Economy. Suwilaay'msga Na Ga'niiyatgm (Teachings of Our Grandfathers)*, Vol. 1. Prince Rupert, BC: The Tsimshian Chief for Tsimshian Children Present and Future.

———. 2000. *Defending the Mouth of the Skeena: Perspectives on Tsimshian Tlingit Relations*. Prince Rupert: Tin Ear Press.

———. 2002. "Adawx, Spanaxnox, and the Geopolitics of the Tsimshian." *BC Studies* 135 (Autumn 2002). 101–35.

Marsh, James H. 2006. "Grand Trunk Railway of Canada." *The Canadian Encyclopedia*. https://www.thecanadianencyclopedia.ca/en/article/grand-trunk-railway-of-canada.

Marshall, Yvonne. 2006. "Houses and Domestication on the Northwest Coast." *Household Archaeology on the Northwest Coast*. 1st ed. Sobel, Elizabeth A., D. Ann Trieu Gahr, and Kenneth M. Ames, eds. Ann Arbor, MI: Berghahn Books. 37–56. https://doi.org/10.2307/j.ctv8bt3gt.

Martindale, Andrew. 1999. The River of Mist: Cultural Change in the Tsimshian Past. University of Toronto Doctor of Philosophy Thesis.

———. 2009. Entanglement and tinkering: Structural history in the archeology of the Northern Tsimshian. *Journal of Social Archaeology*, 9(1). 59–91.

Martindale, Andrew, Bryn Letham, et al. 2009. "Mapping of Subsurface Shell Midden
    Components through Percussion Coring: Examples from the Dundas Islands."
    Journal of Archaeological Science 36(7):1565–75.

Martindale, A., Letham, B., et al. 2017. "Urbanism in Northern Tsimshian Archaeology."
    Hunter Gatherer Research 3:1. 133–63.

Martindale, A. and Susan Marsden. 2003. "Defining the Middle Period (3500 BP to
    1500 BP) in Tsimshian History through a Comparison of Archaeological and Oral
    Records." BC *Studies* 138/9 (Summer/Autumn 2003):13–50.

McDonald, James. 1990. "Bleeding Day And Night: The Construction Of The Grand
    Trunk Pacific Railway Across Tsimshian Reserve Lands." *Canadian Journal of
    Native Studies* 10(1): 33–68.

McElhanney. 2022. "Watson Island Redevelopment Project." https://www.mcelhanney.
    com/project/watson_island/.

McGovern, P.C. 1960. "Prince Rupert, British Columbia: A new town that never grew
    up." *Ekistics*, 10(59), 148–151. https://www.jstor.org/stable/43621409.

McIntosh, Andrew and Shirlee Anne Smith. 2006. "Rupert's Land." *The Canadian
    Encyclopedia.* https://www.thecanadianencyclopedia.ca/en/article/ruperts-land.

McIver, M. 1985. "A superdrought in the West." *Maclean's.* https://archive.macleans.
    ca/article/1985/7/29/a-superdrought-in-the-west.

McLaren, Duncan. 2008. "Sea Level Change and Archaeological Site Locations on
    the Dundas Island Archipelago of North Coast British Columbia." PhD thesis,
    University of Victoria.

Meilleur, Helen. 1980. *A Pour of Rain: Stories from a West Coast Fort.* Victoria: Sono
    Nis Press.

Meissner, Dirk. 2017. "Culture flourishes at Prince Rupert's All-Native Basketball
    Tournament." CTV News, February 10, 2017. https://www.ctvnews.ca/canada/
    culture-flourishes-at-prince-rupert-s-all-native-basketball-tournament-1.3279229.

Melegrito, Fidez Sotto. 2015. "Featured Association: The Filipino Canadian
    Association Of Prince Rupert Moves Forward." Metrovan Independent News,
    September 16, 2015. https://metrovanindependent.com/2015/09/featured-
    association-the-filipino-canadian-association-of-prince-rupert-moves-forward/.

Memory BC. 2023. "Lester, Peter." The British Columbia Archival Information Network.
    https://www.memorybc.ca/lester-peter-and-mary.

Memory BC. 2023. "Sons of Norway Vinland Lodge No. 28." The British Columbia
    Archival Network. https://www.memorybc.ca/sons-of-norway-vinland-lodge-no-28.

Menzies, Charles. 2008. "Report on Gitxaała Use and Occupancy of the Area Now
    Known as Prince Rupert Harbour with specific reference to the site of the Prince
    Rupert Container Port Development." UBC Blogs. https://blogs.ubc.ca/ecoknow/
    files/2009/04/Port_Sept19_2008.pdf.

———. 2016. *People of the Saltwater: an ethnography of Git lax m'oon.* Lincoln, NE:
    University of Nebraska Press.

Menzies, Charles and Caroline Butler. 2008. "The Indigenous Foundation of the
    Resource Economy of BC's North Coast." *Labour / Le Travail* 61 (2008): 131–49.

Mickleburgh, Rod. 2000. "Miller provides oasis of calm in stormy B.C." *The Globe
    and Mail*, February 15, 2000. https://www.theglobeandmail.com/news/national/
    miller-provides-oasis-of-calm-in-stormy-bc/article1036852/.

Millar, Kimberly. 2020. "States of local emergency suspended by province." *Prince
    Rupert Northern View*, March 26, 2020. https://www.thenorthernview.com/news/
    states-of-local-emergency-suspended-by-province/.

———. 2020. "Rainbow resilience in Prince Rupert." *Prince Rupert Northern View*, April 12, 2020. https://www.thenorthernview.com/news/rainbow-resilience-in-prince-rupert/.

———. 2021. "City to receive part of $20 million for waterfront development." *Prince Rupert Northern View*, February 23, 2021. https://www.thenorthernview.com/news/city-to-receive-part-of-20-million-for-waterfront-development/.

———. 2022. "Seal Cove Salt Marsh opens with $4 million Prince Rupert Port Authority Investment." *Prince Rupert Northern View*, April 28, 2022. https://www.thenorthernview.com/news/seal-cove-salt-marsh-opens-with-4-million-prince-rupert-port-authority-investment/.

———. 2022. "Prince Rupert wins national brownfield award with Watson Island reinvention." *Prince Rupert Northern View*, November 17, 2022. https://www.terracestandard.com/news/prince-rupert-wins-national-brownfield-award-with-watson-island-reinvention/.

———. 2023. "Dam construction positions Prince Rupert for the future." *Prince Rupert Northern View*, April 8, 2023. https://www.thenorthernview.com/local-news/dam-construction-flows-prince-rupert-into-the-future/.

——— . 2023. "Prince Rupert taxpayers may be on hook for millions with Port and City disputing land value." *Prince Rupert Northern View*, January 11, 2023. https://www.thenorthernview.com/news/prince-rupert-taxpayers-may-be-on-hook-for-millions-with-port-and-city-disputing-land-value/.

Millenium Research Limited. 2014. "Archaeological Investigations at Ya asqalu'i/Kaien Siding, Prince Rupert Harbour." http://millennia-research.com/wp-content/uploads/2019/07/Kaien_Siding_Archaeology_Final_Report_Website-copy.pdf.

Miller, Holly and Michael Reese. 2020. "Indians and Europeans on the Northwest Coast, 1774–1812: A Curriculum Project for Washington Schools." Center for the Study of the Pacific Northwest. University of Washington Department of History.

Miller, Jay. 1998. "Tsimshian Ethno-Ethnohistory: A 'Real' Indigenous Chronology." *Ethnohistory*, 45(4): 657–74. https://doi.org/10.2307/483299.

Moss, Madonna, Dorothy Peteet, and Cathy Whitlock. 2007. "Mid-Holocene Culture and Climate on the Northwest Coast of North America." *Climate Change and Cultural Dynamics: A Global Perspective on Mid-Holocene Transitions*. David G. Anderson, et al, eds. 491–521. Amsterdam: Elsevier.

Moyer, E. 1954. "Mussallem Means 'Peaceful Man.'" *BC Magazine*, March 6, 1954. https://mapleridgemuseum.org/mussallem-means-peaceful-man/.

Mulder, Jean. 1994. *Ergativity in Coast Tsimshian (Sm'algyax)*. Berkeley, CA: University of California Press.

Murphy, Gavin. 1993. "Canada's Forgotten Railway Tycoon." *The Beaver* 73(6): 29.

———. (1992). "Titanic Disaster Claims Canadian Railway Legend Charles Melville Hays." The Historical Society of Ottawa. Bytown Pamphlet Series No. 58.

Murray, Peter. 1985. *The Devil and Mr. Duncan*. Winlaw, BC: Sono Nis Press.

Mussett, B. 2021. "Vietnamese Refugees Arrive." British Columbia: An Untold History. https://bcanuntoldhistory.knowledge.ca/1970/vietnamese-refugees-arrive.

Thomas, Shaun. 2006. "Developer purchases turbines for Mount Hays wind farm." *Prince Rupert Northern View*, November 29, 2006. https://www.wind-watch.org/news/2006/11/29/developer-purchases-turbines-for-mount-hays-wind-farm/.

Nayar, Kamala E. 2012. *The Punjabis in British Columbia: Location, Labour, First Nations, and Multiculturalism*. Montreal: McGill-Queen's University Press.

Nelson, Stuart and Bruce Turris. 2004. "The Evolution of Commercial Salmon Fisheries in British Columbia." Report to the Pacific Fisheries Resource Conservation Council. https://psf.ca/wp-content/uploads/2021/10/Download-PDF679-1.pdf.

Neylan, Susan Lynn. 1999. "'The Heavens Are Changing': Nineteenth century protestant missionization on the North Pacific Coast." PhD thesis, University of BC.

———. 2000. "Longhouses, Schoolrooms, and Workers' Cottages: Nineteenth-Century Protestant Missions to the Tsimshian and the Transformation of Class Through Religion." *Journal of the Canadian Historical Association* 11(1): 51–86.

Norris, Mary Jane and Stewart Clatworthy. 2010. "Urbanization and Migration Patterns of Aboriginal Populations in Canada: A Half Century in Review (1951 to 2006)." *aboriginal policy studies* 1:1 (2011). Chris Andersen, ed. https://doi.org/10.5663/aps.v1i1.8970.

Northern British Columbia Archives & Special Collections. 2009. The Honourable Iona Campagnolo Fonds. https://search.nbca.unbc.ca/downloads/honourable-iona-campagnolo-fonds.pdf.

The Northern View. 2011. "Prince Rupert Port Authority announces restricted access to Ridley Island." August 1, 2011. https://www.thenorthernview.com/news/prince-rupert-port-authority-announces-restricted-access-to-ridley-island/.

Nuffield, Edward W. 1990. *The Pacific Northwest: its discovery and early exploration by sea, land and river.* Surrey, BC: Hancock House Publishers.

Olesiuk, Peter, Graeme Ellis, and John Ford. 2005. "Life History and Population Dynamics of Northern Resident Killer Whales (*Orcinus orca*) in British Columbia." Canadian Science Advisory Secretariat. https://waves-vagues.dfo-mpo.gc.ca/library-bibliotheque/324059.pdf.

Ombudsman of British Columbia. 1985. "The Nisgha Tribal Council and Tree Farm License No. 1, Public Report No. 4." https://bcombudsperson.ca/assets/media/Public-Report-No-04-The-Nishga-Tribal-Council-and-Tree-Farm-Licence-No.-1.pdf.

Ormsby, M. 1962. "T. Dufferin Pattullo and the Little New Deal." *The Canadian Historical Review* 43(4): 277–97.

———. 1971. *British Columbia: A History.* Toronto: MacMillan Canada.

———. 2008. "Sir James Douglas." *The Canadian Encyclopedia.* https://www.thecanadianencyclopedia.ca/en/article/sir-james-douglas.

Orton, Tyler. 2014. "Port and energy boom reignites Prince Rupert's economy." *Business in Vancouver*, June 1, 2014. https://biv.com/article/2014/06/port-and-energy-boom-reignites-prince-ruperts-econ.

Packman, Glen A. 1979. "Pulp Mill Environment Assessment: Canadian Cellulose Limited Northern Pulp Operations Port Edward, British Columbia." Regional Program Report. https://publications.gc.ca/collections/collection_2019/eccc/en40-240/En40-240-79-7-eng.pdf.

Patton, Anna K.B. 2011. "Reconstructing Houses: Early Village Social Organization in Prince Rupert Harbour, British Columbia." PhD thesis, University of Toronto.

Peebles, Frank. 2021. "From Titanic to Titan." *The Orca*, June 17, 2021. https://www.theorca.ca/visitingpod/from-titanic-to-titan-6400436.

Pembina. 2021. "Pembina's successful remediation at Prince Rupert Terminal." April 22, 2021. https://www.pembina.com/sustainability/stories/pembina%E2%80%99s-successful-remediation-at-prince-rupert-/.

Perry, Martina. 2014. "Ship access being examined for Watson Island LNG terminal." *Prince Rupert Northern View*, July 25, 2014. https://www.thenorthernview.com/business/ship-access-being-examined-for-watson-island-lng-terminal/.

Peterson, Jan. 2012. *Kilts on the Coast: The Scots Who Built BC*. Victoria: Heritage House Publishing.

Pethick, Derek. 1976. *First Approaches to the Northwest Coast*. Vancouver: J.J. Douglas Ltd.

Pettigrew, William A. 2013. *Freedom's Debt: The Royal African Company and the Politics of the Atlantic Slave Trade, 1672–1752*. Chapel Hill, NC: University of North Carolina Press.

Pinkerton, Evelyn, Eric Angel, et al. 2014. "Local and regional strategies for rebuilding fisheries management institutions in coastal British Columbia: What components of co-management are most critical?" Ecology and Society 19(2): 72 (2014). http://www.jstor.org/stable/26269574.

"plunder." 2024. Oxford Reference. https://www.oxfordreference.com/view/10.1093/oi/authority.20110803100332360.

Pounds, Norman J.G. 1972. *Political Geography*. New York: McGraw-Hill.

Powell, J.V. and Sam Sullivan. 2006. "Chinook Wawa." *The Canadian Encyclopedia*. https://www.thecanadianencyclopedia.ca/en/article/chinook-jargon.

Powroznik, Gary and Robert J. Sandy. 1993. "Prince Rupert Fishermen's Cooperative: an assessment of its restructuring plan and viability." Report to the job protection commission Province of British Columbia. https://www.for.gov.bc.ca/hfd/library/documents/Bib93230.pdf.

Price, T. Douglas. and James Brown. 1985. *Prehistoric Hunter-Gatherers: The Emergence of Cultural Complexity*. Orlando: Academic Press

Prince Rupert Airport. 2021. "Air Canada announces temporary suspension of air service effective Jan.18 2021." YPR news release. January 13, 2021. http://ypr.ca/2021/air-canada-announces-temporary-suspension-of-air-service-effective-jan-18-2021/.

Prince Rupert City & Regional Archives Society. 2010. *Prince Rupert: an illustrated history*. Prince Rupert, BC: P.R.S & R.A.S.

Prince Rupert Daily News. Microfilm. Prince Rupert Public Library, Prince Rupert, BC: 1911, 1914, 1916–17, 1919–23, 1927, 1929–35, 1939, 1941–45, 1947–50, 1953, 1956–66, 1968–69, 1971–87, 1990–97, 1999, 2003–2006, 2008–10, 2013.

Prince Rupert Economic Development Commission. 2002. *A Socio-Economic Impact Analysis of Skeena Cellulose Inc.* Prince Rupert, BC: Prince Rupert Economic Development Commission.

Prince Rupert Journal. 1910. "Addressed Open Air Meeting of Citizens." August 23, 1910. Vol. 1, No. 20.

Prince Rupert Port Authority. 2021. "2021 Economic Impact Assessment: The Port of Prince Rupert and the Prince Rupert Gateway Make Northern BC Work." https://www.rupertport.com/economic-impact/.

———. 2021. "Our Advantages." https://www.rupertport.com/our-advantages/.

———. 2022. "Strong Return for Cruise Tourism in Prince Rupert." Press Release. October 26, 2022. https://www.rupertport.com/strong-return-for-cruise-tourism-in-prince-rupert/.

———. 2023. Smart, Sustainable Investment. https://www.rupertport.com/smart-sustainable-investment/.

———. 2023. "Terminal Expansion to 1.8M TEU Capacity (2 Stages) - Fairview Container Terminal Expansion." https://www.rupertport.com/active_project/fairview-container-terminal/#:~:text=Today%2C%20Fairview%20Container%20Terminal's%20sustainable,projected%20into%20the%20foreseeable%20future.

Province of BC. 1942. "Bylaw No. 946: A Bylaw to Authorize the Execution of Three Indentures Referred to as a Lease, A Principal Agreement and a Collateral Agreement, and to be made by the Corporation of the City of Prince Rupert Respectively with His Majesty the King in Right of Canada, and Wartime Housing Limited." https://www.bclaws.gov.bc.ca/civix/document/id/oic/arc_oic/0470_1942.

———.1999. "The History of Tree Farm License 1." https://www2.gov.bc.ca/assets/ gov/farming-natural-resources-and-industry/forestry/timber-tenures/tree-farm-licence/management-plans/tfl_01_mp9_appendix_12_tfl_history.pdf.

———. 1999. "Skeena Cellulose will Modernize Mill." Ministry of Employment and Investment, Ministry of Energy and Mines, and Ministry Responsible for Northern Development. Press Release. May 26, 1999. https://archive.news.gov.bc.ca/releases/ archive/pre2001/1999/nrs99/050nr99.asp.

———. 2018. "Facilitator named for logging contractor sustainability review." *BC Government News - Ministry of Forests, Lands, Natural Resource, Operations and Rural Development.* August 22, 2018. https://news.gov.bc.ca/17849.

———. 2019. "New supportive homes for people in need in Prince Rupert." *BC Government News—Ministry of Municipal Affairs.* March 8, 2019. https://news. gov.bc.ca/19101.

———. 2002. "Skeena Cellulose Sale Complete." *Ministry of Competition, Science and Enterprise news release.* April 30, 2002. https://archive.news.gov.bc.ca/releases/ archive/2001-2005/2002cse0011-000101.htm

———. (2023) "Lax Kw'alaams." *BC Geographical Place Names.* https://apps.gov. bc.ca/pub/bcgnws/names/39283.html#:~:text=Origin%20Notes%20and%20 History%3A&text=Name%20changed%20to%20Lax%20Kw,name%20of%20 their%20post%20office.

Putnam, Robert., Frank Taylor, and Phillip Kettle. 1970. *A Geography of Urban Places.* London, UK: Routledge.

Raedenmaecker, Fien De. 2003. "A GIS approach to compare intertidal diversity and contaminant loading in the marine receiving environment of two pulp mills in British Columbia, Canada." MSc. thesis. Belgium: Universiteit Gent. http://www. ecotoxicology.ca/csi/FienThesis.pdf.

Raptis, Helen. 2014. "Exploring the Factors Prompting British Columbia's First Integration Initiative: The Case of Port Essington Indian Day School." *History of Education Quarterly.* 51:4. 519–43. http://www.jstor.org/stable/41303899.

Regehr, Theodore D. 2003. "Hays, Charles Melville," *Dictionary of Canadian Biography.* 14. Toronto: University of Toronto/Université Laval. http://www. biographi.ca/en/bio/hays_charles_melville_14E.html.

Report of Select Standing Committee. 1906. "Kaien Island Investigation." March 7, 1906. 6(7). https://archives.leg.bc.ca/civix/document/id/leg_archives/legarchives/ 1073712468.

Rettig, Andrew. 1980. "A Nativist Movement at Metlakatla Mission." *BC Studies: The British Columbian Quarterly.* Summer 1980. 46:28–39.

Richesson, Brian. 2021. "Pembina opens first LPG export facility." *LPGas Magazine.* May 4, 2021. https://www.lpgasmagazine.com/pembina-opens-first-lpg-export-facility/.

Roach, John. 2020. "Microsoft finds underwater datacenters are reliable, practical and use energy sustainably." *Microsoft News.* September 14, 2020. https://news.microsoft. com/source/features/sustainability/project-natick-underwater-datacenter/.

Rowse, Sue. 2006. "Birth of a City: Prince Rupert, BC." Research Triangle, NC: Lulu. com.

Roy, Patricia. 1989. *A White Man's Province: British Columbia Politicians and Chinese and Japanese Immigrants 1858-1914*. Vancouver BC: UBC Press.

———. 2008. "Iona Campagnolo." *The Canadian Encyclopedia*. https://www. thecanadianencyclopedia.ca/en/article/iona-campagnolo.

Rupert Cold Storage Fonds. 2023. Prince Rupert City & Regional Archives Society. https://princerupertarchives.ca/search/detail-bare.php?ID=630.

Ryser, Laura. Kyle Kusch, Greg Halseth, and Don Manson. 2008. "Northern British Columbia Service Industry Sector Study Population Background and Trends Report." Community Development Institute, University of Northern British Columbia. April 2008. https://www2.unbc.ca/sites/default/files/sections/ community-development-institute/service_canada_population_report_working_ draft_april_2008.pdf.

Salmon, Lynn. 2014. "Charles M. Hays - A Titanic Loss." *The Nauticapedia*.ca. 2014. https://www.nauticapedia.ca/Articles/Hays_Charles.php.

Sanchez, Antonio. 2004. "Spanish Exploration: Juan Perez Expedition of 1774 — First European Discovery and Exploration of Washington State Coast and Nueva Galicia (the Pacific Northwest)." *Historylink.org*. Essay 5677. April 7, 2004. https://www.historylink.org/File/5677.

Savage, John "Mac." 2012. "The WWII American Sub-port of Embarkation, Prince Rupert: An Understanding of Why the Americans Were in Northern BC." Unpublished Manuscript.

Schneider, Howard. 1997. "Economic Crisis Tests Pacific Bloc." *Washington Post Foreign Service*. November 23, 1997: A24. https://www.washingtonpost.com/ wp-srv/inatl/longterm/canada/stories/asiacrisis112397.htm.

Sea Breeze Power Corp. 2023. "Mount Hays and Mount Oldfield Windfarm Projects: Terrain Stability and Geohazards Baseline Report." https://seabreezewind. com/?page_id=704.

Seigel, Leah. 2023. "Chief Legaic's Legacy: A line of Tsimshian chiefs head an impressive trade network along the northwest coast." *British Columbia's Untold History*. https://bcanuntoldhistory.knowledge.ca/1830/chief-legaics-legacy.

Senate of Canada. 1888. "Appendices to the Twenty-Second Volume of the Journals of the Senate of Canada." Ottawa, ON: B. Chamberlin, Queen's Printer.

Sewell, Cookie. 2005. "The Armoured Train in Canadian Service Book Review." *Cybermodeler Online*. (March 2005) https://www.cybermodeler.com/hobby/ref/ sp/book_sp_train.shtml.

Sexty, Robert. 1981. "Canadian Cellulose Company Limited: A Case Study of Government Rescue and Turnaround." The Institute of Public Administration of Canada. IPAC Case Study Program. http://archives.enap.ca/bibliotheques/2012/ 06/030302677.pdf.

Shannon, Anne. 2012. *Finding Japan: Early Canadian encounters with Asia*. Victoria, BC: Heritage House Publishing.

Siegel, Leah. 2023. "Prince Rupert's Wobblies: a riot breaks out at a protest organized by the Industrial Workers of the World Union." *British Columbia's Untold History*. https://bcanuntoldhistory.knowledge.ca/1910/prince-ruperts-wobblies.

Skelton, Oscar. 1965. *Life and Letters of Sir Wilfrid Laurier: Volume 2 1896-1919*. Montreal, QC: McGill-Queen's University Press. https://www.jstor.org/stable/j. ctt1w6tcqj.

Bibliography 243

Spelter, Henry. and Matthew Alderman. 2005. "Profile 2005: Softwood Sawmills in the United States and Canada." United States Department of Agriculture Forest Service. Research Paper FPL-RP-630. https://intrans.iastate.edu/app/uploads/2018/08/fpl_rp630.pdf.

Spencer, Charles. 2007. *Prince Rupert: The Last Cavalier*. London, UK: Orion Publishing Co.

Stacey, C.P. 1948. "The Canadian Army, 1939–1945: an official historical summary." Department of National Defence. Ottawa: King's Printer.

Stanger, Nicholas. 2013. "Iona Campagnolo visits her childhood home at North Pacific Cannery." Nicholas Stanger. Oct 27, 2013. https://www.youtube.com/watch?v=sk7fwGQHU3E.

State of Alaska. "History of AMHS." Alaska Marine Highway System. Accessed in 2023, https://dot.alaska.gov/amhs/history.shtml.

Statistics Canada. 2006. "Selected trend data for Prince Rupert (CY), 1996, 2001 and 2006 censuses." https://www12.statcan.gc.ca/census-recensement/2006/dp-pd/92-596/P1-2.cfm?Lang=eng&T=CSD&GEOCODE=47012&PRCODE=59&TID=0.

———. 2007. "Prince Rupert, British Columbia (Code5947012) (table). 2006 Community Profiles. 2006 Census." *Statistics Canada Catalogue* no. 92-591-XWE. Ottawa. March 13, 2007.https://www12.statcan.gc.ca/census-recensement/2006/dp-pd/prof/92-591/index.cfm?Lang=E.

———.2010. "Population and Demography." Catalogue no. 11-402-X:313–326 https://www150.statcan.gc.ca/n1/en/pub/11-402-x/2010000/pdf/population-eng.pdf?st=r4ZuxıjG.

———. 2013.

———. 2015.

———. 2018. "Prince Rupert, CY [Census subdivision], British Columbia (table). Aboriginal Population Profile. 2016 Census." *Statistics Canada Catalogue* no. 98-510-X2016001. Ottawa. Released July 18, 2018. http://www12.statcan.gc.ca/census-recensement/2016/dp-pd/abpopprof/index.cfm?Lang=E.

———. 2023. "(table). Census Profile. 2021 Census of Population." *Statistics Canada Catalogue* no. 98-316-X2021001. Ottawa. Released November 15, 2023. https://www12.statcan.gc.ca/census-recensement/2021/dp-pd/prof/index.cfm?Lang=E.

Stirling, Jim. 2005. "What's Next for BC's Northwest? the Long, Drawn-Out Story of New Skeena Forest Products and its Predecessor Companies has Come to a Close, with the Focus Now Switching to what Comes Next for the Forest Industry in Northwestern BC." *Logging & Sawmilling Journal* 36:1 (February 2005). 4.

Supernant, Kisha, and Corey Cookson. 2014. "Mapping Social Cohesion in Prince Rupert Harbour, BC: A Social Application of GIS to the Archaeology of the Northwest Coast." *Canadian Journal of Archaeology*. 38:1. 179–210. http://www.jstor.org/stable/43967082.

Supreme Court of British Columbia. 2012. Sun Wave Forest Products Ltd. v. City of Prince Rupert. BCSC 1908 (CanLII). https://canlii.ca/t/fvboj.

———. 2013. Sun Wave Forest Products Ltd. v. Prince Rupert (City). BCSC 1235 (CanLII). https://canlii.ca/t/fzlp4.

———. 2015. Watson Island Development Corp. v. Prince Rupert (City). BCSC 1474 (CanLII). https://canlii.ca/t/gkrf2.

———. 2019. Sun Wave Forest Products Ltd. v Prince Rupert (City). BCSC 415 (CanLII). https://canlii.ca/t/hz9cl.

Supreme Court of Canada. 2007. Lax Kw'alaams Indian Band v. Canada (Attorney General), 2011 SCC 56 (CanLII), [2011] 3 SCR 535. https://canlii.ca/t/fnr69.

Tattersfield, David. (2021). "Cyrus Peck, Piper Paul, and the Canadian Scottish at Amiens." *Western Front Association.* https://www.westernfrontassociation.com/world-war-i-articles/cyrus-peck-piper-paul-and-the-canadian-scottish-at-amiens/.

Tattrie, Jon. 2014. "British Columbia and Confederation." *The Canadian Encyclopedia.* https://www.thecanadianencyclopedia.ca/en/article/british-columbia-and-confederation.

Taylor, Carole. 2022. "Iona Campagnolo - The Woman of Firsts." BC Legends with Carole Taylor. Sep 22, 2022. https://www.youtube.com/watch?v=73jTNMmQdjU.

Thomas, Shaun. 2011. "Community and provincial leaders meet to discuss Tsimshian Access Project." *The Northern View.* Jun 22, 2011. https://www.thenorthernview.com/news/community-and-provincial-leaders-meet-to-discuss-tsimshian-access-project/.

———. 2011. "UPDATE: JS McMillan Fisheries announces closure of Prince Rupert processing plant." *The Northern View.* Jul 5, 2011. https://www.thenorthernview.com/news/update-js-mcmillan-fisheries-announces-closure-of-prince-rupert-processing-plant/.

———. 2012. "Ocean's Fish plant in Prince Rupert closing down." *The Northern View.* Apr 18, 2012. https://www.thenorthernview.com/news/oceans-fish-plant-in-prince-rupert-closing-down/.

———. 2012. "City of Prince Rupert asks court to throw out Watson Island litigation in new filing." *The Northern View.* November 12, 2012. https://www.thenorthernview.com/news/city-of-prince-rupert-asks-court-to-throw-out-watson-island-litigation-in-new-filing/.

———. 2012. "BC Supreme Court decision gives the go ahead to Watson Island sale." *The Northern Connector.* December 28, 2012, 7:25. A3. https://issuu.com/blackpress/docs/i20121228070944502/3.

———. 2014. "UPDATE: Court filing alleges City of Prince Rupert seeking other buyers for Watson Island." *The Northern View,* March 27, 2014. https://www.thenorthernview.com/news/update-court-filing-alleges-city-of-prince-rupert-seeking-other-buyers-for-watson-island/.

———. 2014. "Details emerge around failed Watson Island sale: Lax Kw'alaams 'threatened' city, remediation tops $50 million." *Prince Rupert Northern View.* May 28, 2014. https://www.thenorthernview.com/news/details-emerge-around-failed-watson-island-sale-lax-kwalaams-threatened-city-remediation-tops-50-million-5938974.

———. 2014. "City of Prince Rupert offers Watson Island LNG exclusive rights to former pulp mill site." *The Northern View.* July 16, 2014. https://www.thenorthernview.com/news/city-of-prince-rupert-offers-watson-island-lng-exclusive-rights-to-former-pulp-mill-site/.

———. 2014. "WatCo backer lashes out at Prince Rupert city council." *The Northern View,* August 6, 2014. https://www.thenorthernview.com/news/watco-backer-lashes-out-at-prince-rupert-city-council/.

———. 2014. "LNG Additions." *Need to Know,* September 2014. 1(6):15 https://issuu.com/blackpress/docs/i20150113111004777.

———. 2014. "UPDATE: Prince Rupert mayor, WatCo CEO comment on Watson Island ruling." *The Northern View,* December 19, 2012. https://www.thenorthernview.com/news/update-prince-rupert-mayor-watco-ceo-comment-on-watson-island-ruling/.

———. 2015. "Contract awarded for Watson Island cleanup." *The Northern View,* August 5, 2015. https://www.thenorthernview.com/news/contract-awarded-for-watson-island-cleanup-5939119.

Thomson, Duane. 2016. "The Ethno-Genesis of the Mixed-Ancestry Population in New Caledonia." *BC Studies.* 191: 57-84. https://doi.org/10.14288/bcs.voi191.185094.

Trillium Business Strategies Inc. 2003. "Planning and Feasibility Study: Digby Island / Tsimshian Peninsula Access Project." http://docs.openinfo.gov.bc.ca/Response_Package_2_TRA-2015-54374.pdf.

Tucker, Gilbert. 1952. *The Naval Service of Canada: its official history—Volume II Activities on Shore During the Second World War.* Ottawa, ON: King's Printer.

Turunen, Carrie and Jukka Turunen. 2003. "Development History and Carbon Accumulation of a Slope Bog in Oceanic British Columbia, Canada." *The Holocene* 13:2. 225–38. https://doi.org/10.1191/0959683603hl609rp.

Union of BC Municipalities. 2014. "Port Property Tax Caps. Convention & Resolutions." https://www.ubcm.ca/convention-resolutions/resolutions/resolutions-database/port-property-tax-caps.

Urbas, Daniel. 2019. "BC – corporation unsuccessfully uses indoor management rule and alleged forgery to challenge arbitration result – #181." *Arbitration* Matters, March 28, 2019. https://arbitrationmatters.com/b-c-corporation-unsuccessfully-uses-indoor-management-rule-and-alleged-forgery-to-challenge-arbitration-result/.

Usher, Jean. 1969. "William Duncan of Metlakatla: A Victorian Missionary in British Columbia." PhD thesis. University of British Columbia. http://dx.doi.org/10.14288/1.0058241.

Vassallo, James. 2004. "Landmark lost to flames." *The Prince Rupert Daily News.* November 10, 2004. http://www2.citytel.net/~nivlact/landmark_lost_to_flames.htm.

———. 2006. "Natives could throw wrench into port plan." *Prince George Citizen,* April 15, 2006. http://pgnewspapers.pgpl.ca/fedora/repository/pgc:2006-04-15/-/Prince%20George%20Citizen%20-%20April%2015,%202006.

Vickers, Patricia. 2008. "Ayaawx: (Ts'msyen ancestral law): the power of transformation." PhD thesis, University of Victoria. http://hdl.handle.net/1828/1299.

Victor, Olivier. 2006. "Lester was B.C.'s longest-serving." *The Free Library,* March 25, 2024. https://www.thefreelibrary.com/Lester+was+B.C.%27s+longest-serving+mayor.-a0153191202.

Vopak. 2023. "Vopak and AltaGas form a new joint venture for large-scale LPG and bulk liquids export Terminal in Prince Rupert, Canada." April 26, 2023. https://www.vopak.com/newsroom/news/vopak-and-altagas-form-new-joint-venture-large-scale-lpg-and-bulk-liquids-export?language_content_entity=en

Wahl, Ryan. 2008. *Legacy in Wood: The Wahl Family Boat Builders.* Madeira Park, BC: Harbour Publishing.

Wainwright, Alfred. 2003. *A Coast to Coast Walk: A Pictorial Guide.* Wainwright Pictorial Guides. London, UK: Frances Lincoln.

Waldichuk, Michael. 1962. "Observations in marine waters of the Prince Rupert area, particularly with reference to pollution from sulphite pulp mill on Watson Island." *Fish Research Board Canada Manuscript Series,* 733.

Warman, Cy. 1908. "Prince Rupert." *The Canadian Magazine.* 30:5. 395–401

Wentworth, Elaine. 1968. *Mission to Metlakatla.* Boston, USA: Houghton Mifflin Company.

Whiteley, Don. 2007. "Prince Rupert: Prince of Ports." BC *Business Magazine*, July 2, 2007. https://www.bcbusiness.ca/prince-rupert-prince-of-ports.

Wilson, Gary, and Tracy Summerville. 2008. "Transformation, Transportation or Speculation? The Prince Rupert Container Port and Its Impact on Northern British Columbia." *Canadian Political Science Review*. 2:4 (2008). 26–39. https://doi.org/10.24124/c677/200879.

Wood, Chris.1997. "Darn Yankees! Ottawa fashions a truce in the salmon war, but Victoria sees only an empty gesture." *Maclean's*. 110:41. 12–17. https://archive.macleans.ca/article/1997/8/4/darn-yankees.

Wouters, Liz. 2018. "Renewable Energy Charging Forward." *Haida Gwaii Trader*, July 28, 2018. https://haidagwaiitrader.com/index.php?option=com_content&view=article&id=286:renewable-energy-charging-forward&catid=45:articles&Itemid=121.

Zuehlke, Mark. 2017. "Cy Peck, vc, the Prince Rupert Company, and the Great War." *The Northern Review*. 44 (2017): 347–35.

INDEX

ABOUT THE AUTHOR

CHELSEY ELLIS PHOTOGRAPHY

Blair Mirau is a born-and-raised Rupertite and former Prince Rupert city councillor. Since 2016, he has served as the chief executive officer of the Gitmaxmak'ay Nisga'a Society, which has been recognized with the BC Indigenous Community-Owned Business of the Year Award. In 2018, Mirau was named one of BC's Top 30 Under 30 by *BC Business* magazine. He holds a master's in Interdisciplinary Studies and a graduate certificate in Sustainable Community Development from Royal Roads University, as well an undergraduate degree in International Development from the University of Winnipeg.